The Civilization of the American Indian Series

The Navajos

The Navajos

RUTH M. UNDERHILL

University of Oklahoma Press : Norman

By Ruth M. Underhill

Autobiography of a Papago Woman (*Memoir* of American Anthropological Association No. 48, 1936)

First Penthouse Dwellers of America (New York, 1936)

Singing for Power (Berkeley, 1936)

Social Organization of the Papago Indians (New York, 1939)

Hawk Over Whirlpools (New York, 1940)

Indians of Southern California (U.S. Indian Service, 1941)

The Papago Indians and Their Relatives the Pima (U.S. Indian Service, 1942)

The Northern Paiute Indians (U.S. Indian Service, 1943)

Pueblo Crafts (U.S. Indian Service, 1944)

Workaday Life of the Pueblos (U.S. Indian Service, 1945)

Here Come the Navaho (U.S. Indian Service, 1953)

Red Man's America (Chicago, 1953)

The Navajos (Norman, 1956)

International Standard Book Number: 0-8061-0341-8

Library of Congress Catalog Card Number: 56-5996

To Gladys A. Reichard

LONG-TIME FRIEND AND INTERPRETER

OF THE NAVAJOS

Foreword

THESE PAGES DESCRIBE as faithfully as possible the experiences of the Navajos, as an American Indian tribe, as they changed from food-collecting nomads to gardeners and pastoralists to, finally, modern wage earners. Since much of the Navajo history has taken place within the past five hundred years and in well-known territory, these people afford an excellent example of the complex transition facing the modern American Indian. There are gaps in the narrative at some strategic points. Nevertheless, the student of human relations can catch here invaluable glimpses of the circumstances under which new ways are accepted and the mechanism of acceptance with its inducements and restraints.

The Navajos' education in the Southwest began among the agricultural Pueblo Indians. Then came importations from the Spaniards, often filtered through a Pueblo medium. Finally, the United States spent millions of dollars in attempting to change the Navajos' ways. However, the Earth People, as the Navajos call themselves, learned only what they chose and in their own good time. The history of this learning process follows United States relations with the Navajos from the time when a mere presentation of the white man's way was thought to mean salvation for the Indian to the present, when prolonged friction between peoples has produced some deeper understanding of human needs and of the measures required if varied groups are to share the earth.

The materials for this volume were collected during the years of 1945–48 while the author was completing a thirteen-year period of employment with the United States Indian Service. On behalf of the Education Department of the service, she undertook the writing of a children's history of the Navajos, for use in Indian schools. This required the omission of much material that would be interesting to adults, so the present volume was later undertaken and is now presented. It has been planned and constructed from archaeological monographs; from Spanish reports; from reservation records at Window Rock; from original documents in government archives; and from the innumerable documents, printed and mimeographed, which circulate through the Indian Office. The local incidents and conversations included here are the contributions of Indian informants, some of whom were patient during days of interrogation and some of whom, during long drives over the reservation or desultory chats at "sings," brought out colorful traditions to complete the desired picture. It may be that the statements attributed to Barboncito or to Red Shirt have become as stylized as our own tale of Washington and the cherry tree. Still, this is how the Navajo thinks of his past, and the recording of his own attitude surely should be part of the picture.

Many organizations and individuals have assisted in the compilation of this material. The University of Denver lightened my teaching load during the writing. Harry Hoijer allowed the use of his translations from the Navajo, mentioned in the bibliography. Gladys Reichard, well-known specialist on the Navajo, allowed quotations from her unpublished material. F. H. Douglas of the Denver Art Museum permitted free and constant use of his library. Dorothy Field and Dorothy Ellis did valiant work in typing, proofreading, and indexing.

Officials of the Indian Office gave access to unpublished materials and to their own information. I owe a special debt to Willard Beatty, director of Indian Education, Washington, and to Allan Harper, area director at Window Rock, and to his staff. Teachers, doctors, nurses, and others were most helpful both in sharing personal experiences and extending hospitality. Milton Snow provided photographs and drove me to difficult localities. Richard Van Valkenburgh, at one time in the United States Indian Service, now employed by the Navajo tribe, helped with information on old Navajo sites. My Navajo acquaintances mounted into the hundreds, among whom I can name especially Messrs. Sam Akeah, Paul Jones, Jake Morgan, Chee Dodge, and his son Thomas Dodge. They are, of course, not responsible for any of the opinions expressed here on the Navajo situation.

RUTH UNDERHILL

Denver, Colorado

Contents

Illustrations

Maps

The Navajos

1: Navajo Ancestors

THE LARGEST INDIAN tribe in the United States today is the Navajo, numbering some seventy thousand. Living among the rocky canyons and desert plateaus of New Mexico and Arizona, they are famous shepherds and horsemen. Their brilliant costume, with velvet blouse and hand-wrought silver ornaments, stands out in any Indian pageant. Their colorful, handmade blankets and their silverwork, in bold, simple patterns, are sold all over the country. Art lovers are fascinated by their symbolic dry paintings made with pollen or powdered rock. In these days, when Indian customs and ceremonies are changing, the Navajo stands out in many minds as the typical, unspoiled Indian.

Yet, six or seven hundred years ago, there were no Navajos, at least by that name. There were, of course, the ancestors of the present tribe, little groups of half-naked hunters, who were, perhaps, just penetrating the Southwest. They had none of the arts which make them famous today and almost none of the ceremonies. All of these things have been acquired within a few hundred years, for the Navajos are some of the greatest learners and adapters among American Indians. The old idea that the red man is a born conservative, unable or unwilling to change,

3

has long been known as false, but no tribe has proved its untruth more conclusively than the Navajo.

The name Navajo is comparatively recent, and not even in the "Navajo" language. They, along with their blood brothers, now known as Apaches, speak of themselves as Dineh, or Dené, the People. Their tales qualify this as Earth People or Earth Surface People, for, in the long, poetic myth which is their bible, they climbed up to the earth's flat disk from her dark, underground womb. The later names were given them by the farming Tewa Indians of New Mexico, who used the word "Apachu" to mean strangers, or enemies, much the same thing in ancient days.[1] It was later yet that one of these small groups of strangers settled to agriculture and became known as *Apaches de Nabahu,* or "Strangers of the Cultivated Fields."

The Earth People speak a language entirely different from others in the Southwest. To the surprise of students, it was finally identified as Athapascan, a northern tongue, first met around Lake Athapasca, in Canada's Northwest Territory. It was by means of this language that these desert horsemen, who abhor fish as something strange and inedible, were traced to a home in the north woods where fish is the usual food and travel is by canoe. It has been proved that the Athapascans of the Southwest can actually understand some words used by Indians of British Columbia, the Sekani, Beaver, Carrier, Slave and Chippewyan. Pronunciation may be different, but when words from the north were submitted to them, old Navajos have been known to clap their hands and exclaim: "That is the way we *used* to say it!"[2] What unremembered changes have taken place when a northern word for horn spoon means, to the Navajos, gourd

---

[1] Information from John Harrington, Bureau of American Ethnology. According to Erik Reed, National Park Service, the word has the same meaning in Zuñi.

dipper! Though they may have never seen a boat, the Navajos can describe the gliding flight of an owl by a word which, in the north, means to paddle a canoe. They have been planting corn for centuries, yet one of their words for corn can be analyzed to mean food of the strangers.[3] So, perhaps, the People called the new grain by this term when they first entered the Southwest.

These ghostly reflections of their past would indicate that they came from the southern edge of the great Athapascan area, which stretches through western Canada and central Alaska. If we suppose, as most students now do, that the American Indians entered Alaska from Siberia and streamed down through Canada, then the country of the Athapascans covers most of the northern part of their route. It would look as though the Athapascans might be late comers, camping along the trail, while earlier arrivals had moved on. The supposition has fascinating possibilities, but it is still in the realm of theory.

These Athapascans of Canada and Alaska are among the most primitive tribes on the continent. Camped along the lakes and streams of the great north woods, they lived, before the white man's day, by hunting the caribou, moose, and bear, and by trapping fish. Their homes were shelters of poles, covered with bark and earth. Most of them made no pottery or baskets. They led a wandering life, with little organized government. Their ceremonies were only the few, irregular ones which called the wild game. Their medicine men were solitary visionaries, with no established ritual.

[2] A. G. Morice, "The Unity of Speech among the Northern and the Southern Dene," *American Anthropologist,* Vol. IX, No. 4 (October–December, 1907), 729–30.

[3] Edward Sapir, "Internal Linguistic Evidence Suggestive of the Northern Origin of the Navaho," *American Anthropologist,* Vol. XXXVIII, No. 2 (April–June, 1936), 225–32.

Yet these primitive hunters have been enterprising travelers and colonizers. Some of their offshoots are the famous canoe and totem-pole builders of the Alaskan coast, known as Tlingit and Haida. The language of these wealthy woodworkers is as far from Athapascan as English is from Greek. Yet the two seem to have a common origin, just as English and Greek have. Some small band of adventurers must have wandered out to the coast, mixed with other peoples, learned from them, and then developed their learning magnificently.

Over and over again, this has happened. There are groups of Athapascans on the shores of Bering Sea, sharing the arts and customs of the Eskimos. Others have been found in Oregon, hunting the elk and paddling river canoes with the Sahaptin Indians. Some, in California, have made elaborate baskets and danced the White Deer dance with the Yurok. In fact, these colonizing northerners remind one of the Norsemen in the Old World, even though their travel was by land and not by sea. Over and over again, European history tells of the movements of the Scandinavians into Britain, France, or Italy. Each time, the wanderers learned the customs of the new country and took a place among its foremost citizens, as Saxons, Normans, or Varangians. So the Athapascans of the north woods poured their vigor into Indian cultures up and down western North America.

Most famous of their migrations was the one which took band after band of Indians to the Southwest, to become the Navajos and Apaches.

What manner of people were they to begin with, and what equipment did they bring, material and psychological? Anthropologists are still working on this subject and with very few hints to go on. The Athapascans of British Columbia, now flannel-shirted trappers, have little to tell about ancient days. We do know that they had skin clothing and moccasins, and this, at least, is a clue. Indians of the Southwest and California, in the days when the People were making their journey, usually went barefoot or protected their feet with sandals. So, when moccasins are found in any quantity along their probable route, archaeologists scent an Athapascan.

The northern Athapascan dwelling was a type of structure common in the north woods, a conical frame made of tall poles leaned together and covered with any material at hand. In Maine and eastern Canada, the covering was birchbark; on the plains, buffalo hide; with the Sekani of British Columbia, linguistic kinsmen of the Navajos, it was bark and leaves.[4] The Navajos probably kept to this dwelling throughout their journey. True, they added an extension, and as they reached drier country, their covering was earth, not leaves. Still, the earliest Navajo ruins yet found are of this type of house. Even yet it is built in parts of the reservation, and the Navajos call it the "forked-stick hogan," their oldest and most revered habitation. Perhaps along with it went the "sweathouse"—that tight little hut wherein a bather poured water on hot stones until the dirt and perspiration could be rubbed off his body together. It was an American Indian version of the Turkish bath and a highly efficient device where water was scarce.

Another valuable piece of equipment was the sinew-backed bow. This strong, short weapon, well known in the north, is thought by some students to have been brought from Asia by some of the late comers to American shores. Made of wood or horn, often in the double curve known to whites as a Cupid's bow, it is reinforced with sinew glued to its back and sometimes wound around its length. Such a bow with its powerful spring would seem a formidable weapon to earlier Indians of the South-

[4] Diamond Jenness, *The Sekani Indians of British Columbia,* 32. John S. Honigman, *Ethnography and Acculturation of the Fort Nelson Slave,* 50.

west, whose bow was a simple stick of wood bent into shape by the bow string. It may be, too, that the Athapascans even used a kind of armor, consisting of a heavy shirt of elk or moose hide.[5] Certainly the historical Navajo had something of the sort.[6]

The rest of the pioneering baggage resolves itself into a series of questions whose answers, we hope, will be unearthed in the next few years. Did they have pottery? There is scarcely a sign of the art among their northern relatives, and indeed such heavy and breakable containers are of little use to a hunting or migrant people. Yet the Navajos and many Apaches, up to today, make a tall, gray pot, with a pointed bottom which they say is "from the beginning." Would that it were possible to trace that beginning, for this pot is unlike most of those made in the Southwest. Instead it follows a style long known in the eastern woodland country and thought by some students to have been brought from Asia. As we follow the wanderings of the People, the question of where and when their women learned to make pottery takes a key position.

Even more revealing would it be to know the social customs with which the wanderers started, but here the trail is obscure indeed. The northern Athapascans and the others, scattered through Oregon and California, show varieties of behavior adapted, often, to the customs of their neighbors. However, it is believed that, like the Navajos and Apaches today, they may have counted their descent through women.[7] Their mother-right families may even have been gathered into clans (groups thought to be descended from a common female ancestress).[8] The custom is none too common in the north, yet

---

[5] C. Hill-Tout, *British North America*, 50.
[6] W. W. Hill, *Navaho Warfare*, 29.
[7] Hill-Tout, *British North America*, 147.
[8] *Ibid.*, 143–45.

clue hunters sniff the air avidly when they hear the name of one Navajo clan. Doing some violence to the native spelling, I may call it *sinna jinny*. This is a word which the Navajos cannot translate, although they offer various theories. How surprised they would be to visit their relatives the Sekani and find that, among them, *sinna jinny* is the regular term for any group of clans![9]

Perhaps the young husband among these wanderers went to live with his wife's family, as some northern Athapascans do, and as Navajos and Apaches do today.[10] Did he also practice mother-in-law avoidance, the age-old device for keeping peace in a family? Today, no Navajo man will stay in the room with his wife's mother, nor even speak to her directly. If this rule were disregarded, the mother-in-law, herself, would be offended, and sometimes both she and her son-in-law believe that the penalty would be insanity, forcing them to jump in the fire. An Apache husband goes even further and practices a kind of semi-avoidance toward his wife's father, sisters and brothers. The custom is not a Southwestern one, but evidence of it is found among other Athapascans. This, too, may be an item of psychological baggage brought from the north.[11]

[9] Jenness, *Sekani,* 47.

[10] Hill-Tout, *British North America,* 148.

[11] The Athapascan Sarsi of Alberta, Canada observed the taboo, as did their neighbors of Algonkian speech, the Blackfeet; and so did the Cree, although they were late comers to the area. The Athapascan Beaver of Alberta, Canada have only a respect language between son-in-law and father-in-law and between mother-in-law and daughter-in-law. There is no mention of the avoidance among Athapascans who moved to Oregon, and only faint indications among California Athapascans. Jenness, *The Sarcee Indians of Alberta,* 26; Clark Wissler, *The Social Life of the Blackfoot Indians,* 12–13; E. S. Curtis, *The North American Indian,* XVIII, 41, 74; Goddard, *The Beaver Indians,* 221–22. See the following culture element distributions, in the University of California Anthropological Records: H. E. Barnett, *Oregon Coast;* Verne F. Ray, *Plateau;* H. E. Barnett, *Gulf of Georgia;* Philip Dracker, *Northwest Coast Salish.*

A custom about which we feel more certain is the mysterious rite to tame the supernatural power that is thought to take possession of a maiden at maturity. Ceremonies for this purpose are common among northern Indians and through a great part of the west.[12] The Navajos and Apaches, who have these ceremonies in more elaborate form than most Southwestern Indians, perhaps inherited them from their northern ancestors.[13]

One more item of emotional or intellectual baggage probably brought from the north was a fear of the dead and all their possessions. This fear of magical contamination causes many Navajos, even today, to desert the hut where anyone has died and never to approach it afterward. Here, again, is a trait well known in the north, among Athapascans and other Indians.[14] It has spread down the western coast and through California, but has not penetrated very far into the Southwest. From the importance which the Athapascans give to this belief, it seems likely that it was well entrenched in their tradition before their arrival in the Southwest. Of more important religious ceremonies, for which the Navajos were later so famous, nothing is known. A guess at the spirits in which they believed would suggest birds and animals, appearing in visions, as they did to many northern hunters.[15] In a variety of these visions of northern tribes, these imaginary beings took a human dreamer to visit their village, and this event is a part of later Navajo ceremonies, intertwined with southern elements.

By what route did they travel and when? So far, the state-

---

[12] Harold E. Driver, *Girls Puberty Rites in Western North America,* 23–34; John J. Honigman, *Fort Nelson Slave,* 85; J. Alden Mason, *Notes on the Indians of the Great Slave Lake Area,* 31; Jenness, *Sekani,* 56.

[13] Driver, *Girls Puberty Rites,* 62.

[14] Hill-Tout, *British North America,* 193; Jenness, *Sekani,* 59; Honigman, *Fort Nelson Slave,* 87.

[15] Hill-Tout, *British North America,* 172–76.

ments on this subject are mostly hypotheses, though, any year, some new discovery may bring the whole story to light. If the start was made from British Columbia, a likely route would be along the eastern foothills of the Rockies. Indeed, the Navajos and most Apaches, to this day, have the traditions of mountain people and dislike the lowlands. They did not, of course, travel in a great army. Since they were living off of the country, they had to stay in small bands, so as not to scare the game animals and exhaust the wild plants. Bands may have consisted of only a few families who camped for generations in one place.

Did some of them stray east to visit the buffalo plains? When Coronado, first white explorer of the area, reached Kansas in 1541, he found Indians there "living in skin tents like Arabs."[16] Were these wandering Athapascans Apaches who had strayed farther east than their kinsmen? Buffalo herds, in those early days, roamed not only in Kansas but as far as the foothills of the Rockies in Colorado. Navajo myths say nothing about hunting the bison, which, indeed, was an arduous matter in those horseless days. It meant creeping up on the animals from ambush or collecting a number of men who could fire the grass around them or drive them over a cliff. Perhaps a few Athapascan bands worked out such devices or met other Indians who used them, for surely they did not always travel in isolation. And perhaps they acquired mates who perpetuated the buffalo tradition, marriage being one of the surest ways of engrafting new ideas in a group.

Certain it is that Navajo tradition shows a reverence for the buffalo which savors more of the plains than of the Southwest, where the game animal is the deer. The hero of the Shooting Chant visits a buffalo village to learn magic in true northern fashion. In the Enemy Way, the only Navajo ceremony with-

[16] Herbert E. Bolton, *Coronado, Knight of the Pueblos and Plains,* 246–47.

out Southwestern pageantry, and thought by Berard Haile to be a very old one, the rattle used must be of buffalo scrotum.

Other bands may have found their way through mountain passes into the desert country of Utah and Nevada. The myth of Sontso (Big Star) describes some Navajo ancestors who lived very much like the early Paiutes. ". . . in a cave lived a family consisting of father, mother, daughter and two sons . . . . Their way of hunting was to make traps of their hair to catch birds which they roasted on spits for they had no pots to boil anything . . . . The women wore skirts of woven yucca and the men only G strings." So some Navajo ancestors were Paiutes or Athapascans living like Paiutes.[17]

In spite of these offshoots, there was surely a large number which kept to the foothills and which approached the Southwest by way of Colorado. Scattered through the southern part of this state and of near-by Utah, there are ruins of simple, stone dwellings of the kind the Navajos built later, when they could not get wood. True, various wandering people passed this way, at different dates, so the ruins may be Ute or Comanche. Still, it has been suggested that some rings of stones, whose date is estimated to be about A.D. 1100, may have been left by the People.[18] There are fragments of gray-black pottery too, but whether these, also can be connected with the Athapascans is a question for future solution.[19]

In any case, it should be clear that we cannot think of the Navajos as marching south by any one route. The foraging, camping, and marrying which constituted their journey spread over many kinds of country and involved many contacts. It

[17] Mary C. Wheelwright, *Myth of Sontso,* 1; *Water Chant,* 11.
[18] Betty H. Huscher and Harold A. Huscher, "Athapascan Migration via the Intermontane Region," *American Antiquity,* Vol. VIII, No. 1, July, (1942).
[19] *Ibid.*

probably brought them to the Southwest at different points and with different traditions. In fact, "the Navajos" are a number of distinguishable groups, even today, each specializing in certain traditions, skills, and even dialects. In fact, the next historical study among them should include traditions from the different areas and the hints of travel which they give.

Whatever had been the People's experience, in plains, mountain, or desert, it was due for epoch-making change as they neared the Southwest. Up to that time, as far as we can tell, they knew nothing of planting. They had no idea of the permanent homes, the farming equipment, and the settled organization which come with a stationary food supply. Now a new way of life was to confront them, and, according to their own tradition, it would constitute an act of pure magic. They were nearing the country of the corn growers.

2: The Navajos Arrive

WHEN GROUPS of the Dené, the People, first glimpsed the "food of the strangers" growing in southern Colorado or northern New Mexico, they could have had no understanding of the vast stretch of agricultural country which now lay before them. South of these states, through Mexico, Central America, and far into South America, were scattered villages, towns, and even empires—all made possible by the growth of corn. Thousands of years before the Christian era, the nutritious grain had been developed, perhaps from several wild plants. From tribe to tribe its use had spread, producing new varieties on the way and taking precedence over all other crops. As the Indians were freed from wandering, they took their first steps toward civilization. By A.D. 1100, these steps had resulted in the empires of the Inca, the Toltec, and the Maya. Farther north, some of the civilizations of Arizona and New Mexico were also reaching their apogee. These were the small city-states of the Pueblo Indians, later to be known to the Navajos as victims, teachers, and spouses.[1]

[1] The Spanish word pueblo is spelled with a capital when it indicates tribal groups, but the lower case is used when it simply refers to a village of these Indians.

If any lone-wolf huntsman from the north or any group of wandering families caught a glimpse of the Pueblo village, cornfields, and ceremonies, they must have seemed almost supernatural. Through the northern part of Arizona and New Mexico, into Colorado and Nevada, and down the Río Grande were scattered the villages of stone or clay, sometimes in the form of one or more great, terraced apartment buildings housing some two hundred people. The men tended the near-by fields of corn with its six colors and other crops of beans, squash, sunflowers, and sometimes tobacco and cotton. In the village, the women ground corn into flour on their mealing stones and cooked it in a score of different ways. They made mats and baskets and their famous pottery, smoothly polished and patterned in black and white or black and red. Men and perhaps women, too, wove cotton into garments which might be decorated in paint and some embroidery. In the plaza, at the base of the multistoried houses, there was a constant round of sacred pageants, where masked and kilted men represented the rain-bringing spirits. Navajo sand paintings to this day picture their gods in the kilted Pueblo costume quite unlike the breechclout of the hunter.

There is no evidence of the exact date when the first infiltration of the People may have begun, but it is known that about A.D. 1100 the Pueblo farmers began to concentrate their scattered settlements into larger towns. Does this indicate a fear of prowling strangers with sinew-backed bows? Appearing and disappearing gypsylike, in little groups, they could hardly have seemed very dangerous. Yet they may well have used their skill to steal just what they stole later—corn and women. What other reason could there be for building dwellings halfway up a cliff, like those at Mesa Verde, Colorado? Surely no people would daily carry water and provisions up a ladder for any reason other than protection. Moreover, in the years between A.D. 1100 and

1400, there was movement all along the frontiers of Pueblo country from southern Arizona to Colorado. In spite of very good arguments about climate and internal squabbles, it seems feasible that the village dwellers were huddling together for protection.

Here it may be asked how can one speak so confidently about dates among a people without written history. The information comes from the new science of dendrochronology, or the study of tree rings. Only a short time ago it was realized that the rings of sapwood which a tree adds to its circumference every year serve as an infallible time marker. Conifers give the best result, for rings of certain trees of this species will show what the tree has received in the way of moisture or food during a given year. Conifers of the same kind cut in similar locations give a similar picture. Their inner rings, made when the tree was young, may correspond with the outer rings of older trees. These can be compared with beams from ancient houses and other ruins which are older still. By such means, specialists are able to name the years represented in any section of wood back, with a few gaps, to the beginning of the Christian era.[2]

Along the eastern frontier of Pueblo country had grown up a crude type of settlement, part Pueblo (so the pottery would indicate) and part due to some unknown people perhaps drifting across the southern plains from Texas and Oklahoma. Such settlements came and went, but what interests a student of the Navajos is the group which existed in the Largo and Gallina canyons from A.D. 1106 to 1254. These people had pottery which one might almost mistake for Navajo.[3] Could there, at that early date, have been Athapascans among them, bringing pottery

[2] W. S. Stallings, *Dating Prehistoric Ruins by Tree Rings.*
[3] Frank C. Hibben, "The Pottery of the Gallina Complex," *American Antiquity*, Vol. XIV, No. 3 (January, 1949), 197.

from the north,[4] or did the gray jars come from the east across the plains, to be acquired by the People later?[5] This is one of the most obscure points of Navajo history and an intriguing puzzle to archaeologists.

Whoever were the dwellers in these outlying settlements, they lived in fear of enemies. Their small, separate dwellings stood on the edge of cliffs, and generally, in the most prominent spot, there was a stone tower some twenty feet high, with double walls and a roof, which might have been used as a firing platform. They apparently needed such defense, for around the year 1254, the settlements were destroyed. In Gallina Canyon all the houses studied had been burned and, in some, skeletons lay on the floor with arrowpoints among the bones, as though the defenders had made a desperate last stand.[6] After that, the villages were deserted. Can the Dené be suspected? It is easy to imagine them infiltrating for a century or so, trading and raiding until, by 1254, they were strong enough for an attack. There are female skeletons in the ruins as well as male, yet the attackers may well have followed the usual custom of taking some women prisoners and finally marrying them. The People, then, would have a group of ready-made pottery makers and teachers of agriculture, too.

This is, of course, a theory which, as of now, does not have factual evidence to support it. Yet the area of these frontier settlements would be on the direct route of people traveling south along the eastern foothills or the Rockies. What is needed is factual proof that among the earliest arrivals along this route

[4] E. T. Hall, Jr., "Recent Clues to Athapascan Prehistory in the Southwest," *American Anthropologist,* Vol. XLVI, No. 1 (January–March, 1944), 103–105.
[5] H. P. Mera, *Ceramic Clues to the Prehistory of North Central New Mexico,* 35.
[6] E. T. Hall, Jr., *Early Stockaded Settlements in the Governador, New Mexico,* 102.

were some groups who would later be Navajos. If they were in the Southwest in the twelfth century, and if they settled down with wives bred in the farming tradition, then the Apaches, arriving later, found the area occupied or else passed it and continued to the southern mountains where they were found later. This would help explain why the Navajos have so many arts and ceremonies unknown to their wilder brethren.

The first proven sign of the Navajo is wood from a hut found in Gobernador Canyon, forty miles north of Gallina, where the settlements were destroyed, and dating about 1541.[7] This is the year Coronado came through the Southwest with his brass-helmeted *Conquistadores*. Coronado's scribes say nothing about the presence of any wandering hunters. Still, they did not penetrate the broken ravines and forested hills of north-central New Mexico. Today, this is the Jicarilla Apache reservation, but the People still speak of it as Dinetah, Old Navajoland, and are even willing to state their rights before a United States Claims Commission. Perhaps, indeed, there are hogan ruins scattered along the cliffs and among the junipers and dating earlier than 1541. Many old, white residents believe that this is so and that archaeology will some day confirm it. Navajos are sure that some old myths, dealing with mountainous, deer-hunting country and with a great river, allude to this area and to the San Juan River which here loops down from Colorado to form its northern boundary

Historians have learned to distrust such poetic myths which often turn the centuries upside down or lump the events of a few hundred years in one dramatic scene. Still, they have to admit that the myth has often grown, like a pearl, around a core of fact. Why should all the Navajo ceremonialists tell the same general story, even though each may have his own names

[7] *Ibid.*, 102.

for the clans and places? The Navajo saga, like our books of Genesis and Exodus, always present two main facts. Some of the Navajos were created in the old Navajo country of New Mexico; others were created beside the "western sea" and came east.[8]

"Created" is the word. Never speak to a Navajo about "coming" from the north, for he will be both surprised and insulted. His ancestors were brought into being by the gods themselves, and these gods came out of the earth in Old Navajoland. He can draw you pictures of them, dressed like a Pueblo dancer in mask and cotton kilt. There are long tales of what happened underground, before the first beings climbed out of the earth near Silverton, Colorado, or about there. Since the Navajos moved away from the old country, their memory of sacred places grows dim. Along with the masked gods came the animals, man's older and wiser brothers who, in those days, had the form of men. There was also a couple of supernatural beings, called First Man and First Woman. Among them all, these beings ordered the world and set up the boundaries of Navajoland.

Wanting their new home to look just like the world below, they had brought some earth from the subterranean mountains. This they placed in four piles at the four points of the compass: north, east, south and west, for that is the order in which both Navajos and Pueblos mention the directions. Thus they made the four sacred mountains which bound Navajoland today. Would that Navajos were certain which mountains these are. Most agree that Debentsa, Big Sheep, in the La Plata Range of Colorado, is the northern mountain, once crowned with jet and a black feather. The eastern mountain "with a black horizontal streak" was crowned with white shell, and it may be anywhere from Blanca Peak in Colorado to Pelado in the Jemez Range of

[8] Washington Matthews, *Navajo Legends*, 135–60.

New Mexico. The southern mountain, which objected to its turquoise and its blue feather, is Mount Taylor, or San Mateo, near Grants, New Mexico. It can be identified because, in a bad temper, it produced volcanic splits around its base. The western mountain is San Francisco Peaks, at the western side of Arizona. That makes Dinetah, or Navajoland, take in the greater part of two states, with the western mountain far out of sight of the other three. But the Navajos have plenty of tales about their wanderings over all that country.

The myth abounds with details which would be valuable history if they could be interpreted correctly. Even the most miraculous events are placed on some hilltop or in some canyon which the Navajo can point out. They know the flat-topped mesa on which Ever Changing Woman, who represents Nature, was found wrapped in many-colored light. They know every locality where the evil monsters, which came to infest the land, were killed off by Nature's war-god sons. After these things had happened, the animals took their animal forms and the gods made ready to leave the earth. Only then were the Navajos created. Here the tale branches out in any number of versions, each told by a Navajo clan. Each clan, according to the tale, was a little group who entered Navajoland in some special, dramatic way.

The first clan was created on the spot. This was the *Kiya-ani,* or Tall House People, who lived in a pueblo and raised corn. The Navajos can point out Kinya'a today, a ruined pueblo of the Chaco group, dating 1097–1106.[9] Some say the first clanspeople were brother and sister created by the gods out of ears of corn found in this very pueblo. Spouses were found for them among the gods, those masked and kilted figures who looked like Pueblo dancers, and this became the foremost agricultural

[9] H. S. Gladwin, *Chaco Branch,* 101, 128.

clan. There is an excellent metaphorical picture of two Navajos marrying two Pueblo people, though the dates would cause trouble if taken seriously.

After this miraculous beginning, the tale slips quietly into history, as did an old Navajo when he was telling me the story. Having finished the killing of the monsters, he went on in the same tone of voice: "And later, the White People were having a war across the sea, and they told our young men to go." Truly, the recent world war was no less magical and strange to a Navajo than the war against the monsters.

The Tall House People were joined by various travelers: the Turn-in-a-Canyon People, the Yucca People, who perhaps had been living on yucca fruit in the mountains, and then by others, including a group from near Santa Fé and one from near Zuñi Pueblo.[10] About the arrival of each, there is a circumstantial story which bears the marks of experience. Perhaps the dates are mistaken and misplaced, but it seems more than likely that small bands of Athapascans came wandering in from the canyons or the yucca mountains to join the first arrivals— and the Pueblo people, too. The very physical characteristics of the Navajos, some tall and rangy, some small and plump, indicate a varied ancestry. The story tells how the combined groups moved to the Chaco and then to the San Juan River, still in Old Navajoland. There they were joined by some Utes, Yumans, Mexicans, Apaches, and migrants from three or four pueblos. Washington Matthews carefully recorded the narrative some fifty years ago, and years later Miss Mary C. Wheelwright heard much the same account from a different myth teller.[11] Frederic Webb Hodge carefully examined the dates and determined the

---

[10] Frederic A. Hodge, "The Early Navajo and Apache," *American Anthropologist*, Vol. VIII, No. 3 (July, 1895), 223.

[11] Matthews, *Navajo Legends*.

beginning to be 1485, some fifty years before the first tree ring appears.[12] So perhaps the tale has elements of truth.

The last chapter of the story is one which contains suggestions that the Athapascans came by a western route, for it relates that certain Navajos were "created" in the west and then travelled east to meet their brethren. When the gods left the earth, according to the tale, after the killing of the monsters, Changing Woman was assigned to a home in the West. Here she was to receive the Sun at his setting in a turquoise house floating on the western sea. She was lonely and hated to go, even though her younger son coaxed her, as is told in the Shooting Chant.

"It is very beautifully fixed for you, mother . . . . Are we telling you of clothes made of weeds, or food from seeds of shrubs, or of rabbits and rats for your subsistence?"[13] (This evidently was the usual livelihood of the Navajo in those days.) Instead, Changing Woman was to be clothed in white shell and fed on flower pollen. The poor goddess consented at last, but she was still lonely. So she made people. Rubbing the skin from her breast, her back, and under both arms, she created four clans. Every Navajo knows about these four, or perhaps five, primeval groups, but their names vary according to the informant, for, of course, his own clan must be among them. So they may be any four among the clans called Great Water, Bitter Water, Near Water, Mud, Salt, Folded Arms, or even Tall House.

The tale says that these people, having lived a long time by the western sea, heard about others of their own speech in the east. So they decided to join them. There is a circumstantial story of how they travelled over the desert, tapping it for water with the wands given them by Changing Woman. The clans

[12] Hodge, "The Early Navajo and Apache," *American Anthropologist,* Vol. VIII, No. 3 (July, 1895), 223–40.
[13] Gladys A. Reichard, Story of the Male Shooting Chant, unpublished.

received their names according to the kind of water they brought forth. At last they came to mountains which, the Navajos insist, were the San Francisco Peaks, in Arizona. Near here, they entered a magnificent house and found quivers of arrows hanging on the wall. The arrows turned themselves into people who first entertained and then fought them. Pueblo people? From here on, the story gives full details of the journey past the Hopi mesas, down toward Crown Point, New Mexico, and then up through Old Navajoland to the San Juan. That is a route which a western party might take, fighting the Pueblos on the way and making a long loop south to avoid the mountain ranges. We wait eagerly to have archaeology discover if this route contains any Navajo camps and tools.

From these hints of myth and fact, it is possible to realize the hardy mixture comprising the Navajo tribe—huntsmen from the north, used to privation and fighting; civilized Pueblo farmers, trained to industry; wild warlike Utes; and wanderers from the western desert, skilled in basket making and the finding of food! Every way of life was represented among them, every physical form and every mental attitude. It is no wonder that such people were open to new suggestions and had the energy to try everything. Here was no settled group of conservatives moving along the same channels for centuries. Considering this background, it is not surprising that the Navajos, within the next few hundred years, remade their way of life not only once but twice. They found new ways to support themselves and evolved a new mythology, with pageantry as magnificent as any known to Indians. And the Navajos are still changing.

3: Between the Four Mountains

"THEY STARTED to walking from there toward the west to Hole in the Ground. They kept walking to Swallow's Nest ... then to House under the Rock Spreads Out. Then to Mistletoe Hangs. Then Dead Tree Stands Up. Then to Possessing Fish. Then to Red House. Then to Lake with Weeds on Surface...."[1] Thus Navajo myth sings of the wanderings of one pair of the People as they moved about the country between the four sacred mountains. This means most of New Mexico and Arizona; and as one hears the litanies of place names, one can well believe that the bands or families entering the corn country did "Walk over every stone in it before they settled down."

No one, now, can identify the points so poetically described. Archaeology has found no sure trace of the Navajos except the problematical pots mentioned in the last chapter and the one ruin dating back to 1541. If the People arrived earlier, from various directions, then the chief authority is myth. It is granted that Navajo myths tell mostly of adventures among gods and spirits; nevertheless, before the supernatural panorama begins, there is often a moment of realism.

[1] Clyde Kluckhohn, *Navajo Witchcraft*, 98.

24

Here, for instance, is the picture of a band coming from the west.[2] They passed San Francisco Peaks and came to Gray Mountain, where they found many kinds of wild berries, such as chokecherry, wild grape, and wild plum. Later they came to Navajo Mountain and stayed for four years, living on berries and the seeds of sage and other plants. After hunting to the north for deer and mountain sheep, they went to Denehotso, where they found antelope and drove them into traps in a canyon. They cleaned the skins and made clothing for themselves. "So there was much hair and wool accumulated in that place, and they named it *Arachla*," from wool or wooly. In talking to me, an old Navajo applied that very term to Monument Valley, the wild rocky stretch at the north of present Navajo country.

The band was lucky to find antelope and get skin clothing, for other myths indicate that the wanderers dressed in the standard desert materials—shredded cedar bark or strips pounded from the long, swordlike leaves of the yucca. This was the costume of Indians in Nevada and California. For women, it meant two fringed aprons, a shorter one in front, halfway to the knee, and a longer one behind. Men wore a G string of plaited fibers, or they went without. For warmth, both men and women might wear a dressed deer or antelope skin tied over the shoulders by the forelegs.

Perhaps it was these western immigrants who brought in the art of basketry, a speciality of the seed gatherers throughout Nevada and California. They had the Paiute style of canteen, coiled of willow withes and made watertight by smearing with piñon gum. Such water bottles are still made at Dinehotso in the western Navajo country and by the Apaches. Too, some Navajos made a special kind of basket-bowl, every step of its manufacture

[2] Mary C. Wheelwright, Bead Chant, unpublished.

being surrounded with ceremony and taboo.[3] Experts say that this Navajo basket is the only one still coiled and sewed in the exact manner of the ancient Basket Makers, dwellers in Nevada and around the Four Corners in 1 A.D. No one knows how long some Navajos camped in that western country before entering the land of the corn growers.

The people coming down through the mountains of Colorado had an easier time. Their stories tell of hunting mountain sheep, deer, rabbits, rats, squirrels, and antelope. The hero of Flintway, a chant translated by Father Berard, "never killed game wantonly but always made his choice among the deer he found."[4] He had his own hunting range and knew that if he trespassed on the range of anyone else, he might be killed. This may indicate an established hunting life of long standing, and, if this is so, it is strange that the Navajos cared to give it up. Doubtless the answer is the Utes, who were pressing close behind them. These hunters entered New Mexico clad quite differently from the desert wanderers. The young man of Gladys A. Reichard's Hail Chant wore deerskin shirt and leggings and even had moccasins, a novelty among the sandal-wearing Pueblos.

There were poor and shiftless people among the wanderers as well as good hunters. The family in the Big Star Chant recorded by Miss Wheelwright had nothing to eat but birds, snared in nooses made of their own hair, and they roasted them on spits since they had no cooking pots. The hero of the Hail Chant ran away from his family and deep into Pueblo country. Keeping away from the settlements, he lived on wild raspberries, rose pips, rabbits, and birds. "Pulling cattails, he chewed their

[3] Harry Tschopik, Jr., "Navajo Basketry," *American Anthropologist*, Vol. XLII, No. 3 (July–September, 1940); *Navajo Pottery Making, Papers*, Peabody Museum (1941).

[4] Berard Haile, *Origin Legend of the Navajo Flintway*, 57.

roots and ate their pollen."[5] The youth in Prostitution Way wandered about with his grandmother, never making camp but sleeping on the ground without pots or blankets. He killed rats and rabbits, and his grandmother worked for the Pueblo people.[6]

The tale of this hunter, a Don Juan of magical power, contains one incident which may reflect the pattern of some early courtships between the hunters and the village dwellers. The hero desired as wives two girls from the Hopi pueblo of Walpi in Arizona, known by the name of Light Can't Get To Them.[7] We can imagine how people living in the terraced stone dwellings, whose lower rooms were dark, must have impressed the outdoor Navajos. To pay for his wives, the youth first killed twelve then fourteen, then thirty, and then fifty antelope which he presented to their father. Reduce these magical figures to an antelope a day, or even just one antelope, and you may see the method used by the wild hunter in courting the secluded village maiden.

Here we are getting close to the contact which resulted in their learning to grow corn, although no Navajo will admit that the learning came by human means. The tale sketched in the last chapter tells how the clan usually known as Tall House was created from grains of corn. The first two beings were a brother and sister for whom the gods found spouses among themselves. This statement can easily be translated to read: A Navajo brother and sister married two Pueblo people. In fact, a Navajo once told me that the Tall House clan once lived in perpendicular stone houses like the Pueblos. Then there is the story of a hero who floated down the San Juan River, came to a good planting place, and had corn, bean, and squash seeds shaken out for him

[5] Gladys A. Reichard, *The Story of the Navajo Hail Chant*, 5.
[6] Kluckhohn, *Navajo Witchcraft*, 96.
[7] *Ibid.*, 101.

from the wings of a turkey. The gods, again dressed in Pueblo costume, came to show him how to plant and to harvest.[8]

Closest to fact, perhaps, is the story of a young hunter who came to a lake covered with ice, with a ladder descending into it.[9] Magically helped by the wind, he climbed down this ladder and saw fields of colored corn in the four directions: white in the East, blue in the South, yellow in the West, and black in the North. Behind the corn fields were great houses, in the same colors. Their inhabitants had the form of human beings but were really coyotes. He stayed at each house in turn, and in each he was given two beautiful maidens to wife and four ears of the colored corn. Also, he was taught hunting ceremonies. Finally, complete ceremonies were given for him, so that he qualified as a singer himself. Then he went back to his people, taking samples of the colored corn which he gave them for planting. He himself returned to his coyote wives.

This might well be a myth-covered slice of history telling how one particular hunter visited a pueblo and brought back corn for his people. The myth says he also learned the ceremonies which would make the corn grow, and this we can well believe. No ancient Indians raised corn without ceremony, and most students think that the songs which fostered the magical grain were passed from tribe to tribe along with the grain itself. Of course, they changed as they passed through the imagination of each new people. So the Navajos may have composed their own, in imitation of their Pueblo neighbors as they sang the planting song:

> *I wish to put in,*
> *In the middle of the wide field,*

[8] Washington Matthews, *The Night Chant,* 187.
[9] Mary C. Wheelwright, Coyote Myth, unpublished.

> *I wish to put in*
> *White corn (or yellow, or other color) . . .*
> *I wish to put in.*
> *Good and everlasting one*
> *I wish to put in.*

Or the growth song:

> *It increases and spreads . . . .*
> *In the middle of the wide field . . . .*
> *The white corn, it increases and spreads*
> *Good and everlasting one, it increases and spreads.*[10]

In the sandy bottoms of Gobernador and other canyons leading north to the San Juan River, there was room for small corn fields and later for other crops. In 1541, there was at least one Navajo hut here. The next dated one is a hundred years later, 1656, plus or minus twenty years, which is as near as the tree ring date can come.[11] Surely neither of these dwellings stood alone. There is reason to believe that during the late sixteenth and early seventeenth centuries the farming settlements in Old Navajoland were "increasing and spreading" like their corn. They must have been in touch with Pueblo people by this time and not merely the frontier dwellers of Gallina, whom the Navajos themselves may have driven out. In the sixteenth and seventeenth centuries they were within reach of the historic pueblos and probably had already begun that relationship of trading and fighting which lasted for some four centuries.

Their nearest neighbor was the Pueblo of Jemez, some

[10] W. W. Hill, *The Agricultural and Hunting Methods of the Navajo Indians,* 69.

[11] Dorothy Keur, "A Chapter in Navaho-Pueblo Relations," *American Antiquity,* Vol. X, No. 1, (July, 1944), 84.

twenty-five leagues (roughly sixty-two miles) to the south over bare and waterless country—so said the later Spanish accounts.[12] Since the Navajos had plenty of deer in their country, and since the pueblos had long since used up the game near their habitations, the Navajo hunters probably traveled those sixty miles carrying buckskins or even dried venison for trade. They did not trust the villagers, nor the villagers them. Myth tells of a boy camping near Mount Taylor who was hired by the Jemez to climb a cliff and bring down some eaglets. They promised him jewels, but their intention was to leave him on the cliff to die. Of course the Navajo succeeded in fooling them, dancing into the sky with all their jewels, while the eaglets remained safe.[13]

To the east, across hilly and wooded country, was the important pueblo of Taos, later a trading center for Navajos, Apaches, Comanches, and the village Indians. Early relations with Taos must often have been warlike, for the Navajo Enemy Way, perhaps one of the earliest of the chants evolved in the Southwest, is based on a raid of that pueblo.[14] Omitting the magical elements with which the story bristles, one can see in this legend a faint reflection of Navajo war methods in these early days.

Somewhere across the valley, a short distance above "rock ledge extension," a certain family lived, they say. A man of the Corn People married into this family, and he and his father-in-law decided to make a raid. Said the father-in-law, "Let us go to war somewhere . . . . Let it be Taos," the man decided. After three days, the two men arrived at Taos and lay in ambush at

[12] W. W. Hill, "Some Navajo Culture Changes During Two Centuries," *Smithsonian Miscellaneous Collections,* Vol. C, (1940), 402.

[13] W. W. Hill, "The Legend of the Navajo Eagle Catching Way," *New Mexico Anthropologist,* Vols. VI, VII (1944).

[14] Berard Haile, *Origin Legend of the Navajo Enemy Way,* 141, 145, 153, 163.

the watering place of the house-dwellers. At dawn a certain boy that came for water was grabbed and taken home as a prisoner. They made two more raids, capturing first a girl and then another boy. This hardly satisfied the son-in-law, who was anxious to excel over the older man. He ranted: "Should we always return with only a single enemy? This time everything such as their soft goods (skin and blankets), their jewels, their food, the able-bodied young men and able-bodied maidens, all these should be brought back here. So the man summoned all his clansmen, the Corn People, for a full-sized raid. This time, however, the Taos people managed to encircle the Navajos on a rocky point. "Right where they had encircled them, they began to slay them. A rock point extended out this way from there, with no passage down from it. To this, it seems, they headed and cornered them, while they continued to slay them. There was no hope. The sun set before they finished the slaughter . . . . Not one of them survived."[15]

Of course the tale ends with revenge by the Navajos, who arranged a mass attack under the leadership of their war god himself. Four times they camped and sang songs mentioning "enemies that shall die, of the coyote that shall eat them, of the crow that shall eat them, of the magpie that shall eat their flesh . . . of the wolves that shall eat their flesh and carry away every part of them."[16] This time they reached the pueblo, from which the people began to flee "in a black streak." Then some men ran into the entrances and went along slaying them, some began killing inside below the houses, others in the house terraces, and others along the housetops . . . . Scalp taking continued until all, without exception, were taken.[17]

[15] *Ibid.*, 141–45.
[16] *Ibid.*, 153.
[17] *Ibid.*, 163, 165.

Surely, such raids and counterraids must really have taken place. This account may even be based on a raid that took place as late as the seventeenth century. For we are now approaching the date when the Navajos step out of myth and into history. As early as the 1600's, so later accounts inform us, they were an established people and had achieved a name. Their Pueblo neighbors, the Tewa of the Río Grande, spoke of them as Strangers of the Cultivated Fields, *Apaches de Nabahu*. Even their roving Apache kin called them the Cultivators.[18] So the Spaniards heard, and so they finally launched the name into history. For while the Navajos planted their corn and hunted the deer in their remote canyons, an event had occurred which would change all Indian life in New Mexico.

The Spaniards had come to stay.

[18] Information on both these points comes from Mr. John Harrington of the Bureau of American Ethnology.

Monument Valley, Arizona. This area may have been the scene of the great antelope hunt mentioned in Navajo mythology.
(Courtesy American Museum of Natural History)

San Francisco peaks, the Navajos' sacred mountain of the West.
(Photograph by Milton Snow, Courtesy U. S. Indian Service)

Old-fashioned Navajo hogan in Canyon de Chelley.
(Courtesy American Museum of Natural History)

A forked-stick hogan, the type of dwelling used by the earliest Navajos.
(Photograph by Milton Snow, Courtesy U. S. Indian Service)

4: Second Beginning

SHEEP AND HORSES

NEVER ASK A Navajo how his tribe obtained the sheep and horses which for centuries have furnished the bases of their life. That is, not if you want a factual answer. It is nothing to him that history recounts how the Spaniards rode into the Río Grande Valley with their silver bridle ornaments jingling and how their herds and their ox carts followed. Tell him that up to that time no Indian had owned a horse, and he will answer firmly: "If there were no horses, there were no Navajos."

He is right. The Navajos, as we know them, did not exist until the Spaniards arrived with the animals which were to make them rich. To be accurate, the People were not established as sheepherders and horsemen until almost a century after that. Still, the coming of the white men and their animals was the beginning.

It happened in July, 1598. Don Juan de Oñate, future governor and captain general of the colony of New Mexico, rode up from Zacatecas in Mexico with 130 bearded and armored soldiers,[1] while priests, families, and retainers increased the num-

[1] George P. Hammond, *Don Juan de Oñate and the Founding of New Mexico,* 187–200.

ber to 400.[2] Pueblo people along the way fled and had to be coaxed out of hiding. Not only the beards and the armor of the mounted men appalled them; but even more amazing were the 62 lumbering oxcarts and the herd of 7,000 tame animals, including 1,000 head of cattle, 3,000 sheep for wool, 1,000 for mutton, 1,000 goats, 100 black cattle, 150 colts, and 150 mares.[3]

Up to this time, most Indians throughout the Americas had had no domestic animals but their half-starved, half-wild dogs. Once there had been wild horses in the land, and perhaps the first Indians to arrive, thousands of years before the Christian era, had used them for food. They had died out or migrated long before any native tribe learned to domesticate and train animals. So no Indian had ever ridden a horse. Their enormous journeys over two continents had been performed laboriously on foot with women or, later, dogs as the burden bearers. As for sheep and cattle, the only native creatures of that sort were the mountain sheep and the bison, which no one has ever tamed. Perhaps some half century ago, the fathers of Southwest Indians had looked on Coronado's horses and his few straggling sheep with as much amazement as their sons were showing now. Those animals had passed like a mirage, the horses dying or being ridden south again[4] and the sheep, reduced to a handful, eaten.[5] It was Oñate's cavalcade which introduced the horse and sheep to the American West.

[2] Herbert E. Bolton, *Spanish Explorations in the Southwest, 1542–1706,* 202.

[3] George P. Hammond and Agapito Rey, *Gallegos Relation of the Rodriguez Expedition to New Mexico,* 19.

[4] Francis Haines, "The Northward Spread of Horses Among the Plains Indians," *American Anthropologist,* Vol. XL, No. 3 (July–September, 1938), 429.

[5] Most of Coronado's sheep were lost while crossing the mountains. According to Winifred Kupper (*The Golden Hoof*) four ewes and twenty-eight lambs were left with the priest at Tiguex on the Río Grande. Their fate is unknown.

The colonists meant to set up ranches after the Spanish manner, and indeed the dry, brilliant uplands of the Southwest were so like those of Spain that neither animals nor men were likely to feel much difference. First, however, the country must be subdued and the Indians started on their way to Christianity and civilization. Oñate's contract made him Governor and Captain General of New Mexico, an indefinite stretch of country extending west to the Pacific and east and north as far as he could make it. He was authorized by the king of Spain to distribute land among his colonists, to accept the submission of the Indians, and to see that, for the good of their souls, they rendered homage to both the king of Spain and the Christian God. Most of the Pueblos did. Of Acoma, which did not, Oñate made short and bloody work. He had no knowledge of the distant Navajos, who were, officially, also under his domain. By 1610 or thereabouts, a capital had been established at Santa Fé; great stretches of land around the pueblos had been doled out in ranches; and in many of the villages themselves there were priests and churches. The Pueblo Indians were a subject people.

So far the Navajos in their remote canyons had been untouched and perhaps even unheard of. Undoubtedly the desert gossip had brought them news of the new happenings as monstrous as anything in myth. Probably their scouts had prowled to the Río Grande Valley and watched from behind rocks as some mounted conqueror rode by; or, perhaps, they had mingled, unrecognized, among the Pueblo residents as a brown-robed friar mustered his workers to build a primitive, mud-brick church within the very pueblo. However, their Pueblo neighbors, now known as the "Christian" Indians, had reported on them.

It was 1626 before Father Zarate-Salmeron, in a report to Spain, mentioned the mysterious Apache Indians of Nabaho who lived somewhere in the hinterland.[6] In 1630, Fray Alonso de Benavides, also writing to Spain, distinguished these special Apaches from the wilder ones, who lived farther away. Those others, said Fray Alonso, never planted but lived by the chase, whereas the Apaches of Navajo "are very great farmers," for that is what Navajo signifies—"great planted fields."[7] Thus was the tribe launched into history by its official Spanish name: *Navajo*. There is some argument about the spelling of the name today. The letter *j,* in Spanish, has the sound of *h,* and the good brother wrote the word as he heard it.

Fray Alonso's more detailed descriptions of the Navajos sound very much in character. There is flint in their mountains, he says, and the Christian Indians greatly desire it.[8] They make expeditions to get the stone, but the Navajos, two or three thousand strong, come out to fight them, and there is much killing. So the "Christian" Indians wait until the Navajos have gone on a mass hunt, then sneak into the mountains. The Navajos, however, soon hear about this and come in force (30,000, says the friar!) to attack the villages. Their weapon is the bow and arrow, with which they also fight the other Apaches and the Spaniards.[9] All this sounds familiar. So does the statement that these strange Nabahu, Nabaho, or Navajos live underground. The earth-covered huts of the People have looked to many whites like tunnels bored in hills.

Finally a Navajo chief and his followers really visited Santa Clara, the Río Grande pueblo which was the taking-off place for their western wilderness.[10] Listening excitedly to accounts

---

[6] Charles A. Amsden, *Navajo Weaving,* 127.

[7] Fray Alonso de Benavides, *The Memorial of Fray Alonso de Benavides,* 44, 267, notes.

[8] *Ibid.,* 60.

[9] *Ibid.,* 59, 60.

[10] *Ibid.,* 49.

of the supreme God and of the Holy Mass, they wanted to be Christians, so they said. Many Indians have said the same on first hearing of the white man's splendid Great Spirit. The amount of service He requires, though, usually proves discouraging. The chief did not come to Santa Clara again, even though a mission for the Navajos was hopefully established up there. The People had retired to their ravines and cornfields, out of the Spaniards' way. Yet they knew of the new ways which their Pueblo neighbors learned.

The Spanish domination was not a total loss. True, the villagers had to pay tribute of cloth and produce, did day labor at a fixed price, and were expected to give up their native dances and attend the Christian church. Still, the church had schools to instruct them in the civilized arts, which were to enter deeply into the life of both Pueblos and Navajos. The Spaniards had brought such crops as wheat and watermelons from Spain and chili and indigo from Mexico, and they showed how wheaten bread could be cooked in round, earthen ovens. Both Pueblos and Navajos make such ovens to this day, and no one knows when they learned.

The Pueblo Indians were not allowed to have horses, since this would make them too independent, but they were sometimes given sheep. What a delight in a land where the deer were killed off and the meat food was mostly rabbit! They learned to shear the wool and to dye it with indigo brought from Mexico. Then they spun and wove it like their own cotton. Soon the men were wearing woolen breech cloths and the women a wraparound blanket dress. So excellent were these little dark woolen blankets that the Spaniards began to trade them to Mexico and even set taxes and prices in *mantas* instead of money.

The Navajos, at this time, were not interested in weaving— at least, there is no record of it. Yet they must have watched the flocks of black and white sheep pouring up and down the mesas as they were driven from summer to winter pasture. The sheep which the conquerors had brought was not the lordly *merino,* whose use was reserved for royalty. They were the *churro,* the common sheep of Spain, scrawny, long-legged, and needing little care, but with long straight wool which was almost grease-less and could be woven without washing.[11] Such sheep had grazed on the uplands of Spain perhaps from Neolithic times.[12] They had been driven back and forth to winter and summer pasture until the country was crisscrossed with broad sheep roads where no one was allowed to plant.[13] The Spanish colonists, on their county-sized ranches, soon began to practice the same kind of "transhumance," and when the Navajos got sheep, this was the method they used. When did that event happen? No word of Navajo legend tells us. The myths always soar into poetry when they reach sheep and horses—those gifts of the gods.

The gods, of course, had had the animals from the beginning of time. When they arranged the world and planned the pattern of the stars in the sky, they first laid the glittering objects out on a sheepskin. The Sun, father of the war gods, possessed a flock of sheep in four colors. The beautiful and human myth of the Shooting Chant tells how he offered these to his twin children when they had sought and found him.

> *Well, what did you come for, the white sheep, perhaps?*
> *No. Not the white sheep.*
> *The black sheep? No.*
> *The spotted sheep? No.*
> *The red sheep? Not the red sheep.*
> *The sheep with the thin bladed horns?*
> *That was the sheep he cherished above all.*[14]

11 Winifred Kupper, *The Golden Hoof,* 19–21.

It may have been a relief to the Sun that the twin war gods asked an even loftier boon, for obviously he had the sheep ready for the People as soon as they were created.

In fact, the sun and moon are nothing but immortal beings on horseback carrying bright shields on their arms. There are many stories of how the gods made the gift to men, and one of the most beautiful was recorded by Edward Sapir.[15] It tells how Monster Slayer, the elder of the twin war gods, went looking for this necessary part of man's equipment before there were men on earth. On each of the four holy mountains he inquired, and at each he was told: Had you asked for soft goods (skins and blankets), we could have given them. Had you asked for hard goods (beads and jewelry), we could have given them. But this which you seek is not here.

Finally, Monster Slayer met Mirage Man who took him to his home, from which four doors opened in the four directions. Looking through the door at the east, the war god saw illimitable pastures filled with prancing horses, made from the sacred white shell. White butterflies flew over their heads and a beneficent, mistlike rain was falling. Through the south door, he saw horses of turquoise, with blue jays flying above them and a rainbow above. Through the west door, he saw horses of abalone; and through the north, horses of jet. He gathered the jewels of the different colors and, when he returned to earth, created horses from these, with song and ceremony.

So the Navajos say. It is rather certain that they had seen horses while they lurked in their northern canyons and while the Spaniards rode in lordly state up and down the Río Grande

[12] Hilzheimer, "Sheep," *Antiquity,* Vol. X, No. 38 (June, 1936). Julius Klein, *The Mesta,* 7, 7n.

[13] Klein, *The Mesta,* 18–20.

[14] Reichard, Story of the Male Shooting Chant, unpublished.

[15] Edward Sapir and Harry Hoijer, *Navaho Texts,* 108–126.

Valley. Perhaps they had even stolen a few, and surely they must have managed some sheep. Still, there could not have been many, even of these. (A later Spanish account speaks of 150 sheep among 4000 people.)[16] The miracles had happened. The Navajos had been dazzled by them. But the new animals, gifts of the gods, had not yet been made part of their life. Another happening was needed to set the train of events going, and that occurred in 1680.

The Pueblos revolted.

[16] W. W. Hill, "Some Navajo Culture Changes During Two Centuries," *Smithsonian Miscellaneous Collections,* Vol. C (1940), 405, 407.

5: Learning by Marriage

FOR ONCE IN their history, the Pueblos all joined together to fight. For eighty years, they —at least the ones along the Río Grande—had taken Spanish orders, worked like mill hands to supply the caravans going to Mexico, and been whipped and hanged for continuing the cult of their gods who, to the Spaniards, were no more than devils. Now they wanted to be let alone, free from priests, taxes, and everything belonging to the conquerors. The Apaches helped them. Up to now, these bandits had been raiding the Pueblos, but were willing to change policy when they saw a chance of better loot. It may well have been their presence which made destruction so complete, with ranches plundered and churches desecrated. In the revolt of 1680, some four hundred Spaniards were killed, including women, children, and priests. The rest finally marched down the Río Grande to the Ford, across from where El Paso, Texas now is. There they stayed for twelve years, writing reports to Spain and trying to keep alive.

The Navajos, so most authorities say, took no part in the fight, but hovered on the outskirts, catching the stock which ran away and receiving the refugees. They had always contended that war brings rain and blessing. "Because of it, flowers which have become beautiful exist, they say. Because of it rain exists, they say."[1] Now this war, which was none of theirs, was making them rich and powerful; and before a century had passed, the dominant group in New Mexico would be not the Pueblos but the Navajos.

The Pueblos got very little satisfaction out of their victory. First their crops failed—a sure sign of displeasure from the spirits. Then the faraway Spaniards began making overtures of peace, and village after village succumbed. In 1692, the Spaniards themselves marched back, armed to the teeth and prepared to crush all opposition. They found the more rebellious villages empty, their inhabitants camped on mesa tops. There they prepared to stand siege, without crops and sometimes without water supply. Their stand was heroic but hopeless, for village by village the rebels were starved out. De Vargas, the new governor, announced that all persons captured while fighting against the crown should be sold into slavery in the West Indies, and he made good his threat to the tune of about six hundred people. No wonder the Pueblos were terrified. They were willing to give up their homes, their language, and their village allegiance, and to save their lives and their children, many became Navajos.[2]

The Navajo tribe may have doubled or even tripled at this time, though there is no exact way of estimating its size. Many families, clans, and even villages of Pueblos spent years with the Navajos and at last returned, laden with Navajo ideas and Navajo blood. Others remained permanently, and their members married among the Navajos. Jemez Pueblo revolted in 1696, and history says that practically all its people went to live with the Navajos who had long been their neighbors.[3] According to the

[1] Sapir and Hoijer, *Navaho Texts*, 341.

[2] Ralph E. Twitchell, *The Leading Facts of New Mexican History*, I, 399.

[3] L. B. Bloom and L. B. Mitchell, "The Chapter Elections of 1672," *New Mexico Historical Review*, Vol. XIII, No. 1 (January, 1938), 107.

Navajo tale, the Jemez people merely sent them all their un-
married maidens, with the request: "Do you find husbands for
our girls so that if our pueblo is destroyed the Jemez blood will
be preserved." The accomplished and urbanized maidens did
indeed find mates. After the Navajo custom, by which descent
goes down through women, they were made the founders of a
clan called the Coyote Pass, or Jemez clan. This clan, even today,
according to the Indians, is known for its skill in agriculture
rather than in the Navajo specialty of sheepherding.

Other villages have similar tales. Did one doubt that inter-
mixture of Pueblo and Navajo stocks has taken place on a large
scale, he has but to note the extreme differences in physical type
among today's Navajos, who vary from the tall rangy build suggestive of the plains or the north to the neat, plump figure with
small hands and feet so familiar among the Pueblos. Indeed,
Ales Hrdlicka, famous physical anthropologist, has stated that
the Navajos today "are much more closely related both physically and ethnically to the Pueblos" than to the Apaches.[4]

Archaeology confirms this fact. The wild and wooded country of Old Navajoland is sprinkled with ruins of Navajo and
Pueblo houses intermingled. These were occupied at the same
time, the dates ranging from 1700 to about 1775.[5] The Navajos
were for three-quarters of a century or more under intensive
Pueblo influence. The People were well established in the canyons of Old Navajoland before the influx of refugees began.[6]
After 1656, the archaeologists can identify whole Navajo villages,

[4] Ales Hrdlicka, *Physiological and Medical Observations Among the Indians of Southwestern United States and Northern Mexico,* Bureau of American
Ethnology, *Bulletin* No. 34 (1908), 8.
[5] Dorothy Keur, "A Chapter in Navaho-Pueblo Relations," *American
Antiquity,* Vol. X, No. 1 (July, 1944).
[6] Malcolm Farmer, "Navajo Archaeology of Upper Largo and Blanco
Canyons, New Mexico," *American Antiquity,* Vol. VIII, No. 1 (July, 1942).

with hogans, sweat houses, storage pits, and pottery.[7] Sometimes there are fifty of the old forked-stick hogans grouped together on some level stretch among the trees, with the cornfields in the valley below.[8]

All that was changed when the Pueblo refugees poured in. The first known date for this influx—which means the year when the first known beam was cut—is 1723, almost thirty years after the Spaniards' return. Perhaps earlier beams will be found —or perhaps the villagers went through many stages of change on their way from their settled homes to this frontier wilderness among the barbarians. However, when they had once found this place of refuge, they continued to build there until 1764.[9] No longer were the houses in the grand classical style, four or five stories high and housing some thousand people. The small stone buildings the archaeologists found have been called *pueblitos,* or little pueblos, so small and rough are they compared with the product of the earlier period. Yet the perpendicular stone walls and flat roofs are unmistakable, as are the scraps of pottery lying among them, for these represent styles from every Pueblo, from the Río Grande on the east to the Hopi in the Arizona desert.[10]

These small buildings never equal the number of Navajo hogans, which still retain their old conical style. Sometimes the *pueblitos* stand on cliff tops, after their old custom, separated from the Navajo hogans on the benches below. Sometimes the

[7] Keur, "A Chapter in Navaho-Pueblo Relations," *American Antiquity,* Vol. X, No. 1 (July, 1944), 76, 84.

[8] Edward T. Hall, Jr., "Recent Clues to Athapascan Prehistory in the Southwest," *American Anthropologist,* Vol. XLVI, No. 1, (January-March, 1944).

[9] Keur, "A Chapter in Navaho-Pueblo Relations," *American Antiquity,* Vol. X, No. 1 (July, 1944), 84.

[10] Farmer, "Navajo Archaeology of Upper Blanco and Largo Canyons, New Mexico," *American Antiquity,* Vol. VIII, No. 1 (July, 1942). Also personal information from Stanley Stubbs, Laboratory of Anthropology, Santa Fé, New Mexico.

two kinds of dwelling are huddled close within the same defensive wall, and defense seems to have been necessary. This time the enemy was not the conquering Spaniard, who rarely bothered with this inaccessible spot. Now the Utes and Comanches were bearing down from the north, even as the Navajos had once done, and now it was the Navajos who needed defense against strangers. No longer were the People mere barehanded wanderers with no property but their sinew-backed bows; the few Spaniards who saw them reported them as having fields and flocks.[11]

Having need for defense rather than for attack, they may have learned another early lesson—one whose results were helpful for centuries afterward. This was the art of building in stone. There is no proof that the Navajos had ever used stone before this time, though the possibility has been suggested.[12] The People themselves never mention any ancient type of house but the conical frame of logs covered with earth. Yet the settlements of Old Navajoland, dating *after the Pueblo refugees came*,[13] contain what look like watchtowers as much as four stories high.[14] It is possible that the Pueblo refugees were putting more effort into the building of defensive works than into their own houses. Nevertheless, these towers and walls show a foreign touch, perhaps due to Navajo ingenuity, especially in the unorthodox use of natural boulders as part of the foundation and the unusual loopholes which might be used by archers. The Navajo neigh-

[11] W. W. Hill, "Some Navaho Culture Changes During Two Centuries," *Smithsonian Miscellaneous Collections,* Vol. C (1940), 402, 405, 406.

[12] Betty H. and Harold A. Huscher, *The Hogan Builders of Colorado,* 75–80.

[13] Farmer, "Navajo Archaeology of Upper Blanco and Largo Canyons," *American Antiquity,* Vol. VIII, No. 1 (July, 1942), 71.

[14] Some of these are similar to the watchtowers of the Gallina people, who may have been Navajo victims. Hall, *Early Stockaded Settlements,* 62. Hibben, "The Gallina Phase," *American Antiquity,* Vol. IV, No. 1 (July, 1938).

bors, who perhaps were already fathers and brothers-in-law to some of their visitors, were giving their minds to a new craft.

Sometimes there are signs of round Navajo houses with walls of stone, such as may be seen on the reservation today. These are in the minority[15] in the older Navajo settlements, though later[16] it is possible to find whole groups of circular stone houses with boulders used in their sides. This would be a solution to the housing problem in treeless areas, and perhaps this, along with the urging of the Pueblo spouses, was the reason for the Navajos to build them. Still, the People did not adopt the stone house as a regular thing. That would be an expensive investment for a group who abandoned any building where death had occurred. Even today, the horror of death-contamination is leaving them only slowly, and it must have been one of the chief reasons why they never settled down to be Pueblo dwellers, despite so many good examples.

Yet if the People did not change their house form, they must have changed much else during the time when they lived cheek by jowl with the urbanites. These years, more than anything else, may account for the sharp difference between the Navajos and Apaches, the one group saturated with Pueblo craft and ceremony and the other still savage hunters with only a smattering of new customs. Some families, later counted as Apaches, may have been living with the Navajos at this time and so have learned the colored pottery and the Bear Ceremony, to be mentioned later. For most of the Dené, this was the parting of the ways.

Take, for instance, the famous art of Navajo weaving. If you ask a member of the tribe today when weaving was learned,

15 Keur, "A Chapter in Navaho-Pueblo Relations," *American Antiquity,* Vol. X, No. 1 (July, 1944), 76.

16 *Ibid.* Also Farmer, "Navajo Archaeology of Upper Blanco and Largo Canyons," *American Antiquity,* Vol. VIII, No. 1 (July, 1942), 70–71.

she—for Navajo weavers are women—will tell you that they were taught by Spider Woman, "in the beginning." Yet the Navajo weaving technique, point for point, exactly duplicates that of the Pueblos, who have been weaving since A.D. 600. It is a complicated art, and Navajo girls today need years to learn it from a female relative, practicing every day. It is difficult to believe that the Navajos had worked out the loom, the spindle, and all the other equipment before this era of "learning by marriage." A blanket got in trade, a loom glimpsed on a visit to some pueblo would never have given them enough information. Then there is the problem of sex etiquette, for most Pueblo weavers today are men. Indian proprieties would surely forbid a Navajo woman to receive daily instruction from a strange man. But if she married him! It is possible to imagine the skilled weaver working in a Navajo home, trying to teach his sons who were still wedded to the life of hunting and fighting and, finally, imparting the art to his daughters. That this did not happen too early in Navajo history can be gathered from the fact that all known specimens of Navajo weaving are in wool. Therefore they were made after the Spaniards had come and after the Navajos had sheep. And sheep did not come to the Navajos in any quantity until after the Pueblo revolt.

What a change the possession of woolen cloth would have meant for the hunting people. Spanish reports indicate that the men continued to wear a skin breech cloth, sometimes with leggings and shirt added. For the women, however, there was a new dress which lasted for the next two hundred years. It was made on the style of their Pueblo sisters-in-law, who wore a black woolen blanket wrapped around the body, fastened on the left shoulder, leaving the right one bare, and held at the waist by a sash. Perhaps the Navajo women were bigger, perhaps they needed a wider skirt for their riding and walking,

47

and perhaps they were used to a dress made of two deerskins hanging front and back—at any rate, their black woolen dress was a double blanket, fastened on the shoulders and hanging down front and back.

It was not only in clothing that the Navajo women tried a new style. Ruins indicate that they began to make colored pottery, for along with the usual gray jars, there are scraps of a decorated ware, with a bold careless design which has suggestions of many Pueblos but belongs to none. Navajo women were imitating the work of their Pueblo sisters-in-law, and a few of them, as well as some Apaches, kept up the style until recently.[17]

Another innovation was the origin of new clans, or perhaps of all clans. The custom of mother-descent is so nearly universal with Navajos and Apaches that we can imagine it an old one. Therefore, when a Navajo man took a Pueblo bride, his children belonged to her family. Later, when the refugees began to trickle home, the Pueblo wife and her relatives often chose to remain. Then she and her children must have some clan affiliation, for the Navajo, like most Indians, abhorred living with strangers. So the women might be received into some clan which the Navajos considered allied with her Pueblo clan, or she might be made the ancestress of a new clan as the Jemez women were. One new clan is attributed by myth to a lone Mexican woman brought home by a Navajo

For this period in Old Navajoland, there is authority other than myth and archaeology. As early as 1705, the Spaniards began to send expeditions to the country of "mesas and mountains" near the San Juan River, and these continued, sometimes for military purposes and sometimes to explore for metals, up to 1744.[18] Would that some of the eye witnesses who reported

[17] Keur, *Big Bead Mesa*, 33–34.
[18] Harry Tschopik Jr., *Navajo Pottery Making*, 70.

Escalante's map, showing the "Provincia de Nabajoo" (lower right).
(Courtesy National Archives)

An old warrior with lance and shield. Keams Canyon, Arizona, 1893.
(James Mooney, Courtesy Bureau of American Ethnology)

on this journey had been priests—usually good observers—or else women, so that they might have given details of the houses, dress, and crafts of the Indians they saw. How many, for instance, were Navajos and how many were their Pueblo neighbors and relatives? One report mentions "more than two hundred Christian Indians" living on the mesas.[19] These refugees, of course, would not wish to reveal themselves to their former and potential enemies. Yet the "little houses of stone on the tops of the mesas."[20] sound like *pueblitos* rather than hogans, and the one in "stories" might be a watchtower.[21] The "Navajos" glimpsed by soldiers and prospectors in 1743 were "dressed in the same kind of clothes as the Christian Indians," and all reports say that they made woolen cloth and baskets which they traded to the Indians on the Río Grande.[22]

Were "they" the Pueblo refugees, keeping carefully anonymous by sending their Navajo relatives to trade their cloth along with Navajo baskets?[23] Evidence on this would aid in deciding how soon the Navajo learned to weave In any case, we have a picture of four or five thousand people in the canyons of Old Navajoland raising corn, beans, and squash in the sandy valleys, keeping small flocks of sheep and goats with a few horses and cattle, and, after 1722, being "very peaceful and domestic."[24] The Navajo Hail Chant[25] gives a glimpse of this mixed society

[19] Hill, "Some Navaho Culture Changes During Two Centuries," *Smithsonian Miscellaneous Collections,* Vol. C (1940), 412, 413.

[20] *Ibid.*

[21] *Ibid.*, 402.

[22] *Ibid.*, 406.

[23] *Ibid.*, 407.

[24] *Ibid.*

[25] In 1706, Governor Francisco Curevo y Valdez reported that the Navajos "make their clothes of wool and cotton, sowing the latter and obtaining the former from the flocks they raise." Hackett, *Historical Documents Relating to New Mexico,* 381–83. Obviously the governor made a mistake in crediting the Navajos with sowing cotton, which they never did. He possibly confused them

which might well have been located in Gobernador and neighboring canyons in the year 1743.

"Thus it was, they say. There was a Pueblo settlement, near it was their home, a Pueblo house with a hogan near it. There it was that Rainboy (a typical Navajo name and the hero of the saga) started gambling. Among other things, he lost his moccasins, his leggings, his shirt, his mother's beads, his fathers beads, and even his father's token, that was his father's badge of leadership."[26] Granted that this translation admits of various changes, it pictures a young Navajo in his buckskin clothing, living with his mother, brothers, and sisters (who are of the Water's Edge Navajo clan), and his father, naturally of another clan, in their hogan next to a Pueblo dwelling. There seems to be a village government very unlike that known to any Navajos, for the villagers, in council, decide that Rainboy is to be whipped in the plaza for his misdemeanors. Then follow his adventures with supernatural helpers, and this brings us to one of the most important avenues of learning which were now open to the People. While Navajo women learned about pottery and weaving, Navajo men learned ceremony.

Learning is the wrong word. The Navajos *took* from their Pueblo relatives the skeleton of a mythology and the details of a complicated ritual, and on these they built a structure Wagnerian in its grandeur. Many of the tales are localized in this very country of Old Navajoland, with La Plata Mountains of Colorado and the San Juan River carefully described. Among them move miraculous beings dressed in the Pueblo costume of kilt

---

with the Pueblo people, who *did* sow cotton. Southwestern residents often fail to distinguish the two groups even today, in spite of their obvious differences. The governor may have been mistaken about who did the weaving, also. It is possible that the craftsmen—or women—were Pueblo refugees, hiding among the Navajos or else Pueblo spouses of Navajos.

[26] Reichard, *The Story of the Navajo Hail Chant*, 1–2.

and mask, but how different from any spirits imagined by the villagers! Take, for instance, the twin War Gods, children of the Sun. In the peaceful Hopi pueblos, these beings are miracle workers, although they appear as naughty boys who are a nuisance to their grandmother[27] and are scolded by the town chief. In the Navajo myth they are celestial conquerors riding on the rainbow and armed with the straight and the jagged lightning. The Navajo ritual celebrating these and other beings follows rigidly the pattern of the Pueblos. That means eight days of purification and offerings, these last including the prayer-sticks of the Pueblos and even their "jewels" of white shell, turquoise, red shell, and jet, in proper directional order. It also includes making a colored picture on the ground with sand, ground rock and charcoal. Instead, however, of adopting the simple design used in the pueblos and Southern California and Mexico, the Navajos developed "sand painting" into a high art. This must have taken many years to develop, but it perhaps had its beginning when a Pueblo-trained priest initiated his sister's son into the art of bringing spirits to the ceremony by drawing their symbols.[28] At the end of eight days, when the spirit help was called by purification offering and representation, might come the splendid ninth-day—a night, with the Navajos—when a public spectacle allowed all to partake in the spirit blessing.

Thus far, the Navajo ceremony is more or less a reflection of its Pueblo pattern, but it is far different in its purpose and interpretation. Pueblo ceremonies are community affairs conducted by a hierarchy of priests to bring rain and blessing on the whole village. The Navajo hunters thought little about rain during the crucial fifty years or so when they had no villages. What they cared about was the hunter's own health and well-

[27] Elsie Clews Parsons, *Pueblo Indian Religion*, I, 183.
[28] Ruth Underhill, *Ceremonial Patterns in the Greater Southwest*, 44-46.

being, his one sure possession. Heretofore, this had been secured through a medicine man, whose vision took him to a spirit village where powerful songs and rites were taught him. With these as his only therapy, the visionary came back to sing over one who was sick or unfortunate and thus to effect a cure.

The Navajos kept this idea. The medicine man still sang over a single patient, who paid his fee. But all who heard of the ceremony were invited, fixed their thoughts on good things, and shared in the blessing. The medicine man, instead of his single vision, had now learned some elaborate stories which intertwined elements of Pueblo myth with others from the north. As the tale took him to the villages of magic-working animals, he learned such truly Navajo poetry as:

> *Black horned rattler, young chief*
> *Your sacrifice I have made,*
> *Your smoke I have prepared.*
> *This day I have become your child.*
> *This day your grandchild I have become.*
> *Watch over me.*
> *Hold your hand before me in protection.*
> *Stand before me and arise as my protector.*
>
> *Dewdrops and pollens may I enjoy.*
> *With these may it be beautiful in front of me.*
> *With these may it be beautiful behind me. . . .*
> *All is beautiful again. All is restored in beauty.*[29]

The chanter who recited such rituals during nine days of exacting ceremony was no longer a mere medicine man, but a priest, whose training required years and was scrupulously paid for. He probably did not develop to his full stature during the

[29] Reichard, Story of the Male Shooting Chant, unpublished.

half century of the Navajo-Pueblo merger. Perhaps this period saw only the beginnings of some of the People's present theology, using some of the older chants whose mythic background is located in the neighboring country. The full flowering of Navajo myth, with its interrelated episodes must, I feel, be the work of theologians, who compared and refined their creations over a long period. It is possible that during their first acquaintance with a Pueblo nine-day ceremony, makeshift though that would be under refugee conditions, the Navajos caught the idea of pageantry and began interweaving the new material with that of their own religion. The final result may have been years or even centuries in the making. In fact, modifications of ceremony are still going on. Yet here, where the splendor of a new contact with the spirits first burst upon them, they may have established the outlines for that interesting mythology which included not only the Children of the Sun, but the water creatures, sky creatures, beings of rain, cloud, mist, pollen, corn, and a host of others, like the buffalo, "moving with the sky as mirage, black streak on the earth."[30] If Pueblo ritual furnished the scaffolding for this new ceremony, it was the Navajo thinkers who built the palatial superstructure.

Not all the Navajos spent their time in the canyon occupied with peaceful learning. The young men were usually off on adventure, hunting, fighting, and trading. All their earliest traditions speak of deer hunting, and this was good country for it. Hunters went off in groups, and they used some methods and charms very similar to those of the Pueblos.[31] Especially is the use of unwounded buckskin for ceremonies an ancient Southwestern practice, and other methods, although often enriched by

[30] *Ibid.*

[31] W. W. Hill, *The Agricultural and Hunting Methods of the Navajo Indians.*

Pueblo ceremony, reflect Navajo experience in the plains or the north.[32] Besides deer, they hunted bear and mountain lion, and there were buffalo in Colorado, a little to the north and perhaps in what is now New Mexico, east of the Río Grande.[33] It is likely that the Navajos made expeditions after this valuable food, especially after they had horses. Perhaps they sometimes accompanied the Utes, with whom they made a truce when convenient; or their Pueblo relatives-in-law may have accompanied them and acquired some new techniques in their turn.[34]

Ceremonially, the buffalo became for the Navajo a revered being. Witness the lines from the Shooting Chant just quoted and also the number of buffalo products used in ceremony, from generative organs even to the dust on the animal's tracks.[35] According to Navajo tradition, some of the People, perhaps the more easterly groups, kept up seasonal excursions to buffalo country for a long time, though this may have meant going farther east. Sometimes they could avoid the journey by trading with other hunters, like Utes or Apaches. Trading is a recurrent note in Navajo history and was probably practiced in the days of their first arrival. And now that they had sheepskins to barter, the opportunities must have increased. Trading relations, however, were not always peaceful, and resulted, for example, in a fight with the Pawnee in Kansas in 1697–98.[36]

More remunerative than either hunting or trading was the new practice of slave raiding. The Navajos had been taking captives since those early days when they raided Taos, but early

[32] *Ibid.*, 190.

[33] Frederick A. Hodge, *Handbook of American Indians North of Mexico*, 169.

[34] Franciscan Fathers, *An Ethnologic Dictionary of the Navaho Language*, 309; W. W. Hill, *Agricultural and Hunting Methods*, 374, 392.

[35] Franciscan Fathers, *Dictionary*, 401; Berard Haile, *Origin Legend of the Navajo Flintway*, 18.

[36] Alfred B. Thomas, *After Coronado*, 13–14.

Spanish accounts of the slave trade say little about the Navajos and their part in it. They recognized its lucrative possibilities, and in 1694, some of them raided east into Nebraska. Returning with captive Pawnee children, they offered them for sale to the Spaniards and, when they were refused, calmly beheaded them.[37] This form of pressure on the whites came to be a regular thing with Indian slave traders. For the slave business in New Mexico was only in its infancy and was to flourish for a century or more. True, slavery in the New World was forbidden by royal Spanish decree as early as 1532, but that decree proved impossible to enforce. The Spaniards needed field workers and house servants, but no white man had come to the New World to do that kind of work—and the Indians likewise objected. The best plan was to make use of Indians captured in raids—whether these raids were justified or not. The usual explanation was like that made by Ulibarri, when he distributed eighty-four Picuris Indians among the members of his expedition: "That it was to save their lives by maintaining them that I gave them out as servants."[38] The Indians, who needed little or no justification for raids, soon found that they could act as middlemen, capturing each other and making sales to the whites. The yearly fair at Taos was a recognized occasion for this exchange, when the slave-hungry Spaniards met the horse-hungry Indians.[39] Spanish officials, including the governor of New Mexico himself, got together all the horses they could afford, along with some axes and knives. The Utes and Comanches, at peace for the occasion, could produce Jicarilla captives,[40] while the more distant

[37] *Ibid.*, 13.

[38] *Ibid.*, 50.

[39] Charles W. Hackett (ed.), *Historical Documents Relating to New Mexico, Nueva Viscays and approaches thereto, to 1773*, 486–87.

[40] Thomas, *After Coronado*, 44.

Apaches brought in Pawnees,[41] a partly agricultural tribe who ultimately became captives *par excellence* for all the plains raiders.[42]

The canyons provided very good bases for Navajo raids against the harried Pawnees to the east. Some of their expeditions must have been in force, for once the reports aver that four thousand Navajos were destroyed.[43] In 1699, the Navajos took revenge and appeared at the Spanish fair laden with slaves, jewels, guns, powder flasks, clothing, and even small pots of brass.[44] The People were acquiring goods other than those of their Pueblo relatives, and the influences they received from the whites may sometimes have come overland from the French. A few Navajo forays are reported in the early 1700's, interspersed with Spanish punitive expeditions and intervals of peace.[45] This was mere apprenticeship, however, compared with the proficiency in robbing and raiding that the Navajos later acquired.

In 1764, or thereabouts, the last known Pueblo house beam was cut in Gobernador Canyon, indicating that the refugees had begun to move home. They may have stayed a little later in some of the near-by canyons, but, by and large, the end of the 1700's marks the date when the two peoples separated.[46] They had given and taken all they could. Many a Pueblo woman must have returned to her village with a family of half-Navajo children and perhaps with ideas on war and hunting unknown before. As for the Navajos and the half-Pueblos who remained in the canyons, they were bursting with new ideas, new tech-

[41] *Ibid.,* 14.
[42] Hodge, *Handbook of American Indians,* II, 214.
[43] Thomas, *After Coronado,* 14.
[44] *Ibid.*
[45] *Ibid.,* 71.
[46] Farmer, "Navajo Archaeology of Upper Blanco and Largo Canyons, New Mexico," *American Antiquity,* Vol. VIII, No. 1 (July, 1942), 71.

niques, and new wealth. But they did not remain in the canyons long. By the end of the eighteenth century, Old Navajoland was practically deserted. The People, their apprenticeship over, were streaming out with their sheep, their horses, and their weaving to occupy the country between the four mountains.

6: The Navajos Become a People

EXPANSION AFTER 1690

THE PERIOD OF intimacy with the Pueblos ended in the 1770's. The Navajos emerged as a new people, swollen in numbers, endowed with new crafts and new ideas, and bursting with the energy which results from such stimulus. Yet they had not become pueblo dwellers. Perhaps if urban influences had found them later in their history, when the years of roving were behind them, they might have settled in villages, as some Apaches did.[1]

One group nearly did something of the sort, or at least proposed it. Now that the Navajos are about to spread out and develop differences, it might be fruitful to pause over this segment which went farthest toward Pueblo ways. Its members became known as the Alien, or Enemy Navajos, and even today the children of Cañoncito may hear that insult screamed at them in school. The "Aliens" moved south about 1745, when the merger-settlement at Gobernador was still flourishing. They built no *pueblitos*, for this was not a case of Pueblos and Navajos living side by side. The "Aliens" were one people, though the Pueblo admixture must have been strong. The ruins of the settlement gave plain evidence of how much the Navajos had

[1] Thomas, *After Coronado*, 53.

learned. They were building their hogans of stone oftener than of poles and earth,[2] and some had cribbed roofs, like those of Pueblo ceremonial rooms, and even smoke deflectors.[3] They were farmers rather than sheepmen and neighbors to the Pueblos of Sia and Santa Ana. Surely it was they who requested, in 1750, that they might found a pueblo at Cubero, near Acoma.[4] The pueblo was never founded, but these Navajos grew farther and farther away from their mobile, sheepherding kinsmen. The Spaniards even placed a mission among them, but the Navajos could not change to that extent, and the mission only lasted a few years. Nevertheless, in later times these Navajos of the Cebolleta neighborhood were always known as friends of the whites, and when guides were needed for the remote Navajo regions it was the "Aliens" who obliged. We shall hear of them often.

The rest of the People felt little temptation to settle. It was the flocks and herds, that important movable wealth, which called them into the open and set them roving over the land between the four mountains. Now, for the first time, the Navajos knew the meaning of wealth. For years after their first arrival, the myths show them as almost destitute wanderers. Even after learning to grow corn, they lived on a marginal subsistence, with no accumulated goods. The Spanish accounts of the Pueblo merger speak of small fields dependent on rainwater, and "a few small flocks of goats and sheep" for three or four thousand Indians.[5] It took a while for those flocks to increase and for the Navajo hunters to learn how to care for animals, rather than to kill them. Presumably they learned from their Pueblo relatives,

[2] Dorothy Keur, *Big Bead Mesa,* 33.

[3] *Ibid.*

[4] Letter of Cachupin, in *Historical Documents Relating to New Mexico* (ed. by Charles W. Hackett), 424.

[5] W. W. Hill, "Some Navaho Culture Changes During Two Centuries," *Smithsonian Miscellaneous Collections,* Vol. C (1940), 402.

who had learned from the Spaniards, and the Spaniards perhaps from the Moors.

The same system of animal husbandry was practiced in New Mexico almost to the present day. It involved transhumance, or moving the flock from highland to lowland following the grass. Pueblo people, wedded to their villages, let the flocks graze near them in winter and in summer sent one or two members of the family to camp with them in the hills. Navajo families picked up their goods and moved with the sheep. In the days of Navajo pride, no hogan was complete without the near-by sheep corral, where every night the sheep were kept safe from coyotes and human enemies. To a Navajo, not only does home mean the gleam of firelight through the hogan door, but also it means the soft bleating of sheep and the patter of hooves, as the women or children drive the flock in at dusk.

Navajo sheep, from the outset, were often the property of women. Perhaps this was because they used the wool for weaving, or perhaps because they could guard the sheep near home while the men were off hunting and fighting. It was the women who hacked off the wool for weaving, using any piece of iron they could get in trade, or even a sharp stone. When a sheep was butchered, the Navajos followed the traditions of hunting days and ate every part of the animal, even the small intestines . . . . Winding them about a string of fat, they roasted them on the coals."[6] The Navajos were a well-nourished people, with their wealth increasing around them. The Navajo women, who pass down the clan name to their children, have always played a dignified role. Now that a mother owned sheep, she could give each child his proper portion, see that her daughters were worthily established with their incoming husbands, and even send something with her sons to their new brides.

[6] Sapir and Hoijer, *Navaho Texts,* 413.

Horses belonged to the men. One who sees a Navajo today jogging over the desert on his little nag can easily believe that the two came into being together and that the People have never been without horses. Indeed, when the Spanish ranches were deserted and the horses went wild, the Navajos—as well as the Apaches and Comanches—who caught them got on and rode as though familiar with riding. When the Spaniards returned after the rebellion, they soon found themselves ringed about with wild, mounted Indians. The yearly fair at Taos was thronged with Apaches, Comanches, Utes, and Navajos who came to barter their goods, including slaves, and to obtain horses. Spain regulated the prices, giving one horse for 12–15 skins and two pack horses for a slave girl ten years old. A smaller *pieza* or piece (the Spaniards, in deference to their law against slavery, always spoke of human merchandise by this term) was worth a pack horse and something extra.[7] The Spaniards, unable to get Indians to work for pay, were particularly anxious to buy these slaves and yearly scraped together all the horses they could find.[8]

The Indians were glad to oblige when no other means of getting mounts were at hand, but they found raiding easier than trading. Their practice was to rush on a horse corral at dawn howling like wolves and waving blankets to stampede the herd. By 1775, the herds of New Mexico were so depleted that the province had to send to Spain for fifteen hundred horses to be used against Apaches, Navajos, Comanches, and Utes.[9] Not all the lost horses were in Indian hands, for some had escaped, and soon there were herds of wild, unbroken ponies in the outland for anyone to take who could. The Spaniards called these

[7] *Ibid.*
[8] Hackett (ed.), *Historical Documents,* 486–87.
[9] Archivo General, Library of New Mexico Historical Museum, pieza 6a.

animals *mesteño,* wild, and thus we get our western term "mustang."

To the Navajo, this new property which could move under its own power was a miracle—no more tedious foot journeys of a few miles a day, with the baggage carried on the backs of women! Now all the goods could be loaded on horses, and the whole family could ride, even the baby in its cradleboard hanging to the saddle. Their food, in the form of sheep, could follow behind, and so could their clothing, in the form of wool on the sheep's backs. No urban urge to town building could stand against such a mobile invitation. The Navajos again became rovers, but this was a roving of a very different sort from that of the poverty-stricken stragglers pictured in the myths. The Navajos were now a recognized people, with a name well known both to Spaniards and Indians. Having established a way of life that would suffice them for the next two hundred years, they spread less like prowlers than like conquerors.

The country had been filling up since their arrival, and the possibility of spread was not unlimited. To the north, in the fine hunting lands of Colorado, the Utes had taken possession and already were kidnapping Navajo women and children. To the east were the Pueblos, strung closely along the Río Grande. South of them were groups of the Apaches, kinsmen of the Navajos but no longer friends. They too had acquired Spanish horses and sheep, though the sheep were usually eaten rather than tended. Still, the Apaches were not to be trifled with. The Enemy Navajos, as has been mentioned, did move south, but they were the only ones who cared to stay so close to the Spaniards. The main body of the Navajos moved west, toward the truly empty land.

Here was that area which the Navajos came to regard as their own and which finally became their reservation. The land "between the four mountains" is an expanse of desert, ravine, and table land—the size of New Hampshire, Vermont, and Rhode Island put together. Across this arid country, from north to south, stretch two low mountain ridges, which became landmarks in the People's movements. To the Navajos, these are two great human figures, male and female, and each contains sacred spots where no white must venture.

The eastern figure, slanting southeast (which means head down) across the Arizona-New Mexico border, is the Goods of Value Range,[10] called by the whites the Chuska, Lukachukai, and Carrizo Mountains. These are jumbles of cliffs and boulders with only a few passes between them, which white Americans later found almost insurmountable. The Navajo tale of their arrival in the corn country brings their western contingent in a great sweep south of this range. Even after a tramp of some thousands of miles, the Goods of Value Range must have looked impassable. West of it stretches the colorful land of red rocks and gray desert, with its few fertile patches, growing more barren as it reaches the huge female figure in western Arizona. This one, the Pollen Range, lies with her head, Navajo Mountain, toward the north and just over the state line, while her body, Black Mountain, extends into the Hopi mesas. The Navajos were to occupy many of these lofty spots as well as the flat country between.

As the Navajos moved out of their canyons, they faced the male figure to the west of them across a waterless expanse. Here lay Chaco Canyon, once a center of Pueblo civilization but now dry and deserted, where there are forty-one ancient Navajo dwellings of stone now to be found.[11] Obviously the People had taken their building lessons to heart, as well they might in an

[10] Richard Van Valkenburgh, *Dinebikeyah*, 27, 41.

[11] Roy L. Malcolm, "Archaeological Remains Supposedly Navaho from Chaco Canyon, New Mexico," *American Antiquity,* Vol. V, No. 1 (July, 1939). 6.

almost treeless country. Some Navajos were still building stone hogans in the canyon when visited by white Americans, but the majority had passed on. Gradually the People spilled over the mountains to the wide valley beyond, the present site of reservation headquarters. Here the Chinle carries mountain waters to the San Juan River, which runs through a wide, flat land dotted with mesas and weird solitary rocks. To the south of it, they found meadows, trees, and water at Bear His Spring, which would later be Fort Wingate.

This was a fine, open land, and in it were new pueblos with which the Navajos had few ties of friendship. Pueblos ripe for raiding! The Navajo had no intention of leaving their flocks to increase by the slow process of nature. Finding it easy to take what they wanted and have plenty, they did so, and decided they were never going back to the days of poverty.

Zuñi children, scaring crows in the fields, learned what it was like to see three or four rangy figures in badger-skin caps rise from behind rocks with a wild war cry. In a moment more, their father might be lying scalped and their mother flung across a warrior's saddle, while the flock of sheep plunged away in front of the yelling horsemen. Often the children were carried away, too, for the Navajos now had enough to feed extra mouths, and they liked to have captives to do their menial work. The raiders were rarely caught, even though the Zuñi marched valiantly the thirty or so miles to Bear Spring and came back to boast at the scalp dance how,

> *. . . one of the enemy*
> *In a shower of arrows*
> *In a shower of stones,*
> *In a shower of war clubs,*
> *With bloody head*
> *Reached the end of his life,*[12]

flocks and women were usually taken far from Bear Spring. The Hopis perched on their western mesas also heard the war cry. "When the Navajo were hungry," say the old men, "they went to the Hopi country. The Hopis would treat them well and feed them. When the Navajos had been fed, the Hopis would throw them off the mesa. In revenge the Navajos would organize a war party . . . . Then each people would feel themselves satisfied and a treaty would be made which would last until someone was thrown over the mesa or until a Navajo killed a Hopi in the cornfields."[13] Another Navajo saying is that they took Hopi captives in order to get weavers.

There must have been intervals of peace between the forays, for how else did the Hopis and Zuñis learn so much Navajo? The Big Firebrand society at Zuñi has a series of songs in Navajo and so have the players of hidden ball on the Hopi First Mesa.[14] Even one Hopi ceremonial has a clown play in Navajo,[15] and Hopi women disguise themselves as Navajos in the buffalo dance.[16] When the Spaniard Escalante visited the Hopis in 1776, he was addressed in Navajo, the language which the Hopis used and often use still for talking with foreigners. While the Pueblos were thus learning from their Navajo friends and enemies, how much were the People themselves acquiring? Surely they added to their ceremonial structure, for it is unlikely that they perfected it all at once and then left it untouched. In fact, "the Zuñis and Hopis claim that the Navajos obtained the secrets of Pueblo medicine by intruding upon their ceremonials or capturing a Pueblo and that they appropriated whatever suited their fancy."[17]

[12] Ruth Bunzel, *Zuni Ritual Poetry*, 678.

[13] Katherine Bartlett, "Hopi History, II: The Navajo Wars," *Museum Notes*, Vol. VIII, No. 7 (1936), 35.

[14] Elsie Clews Parsons, *Pueblo Indian Religion*, 650, 742, 1040n.

[15] Elsie Clews Parsons (ed.), *Hopi Journal*, 329.

[16] *Ibid.*, 899.

[17] James Stevenson, *Ceremonial of Hasjelti Dailjis*, 86–87, 286.

Did the magnificent masked pageants of these western pueblos inspire certain Navajo ceremonials, say the Night Chant? Assigning dates is far too tricky a matter, but it is hard to believe that the Navajos observed the Hopi and Zuñi ceremonials in full splendor without profiting by it.

Most of the Navajo moves had skirted the Goods of Value Range whose crags and precipices walled Old Navajoland at the west. Pueblo settlements lay either east or west of this mountain barrier, which the Navajos in their horseless days never tried to cross. Now, however, the People were equipped for exploration. Among the crags they could camp unseen by enemies and even find hidden pastures where sheep could be kept in comfort. They soon began to make use of this untouched territory, and, according to United States Indian Service experts, the pastures in the Chuska Range have had longer continuous grazing than any on the reservation. The range projects on its western side into the magnificent rocky walls of Canyon de Chelley. The name sounds French, but actually it is the Spanish way of spelling *tsegi,* the Navajo word for canyon—as though any letters in the white man's alphabet could represent the deep gargle which is the Navajo *g.*

The famous canyon, which is actually two canyons in the shape of a narrow "Y," is twenty-seven miles long and one hundred to five hundred yards wide. Along its bottom meanders a shallow stream, dead dry in summer, and on each side rise stone walls as high and smooth as those of skyscrapers. Like skyscrapers, they are irregular in height, now jutting into corners, now rising into pinnacles. Here and there, in their walls of black or red sandstone, are arched openings where the ruins of some Pueblo house show their broken windows and towers. Those rock openings have known no drop of moisture since the last geologic change thousands of years ago. On their floors are still preserved shreds of cloth from Pueblo looms and corncobs hundreds of years old. Among the cliffs are hidden storage bins made by the Basket Makers, the very first farmers of this plateau region. For this canyon, say the archaeologists, has been continuously inhabited from A.D. 348 to 1287.

The canyon was empty at the time of the Pueblo rebellion, and the Jemez clan of the Navajos claim it was they who settled it. So *tsegi* became known for its beautiful women, and rough Navajos from the hills came to steal them as brides. It was known also for its rich garden patches of corn, beans, and squash, for the radiation from the rock walls gave an almost greenhouse heat. After the Navajos were established, Hopi refugees who had killed their Spanish priests moved into the canyon. They brought the seeds of peach trees which the priests had given them, and soon the Navajos, too, were raising peach trees, for when did this tribe see any desirable thing without learning to get it for themselves! The Hopis left, but the Navajos spread and flourished. Pictures of deer and men began to appear on the canyon walls, done in the vivid Navajo style which contrasts strongly with the rigid figures of the Pueblos. Domed, wooden huts grew like mushrooms in the sheltered bays among the rocks. Even with stone *pueblitos* all around them as models, the Navajos did not care to build Pueblo houses, but built circular huts of piñon branches covered with earth. The ruins even show one of pine logs in six-sided shape and dated 1770.

As the 1700's drew toward their close, the Navajos were well embarked on their western expansion. A map made by the priests Dominguez and Escalante, in 1776, shows the localities just mentioned, and in 1786 they were listed as follows: (1) San Mateo, northwest of Mount Taylor; (2) Ceboletta and Encinal, southeast of Mount Taylor (settlements of the Enemy Navajos where the temporary missions were placed); (3) Chuska Mountain, the Goods of Value Range; (4) Bear Spring; (5) Canyon de Chelley.[18]

By this time, there was no doubt of Navajo weaving skill. It is granted that perhaps those first Spanish visitors to Gobernador may have seen only Pueblo weaving while Navajo women had scarcely learned the art. Now, however, the parting had taken place, for the Pueblo people had returned to their villages —all but those who chose to remain with the Navajos forever. Any reports of Navajo weaving must go to the credit of the People themselves. There was such a report in 1781, when Teodoro de Croix, military governor of the interior provinces, wrote: "These . . . Navajo, deviating nobly from their race, are inclined to work and to recognize a stable domicile, make their woven stuffs from wool, sow and conserve their crops."[19] We have no specimens of these woven stuffs, for the very earliest known products date after 1800. Some fragments of a very early date show brown and black stripes of natural wool on a white ground, with sometimes a narrow thread of blue, dyed with Mexican indigo—practically a replica of an early Pueblo blanket. The Navajos were still closely tied to their teachers— or were Pueblo weavers still living among them? One of their traditions is that they raided the Hopi towns purposely to capture weavers.

That cannot be the whole story, for now known are a series of Spanish reports, all mentioning Navajo weaving. In the days before the Pueblo rebellion, these reports had extended themselves in praise of Pueblo skill in the textile arts, but now there is not a word of it. In 1776, the Navajos were said to be living

[18] Katherine Bartlett, "Hopi History, II: The Navajo Wars," *Museum Notes,* Vol. VIII, No. 7 (1936), 31.

[19] Alfred B. Thomas, *Teodoro de Croix and the Northern Frontier of New Mexico,* 113.

almost entirely by their weaving since farming was so poor.[20]
"They work their wool with more taste and delicacy than the
Spaniards. Men and women," says the report of 1795, "always go
decently clothed and their captains are rarely seen without silver
jewelry." Also, the report adds (Ah, how mistakenly), "they
are not in a state of coveting sheep, as their own are innumerable."[21] Those last four words were true, but the Navajos were
always in a state of coveting sheep—and they knew where to
get them. They had seen Spanish ranches looted and noticed
how seldom the looters were caught. Now the ranches were
spreading all over New Mexico, which contained our states of
New Mexico and Arizona and an indefinite stretch of country
to the north. Wealth lay open to the Navajos, and they made
freebooting their profession.

At first the Spaniards saw little danger in this growing tribe
which in the days of the Pueblo merger they had reported as
"very tame Indians and peaceful."[22] Their attention was on the
wilder peoples who ringed their settled province of New Mexico: Utes on the north, Apaches on the east and south. The
Comanches, farther east in the plains, swooped in now and then
to kill or capture over a hundred or so of the scattered Spanish
farmers at one blow.[23] In their attempts to play these menacing
tribes off against each other, the Spaniards at first let the Navajos
alone. However, lamented Croix, "in the midst of peace they
will commit small robberies, are accustomed to mix with the rest
of the Apaches in their incursions, and cannot live without robbery because of the extreme sterility of the countries in which

[20] Charles A. Amsden, *Navajo Weaving*, 129–30n.

[21] *Ibid.*, 132.

[22] W.W. Hill, "Some Navaho Culture Changes During Two Centuries,"
Smithsonian Miscellaneous Collections, Vol. C (1940), 409.

[23] Thomas, *Teodoro de Croix*, 111.

they dwell."[24] How long it was to be before the United States recognized this same fact about robbery and the sterile country!

The Navajos did not "deviate" nobly from their Apache kin quite as much as the Spaniards thought. There are reports of their making alliances, now with the Utes,[25] now with the Gila Apaches.[26] When they needed sheep for use or captives for trade, they raided the very pueblos with which they had lived so closely and helped themselves.[27] The Spaniards, desperate with the attacks of the "innumerable and warlike nations of heathen enemies,"[28] only made occasional expeditions against the Navajos. They preferred to keep peace with this one tribe and sent several diplomatic missions to them. The Navajos were to see scores of such missions in the next hundred years, and they came to pay no more attention to them than to passing thunderstorms. The Spaniards, having no premonition of the future, expected that "in a short period of time we may not only enjoy permanent peace but may accomplish their conversion and their settlement into pueblos."[29]

When he voiced this hope, the governor of New Mexico had no idea that soon the Spaniards themselves would be driven out of New Mexico, while the Navajos would grow bolder and stronger. He decided to give some prominent Navajo the title of general and to pay him well to keep his people quiet. Many a white official has tried this same scheme, without realizing that

---

[24] *Ibid.*, 113–14; *Forgotten Frontiers*, 237.

[25] Thomas, *Forgotten Frontiers*, 46, 55–56.

[26] Thomas, *The Plains Indians of New Mexico, 1751–1778*, 46.

[27] *Ibid.*

[28] *Ibid*, 126.

[29] There was a punitive expedition in 1706, after which the Navajos were quiet for at least twenty years. But by 1775, the Spaniards were out again to punish them. Thomas, *Teodoro de Croix*, 173; Hill, "Some Navajo Culture Changes During Two Centuries," *Smithsonian Miscellaneous Collections*, Vol. C (1940), 409.

Indian chiefs are not dictators. The chief whom the Spaniards had picked around 1800 was Antonio el Pinto (the speckled?), an Enemy Navajo. Doubtless he enjoyed the silver medals, the strips of red cloth, the saddles, the sacks of food, and the title. But he had no more authority than a successful oil speculator who urges younger men into the business.

"Over there they sneaked off now and then," an old Navajo told Edward Sapir. "In groups of two and three they sneaked back and forth. The Mexicans' (which means anyone of Spanish descent) horses they stole from them. From over there to here they brought the horses and mules too. It was just that that made them go wild."[30]

For sixty years, they remained wild. The Navajos had at last found their vocation.

[30] Sapir and Hoijer, *Navaho Texts*, 341.

7: Lords of the Soil

THE HEYDAY OF BANDITRY

A PARTY OF Navajos had taken refuge in Canyon de Chelly—or so says a legend repeated
by the United States National Park Service—
from Spanish horsemen who were following them and doubtless for good reason.[1] Navajo warriors with only their bows and
arrows had no taste for fighting the whites with guns, so they
decided to flee after putting the women and children in a safe
place. There was a cave in the wall of a branch canyon, now
known as Canyon del Muerto, Canyon of the Dead, that could
only be reached by climbing to the top of the rocky wall, then
slithering down. Here the men left their families, and then they
themselves disappeared.

The women crouched behind a rampart of stones and
watched the Spaniards ride through the canyon glancing help-
lessly at bare rock walls. Soon they would have passed, but one
old beldame who had been a captive of the whites could not
control herself. Leaning out, she screeched in such Spanish as
she knew: "There go the men without eyes!" She had thought
she was safe. The Spaniards did not know how to reach the
cave, nor could they even get high enough on the near-by rocks

[1] Richard Van Valkenburgh, *A Short History of the Navajo People.*

to shoot bullets into it. But the cave had a sloping roof. They climbed to where they could hit this slanting roof, pitting it with hundreds of bullet marks, which are there today. The bouncing bullets came down in a rain on the trapped women and children. Meantime, some of the Spaniards found how to climb up the cliff walls and get down to the cave. They walked among the wounded, clubbing and bayoneting them. On the reservation today, there is a skull which was found there, crushed by a rifle butt. No wonder this rock shelter in the Canyon of the Dead is known as Massacre Cave! Scattered bones and scraps of clothing lay there untouched until white Americans arrived, for the Navajos wanted no contact with property of the dead. This is where one of the earliest scraps of Navajo weaving was found— a bit of blanket woven in stripes of brown and white, from the natural wool of the sheep. Its owner perished in the winter of 1804–1805.

After that massacre in Canyon de Chelley, the honeymoon of Spaniard and Navajo was over. True, there was a great treaty meeting when Navajos and Pueblos were urged to keep the peace. They often listened to such urging on the part of whites, and sometimes they accepted presents to assure their good behavior. But the whites were no clan brothers of the Navajos, and promises to them were simply words exchanged with an enemy. As the Spaniards came sadly to realize, the Navajos usually made peace in the spring so they could have a quiet summer for raising and gathering their crops. In the winter, when the crops were in, they broke their treaties and started raiding.

Soon there was no need for making treaties with Spain at all. In 1824, Mexico gained her independence, and the vast, indeterminate province of New Mexico became a department of the Mexican Republic. The Indians saw very little difference:

there were the same ranches to plunder; and their important leaders were still summoned to Santa Fé, which the Navajos knew as Bead Water, where they were given titles, gifts, and staves of office, and, say the Navajos, they were killed at the first opportunity. Perhaps the desperate New Mexicans had reasons for their treachery, for the Navajos were killing them, also. During the next forty years, the Navajos became the most dreaded raiders on the plateau. Lords of the Soil, the New Mexicans called them, and so they continued until their collision with the soldiers of the United States.

They started this peak period of their history as a rich and strong people, and as the years went on they grew richer. They were scattered through western New Mexico and eastern Arizona, with only the Enemy Navajos left near their old home east of the mountains. They had decided on their mode of life, which meant that two or three families lived together in round huts of stone, earth, or wood, with pasturage for their flocks nearby. Their country, so barren today, was then lush with grama grass and threaded by clear streams. Nature has her moods in the Southwest, each lasting for a long period of time. Nevertheless, the Navajos already had the habit of moving two or three times a year, following the good pasturage. So, much of the year, they lived in airy shelters of evergreen boughs, built in a day. The stuffy permanence of a Pueblo house was not for them.

The young men for much of the year desired no house at all. Strong was the tradition of movement among these warriors who had scorned to learn weaving. Their traditions speak of hunting, both deer and buffalo, though the game was growing scarcer. For buffalo, at least, they must have had to go ever farther away, and perhaps only a few groups did so. More and more, the pride of the Navajos was in their own animals, sheep and horses.

In 1824, we get the first glimpse of the Navajos through the eyes of a white American, Mr. Samuel Patton, who wrote enthusiastically to the Missouri *Intelligencer:*

Their skill in manufacturing and their excellence in some useful and ornamental arts show a decided superiority of genius over all the other tribes of the Western Continent.

They have fine flocks of sheep, abundance of mules and herds of cattle of a superior kind. (Mr. Patton does not mention how they got the mules and herds). They have gardens and peach orchards. Several articles of their woolen manufacture equal the quality of ours. We have seen a coverlet made by them the texture of which is excellent, the figures ingenious and the colors permanent and brilliant.

Indeed, weaving was progressing at a fast pace during these years when the Navajo women had all the wool they could use. Already they were dropping the simple striped patterns of the Pueblos and graduating to diamonds and zigzags in brilliant colors. Some of these colors were made by the use of vegetable dyes which they had learned from the Pueblos. One colorful tint was indigo blue, brought from Mexico, but most prized of all was the red thread which they unravelled from Spanish cloth, or *bayeta*. This was actually English baize, imported by Spain for trade with her colonies. The Indians, who could not get scarlet with their vegetable dyes, unravelled the threads and respun them, for high lights in their blanket patterns.

Men wore these blankets draped over one shoulder just as New Mexican gentlemen did. In fact, a Navajo "captain" dressed exactly like a white, in short trousers which came halfway down the calf and were split at the knee. Sometimes these trousers were made of Spanish cloth and sometimes of buckskin, "tanned and excellently tanned." They were decorated along the seams with silver buttons, for the Navajos now had no trouble in getting Spanish ornaments or Spanish cloth, either. A young Spanish gentleman reported all this to Mr. Patton. Once on a military expedition "we killed a chief," said the young gentleman, much as a hunter might describe killing a bear and examining the pelt. He "wore shoes, fine woolen stockings, small clothes connected at the sides by silver buttons of a seam, a hunting shirt, and a scarlet cloth cap, the folds of which were also secured with silver buttons." Even the bridles of Navajo horses, says Patton, were ornamented with silver, just like those of the Spanish dons. Probably these very ornaments *had* belonged to the dons, though the Navajos insisted that they were now rich enough to order silverwork made in Mexico without stealing it.

Opportunities for stealing, in these days, were at their best. Spanish soldiers were gone, and the New Mexicans, busy at organizing their young government, had no time to spare for military duties. The Navajos looked upon this fact as white men looked upon a good hunting season. The raiding was good, and they raided.

They had their own elaborate system of warfare, part practical and part religious. No man could volunteer to lead a raid unless he had war power and could,

> Step into the shoes of Monster Slayer (the war god),
> Step into the shoes of him whose lure is the extended bow string,
> Step into the shoes of him who lures the enemy to death.[2]

The Navajo got such power by paying a medicine man to teach him a ceremony, the Enemy Way, and thus make himself

---

[2] Berard Haile, *Origin Legend of the Navajo Enemy Way,* 282.

invulnerable. The two would camp alone in enemy country, and, when the neophyte returned, he considered himself invulnerable. "Those who think in a bad way," sighed the old Navajos, "the men who know what used to be called the Enemy Way, at that time unfortunately there used to be quite a few of them."[3] One of these experts would announce his intentions in the manner of the plains Indians, and three or four ambitious youths would join him. Their elders might object, knowing well that vengeance was likely to follow, but the youths, with their way still to make and their brides to purchase, would sneak away. "They told each other secretly of their intentions. 'I too over there will be.' It was with that they went wild, saying, 'Should not others as well go on the warpath?' "[4]

Before starting on the raid, they spent days in the sweat house purifying themselves, singing songs, and praying to the Wind People and the Sun People.[5] Then they donned the "armor" which they must have learned in the north, for no southwesterners ever wore shirts made of three or four thicknesses of buckskin. They annointed their arrows with magic poison, made of charcoal from a lightning-struck tree. They carried stone-headed clubs and a leather shield bordered with dangling eagle feathers. Over it they threw a pinch of pollen which had been shaken off a live squirrel for this would make them invisible.

Every step of the way was governed by rules about what one must eat, what position he must take in sleeping, and what words he must use in speech. Even with all the skill to which a Navajo warrior was trained, success depended largely on magic and luck. If a coyote crossed their path, they turned back, for

---

[3] Sapir and Hoijer, *Navaho Texts*, 341.
[4] *Ibid*.
[5] W. W. Hill, *Navajo Warfare*, 8–16.

luck was against them. But if all went well, they painted their
bodies with snakes and bear tracks for power and courage. They
hid outside the enemy's camp until just before dawn, then rushed
in with the war cry. The Hopis learned to dread that horrible
ahu! ahu! And Navajo stories tell how the poor villagers stood
weeping on their battlements as the People made off with scalps
and women. The buckskin shoulder straps worn today in the
Navajo war dance were taken in a raid made on the Hopis at
this time. As for the Zuñis, they grew more and more bitter
as their cornfields were plundered and their children taken as
slaves. The Navajos were to rue that bitterness later, when the
Zuñis had the United States to help with their vengeance.

The best plunder, however, was on the white ranches of
New Mexico and even south of the border. The Navajos, on their
fast horses, ranged as far south as Chihuahua, stopping only
when they met the Apaches, bent on a similar errand.

"There were good large ranches in Mexico," an old Navajo
told me, "where we always got our sheep. Sometimes we would
find great flocks of them out on the mesa with only a Mexican
to guard them. So we took them without any trouble—oh, of
course, we had to kill the Mexican."

Sometimes, they aver, the killing was performed by pure
magic. A Navajo told Mr. Kluckhohn how a troop of Navajo
bandits hid on a mesa, lying low by day and swooping down by
night to drive off the flocks. Once they saw a number of men
with a flock and did not care to attack. So their leader, who was
expert in witchcraft, shot a feather out of a basket, straight at
the Mexican foreman. "If we hear a noise, we've got him." They
did hear a yell, and the next morning at daylight, the foreman
died. The others packed up and went away.[6]

[6] Clyde Kluckhohn, *Navajo Witchcraft*, 94.

The Mexicans were no doubt often frightened out of trying to chase Navajos. Soon the cry "Men of the mountain!" was enough to send every shepherd scurrying for his life, leaving the flock unprotected. Two or three thousand sheep were nothing for a band of Navajos to drive off at one time. "But," they say, "we always left a few ewes, so the Mexicans could raise us another flock for next year." The descendants of the conquerors had become sheep herders for the Navajos. Not only herders, but also slaves—many a white child was carried off to spend his life in a Navajo hut or, worse, to be sold in Mexico.

The slave business, with the Indians as middlemen, was now in full swing. Navajos, Apaches, and Utes were raiding the Spanish ranches, the Pueblos, and the peaceful Paiutes of Nevada and Utah, who could now be reached easily on horseback. The Paiutes, who lived by seed gathering and hunting small game, had pretty well exhausted their stores by the end of winter, so they were hunted in the spring, when they were weak. The poor souls had to be fattened before they were salable.[7] The mobile Utes and Apaches, who had little use for servants, usually traded their human loot for horses.[8]

Young Navajo men, with their fortunes to make, also traded for horses, but some older men were so well supplied that they could afford to keep servants. They had food enough for helpers and work for them to do. Women slaves could tend sheep and do menial work, thus leaving the mistress of the house free for her skilled weaving. Often a slave became an extra wife to her master, adding another strain to the mixed blood of the tribe. Men had worse treatment, one writer affirming that they were

[7] Carling and A. Aline Malouf, "The Effects of Spanish Slavery on the Indians of the Intermountain Region," *Southwestern Journal of Anthropology,* Vol. I, No. 3 (Autumn, 1945), 381.

[8] Hackett (ed.), *Historical Documents,* 486–87.

castrated or had their ears cut, like an earmarked horse.[9] However, later accounts tell of a captured Spanish boy who refused to go home when offered the chance. An interpreter and leader among the People in the 1860's was a captured Mexican boy, whose son became one of the richest and most powerful Navajos.

In their turn, the whites made forays into Indian country. Any unarmed group they could find served to satisfy their vengeance and alleviate the servant shortage, so they killed the men and carried off the women and children. In order not to flout the antislavery law too openly, they held to the time honored fiction that these benighted savages were brought into Christian households to be educated and converted. As a matter of fact, Indians were bought and sold in New Mexico much like Negroes elsewhere.[10] But in official documents such human property was delicately alluded to as *piezas*.[11]

Later estimates gave the number of Indian slaves in New Mexico as three, four, or even six thousand, three out of four being Navajos.[12]

It seems worth while to pause over the factor of slavery in Navajo life because, in some ways, it did provide the education the Spaniards claimed. Not, however, in the Christian religion— we hear nothing about Navajos being converted, no matter how long their stay among the whites! Yet they learned arts and customs, which those who returned could bring to the tribe as a new stimulus to progress. A Spanish master and mistress treated their household of retainers much as did a feudal pat-

[9] Malouf, "The Effects of Spanish Slavery on the Indians of the Intermountain Region," *Southwestern Journal of Anthropology*, Vol. I, No. 3 (Autumn, 1945), 382.

[10] H. H. Bancroft, *History of Arizona and New Mexico*, 681n.

[11] See translation of wills, in New Mexico Historical Museum, Santa Fé.

[12] Oscar H. Lipps, *The Navajos*, 105, 113–115. Affidavits by General Carleton and Assistant Surgeon Louis Kennon, 1865.

Navajo group, showing medicine lodge with sand paintings used in curing the sick.
(Courtesy American Museum of Natural History)

A Navajo chant. Sitting on the sandpainting, a patient and her child receive strength from the powerful spirits.
(Courtesy American Museum of Natural History)

Carnero Mucho, Navajo leader and member of the delegation to Washington, 1874.
(Courtesy Bureau of American Ethnology)

Navajo Scout.
(Courtesy Ben Wittick Collection,
Laboratory of Anthropology, Santa Fé, New Mexico)

riarch who felt responsible for the well being of all. True, there was no hope of freedom and little chance for an honorable marriage. Yet a girl taken young enough grew content with her life, more physically comfortable than life in the Indian camps. She found a mate, bore children, and often refused to return to her people, when invited.

It was such captive women who wove the striking and intricate "slave blankets," so different from the usual Navajo product. These brilliantly colored fabrics, often with a hole for the head, like a poncho, were woven by Navajo women, yet with colors and designs foreign to the People.[13] Navajo weavers, supplied by their captors with new dyes and patterns, nevertheless chose to stick by the ancient type of loom, rather than the foot-treadle loom of the Europeans. The new possibilities thus tried out must have given suggestions to those Navajo women who finally returned to their people—usually with a family of children. Perhaps Spanish dress also had its influence, for the dons surely would not tolerate either buckskin leggings and shirt or a blanket dress, swinging open at the sides. Slavery must be accounted one factor—though perhaps a small one—in the Navajo learning process.

Fear of Spanish reprisals and Spanish slavery did not deter the Navajos from their life of freebooting. They were, indeed, living like many Europeans in the Middle Ages who practiced robbery as a business because it was their only road to wealth. Already, among the People, there were *ricos* or rich men, whose flocks ran into the thousands and whose sons would pay forty or fifty horses for a wife. These leading citizens often preferred to stay peacefully in the sheltered canyons avoiding war and would even make treaties with the whites and promise peace, shaking their heads over the unruly behavior of the young men. Much

[13]H. P. Mera, *The Slave Blanket*.

good silver and red cloth was purchased by the New Mexican treasury to pay these headmen, for whites have never got over the idea that the Indians must have powerful chiefs who can make them "toe the line." Doubtless the rich men really did want peace. They were in the position of a nation which has already won an empire and does not want it disturbed, but "they spoke in vain. 'I really at such and such a time shall go raiding, even though you speak so,' said the young men. 'No, my young men. My young men, my children, do not speak in that way.' Wherever there were war dances, wherever a ceremony was held, there in vain the headmen pleaded."[14]

It was no use. The only recourse of the unfortunate *rico* was to make good the losses out of his own flocks.

New Mexico whites began to take the law into their own hands—it was that or go bankrupt. Year by year, the wealth of their once rich province was passing out of their hands into those of the Indians. Ranches were being abandoned, cowboys would not stay, and there was almost no help from the government. The Mexican Republic was scarcely yet organized, and what army it had was busy putting down revolutions. New Mexico, its most distant province, had hardly a soldier. When robbed, the ranchers had government permission to strike out for themselves and recover what they could. So they, too, became expert at the surprise attack, scalping, and the escape with booty.

The Lords of the Soil were not intimidated. When a group of avengers appeared, they leaped on their horses, kept ready with dragging bridle reins, and made for the mountains. They were still fighting with arrows while the whites had guns, but they say they could easily get out of range while the white man was ramming in his powder. They sincerely believed that it would not be long before the whites would leave New Mexico

14 Sapir and Hoijer, *Navaho Texts,* 341.

and the land would be theirs. What really interfered with their plans was not the whites but the other Indians. For Utes and Apaches were also raiding freely. And to have the Utes on your trail was no joke. Even today the word *enemy,* to a Navajo, stands for Ute, and at the Enemy Way ceremony, which frees one from foreign contagion, the symbolic attacking party always comes from the north, the Ute home. Even without guns, the fighting could be deadly. "Arrows alone they depended upon, they say. When they shot at each other with them some were killed. Others just pulled the arrows out of themselves and took the arrows away from the enemy . . . . When they moved in among one another only the stone club and the axe were useful, they say. They clubbed each other to death with them and pounded each other to death, they say."[15]

The Ute hunters, unlike the Navajos, had never taken up agriculture and sheep raising. They wanted horses and captives. So the Navajos, with their flocks to take care of, were at a disadvantage, and even their hidden canyons could not always protect them. Almost every Navajo family tells some tale of an attack by Utes.[16] Just as white Americans can usually find some ancestor who came over during *Mayflower* days, so the Navajos have an ancestress who was captured by Utes. Of course, she escaped. Those who did not, have not come down to history. The Utes used to confine their prisoners by having them lie on the ground with a buffalo robe or a blanket over them and Utes sleeping all around on the edge of the robe. Wild and hair-raising are the tales of Navajo girls who evaded this custody and made their way home over canyon and desert.

Life was becoming pretty unpleasant for the Navajos, at least those engaged in raiding. They no longer dared to build

[15] *Ibid.,* 429.
[16] Sapir and Hoijer, *Navaho Texts,* 341.

permanent houses. Sometimes a family would keep one dwelling on a hill where some member could stay and look for enemies. The rest would move about with the herds, camping in a different place every night and never daring to take the animals into the open for water until after dark. Men, women, and children left their riding horses girt with the sheepskin which was their only saddle. The horsehair rope which served for bridle was left dragging on the ground so it could be stepped on to stop the horse from bolting. For, at any time of the night, they might hear the ominous thunder of a horse stampede and the wild cry of the sentinel: *U-u-tah! U-u-tah!*

To make it worse, the peaceful Hopis and Zuñis would risk a quick attack whenever the chances seemed good. For half a century, these harmless people had suffered raids whenever the Navajos got hungry. Now they watched the movements of the Utes and the Comanches, and when these tribes had the Navajos at a disadvantage, they also got in a blow. The country was a chaos of fighting bands, each prepared to rush out and attack another—provided it had sheep. Even Santa Fé, the capital, and Albuquerque, the largest town, were not safe from sudden raids. In the dark night attacks, no one knew whether the raiders were Navajos, Utes, Apaches, or even whites out for plunder. All were seizing their chances, but when investigations were made one name was always uttered first—Navajo. This was the word that had come to mean thief and robber in New Mexico, and it was the name that frightened workers off the ranches and travelers from the roads. The white residents stated plainly that they could not feel safe until the Navajos were exterminated.

It was into this situation that the United States government entered, promising peace and progress, with equal rights for all.

8: Men with Ears
Down to Their Ankles

UP TO 1846, few Navajos had ever even looked upon a white American. True, the Utes had seen the strange, long-whiskered creatures, tramping down the Colorado streams after beaver or gathering in the little adobe town of Pueblo, which the trappers used as a field headquarters. One Ute had married a Navajo and come to live with her and he reported:

"A certain people are going to come to us. From below where that sun constantly rises, they are going to come to us. Their ears are wider than anything. They extend down to their ankles. And these people at night, covering themselves with those ears of theirs, lie down to sleep." In fact, these people of the east were so miraculous that one of them "habitually builds a fire on his knees and lies down with his back toward it."[1]

This sounded like any other tale about spirits and monsters which Indians told each other around the campfire. They had no idea that, in the spring of 1846, a little army had already started across the prairies, bound for their own country of New Mexico. For the Republic of Mexico had declared war on the United States, and men of the northern republic were "burning

[1] Sapir and Hoijer, *Navaho Texts*, 331.

85

for the battlefield and panting for the rewards of honorable victory."[2] One army was already in Chihuahua, and naval ships were off the coast of California. General Kearny, starting from Fort Leavenworth in Kansas Territory, was out to reinforce them both and, as it transpired, to add large slices of territory to the United States.[3]

Kearny's Army of the West was a scratch affair, about the size of a modern infantry regiment. The men, all volunteers from Missouri Territory, elected their own officers, wore their own clothes, and provided their own horses (except one battalion which walked all the way). With waving banners, presented by the ladies of Kansas, they started "over the regions of uncultivated nature, where the eagle and the stars and stripes never before greeted the breeze."[4] They were to know a great deal more geography and ethnology before the ladies of Kansas welcomed the survivors home.

For the first part of the expedition, all went well. In Santa Fé the governor fled, and the city surrendered. Rather, it accepted gracefully a change of government. There had been no real authority for so long that the inhabitants were delighted to have someone take charge. As Kearny marched down the Río Grande or sat in Santa Fé, he received daily deputations from other towns and from the Pueblo Indians, eager to take the oath of allegiance. The new rulers promised the citizens every privilege they had had under their former government, including protection from raids and restoration of stolen property. So, promptly, they were told about the Navajos.

The thing to do, said the Americans, would be to invite all

[2] W. E. Connelly, *Doniphan's Expedition and the Conquest of New Mexico and California*, 177.

[3] The following account is adapted from *Doniphan's Expedition*, 124–177. Pages are noted for quotations.

[4] Connelly, *Doniphan's Expedition*, 141.

the Indians to come to a conference. They should be told that peace was now established and raiding was against the law, and then their chiefs should sign a permanent peace treaty. So detachments of soldiers were sent out to bring in the Indians. The Pueblos came cheerfully, bearing arms and asking when their help would be wanted in running off the Navajos. Some Apaches came, their chief admitting grimly: "I take your counsel because you are stronger than I am." Even some Utes came. But where were the Navajos? The answer was a raid on the Río Grande pueblos which killed seven or eight men, took as many women and children captives, and drove off sheep, cattle, and mules.

When this happened, Kearny was already off to California on that epoch-making march which is signalized by markers all along the United States highways, and he left New Mexico under the charge of Doniphan, elected colonel of the Missouri volunteers. It was these long-whiskered farm boys from the "Piker State" who gave the Navajos their first encounter with white Americans. The occasion was literally a howling success.

Doniphan, at Santa Fé, was still east of the Goods of Value Range which had held the Navajos in check for so long. He decided to march straight across it into Navajo country and meet the Indians on their own ground. Three detachments started over the range by different routes, and wild were the tales they told afterward about these chunky little hills which to them seemed "high as the Alps and covered with perpetual snow." They had some excuse for the impression since this was November, they had left their tents behind for lightness, and the government had given them no overcoats. When they woke up in the morning covered with snow and with ice in their long whiskers, they considered their exploit equal to that of Hannibal, crossing the Alps, or anyway, Napoleon.[5]

[5] *Ibid.,* 299.

Only one detachment found the Navajos.[6] This was the one ordered to start from Cebolleta, ancient home of the Enemy Navajos and the only settlement of the tribe east of the mountains. These Navajos had long ago thrown in their lot with the whites, they were Catholic, some of them spoke Spanish, and often before they had guided and interpreted for the Spaniards as they now did for the new conquerors. One of their big men, Sandoval, was brought in by a landowner from Laguna Pueblo. He agreed to go and visit the Navajo chiefs, and he disappeared into the impenetrable mountains. Coming back, he reported that the chiefs were well disposed for peace. However, they did not like to come in among the New Mexicans without a pretty strong escort. Moreover, they would like to take a look at the new conquerors before making a decision. Why did not the Americans come to them? The Missourians were game and even delighted. Captain Reid volunteered for the trip with thirty picked men. Reid was the freeborn American who had faced out General Kearny in the matter of his men wearing coats on a hot day's march. "My men, sir," he had told his commanding officer, "came not to dress but to fight the enemies of their country."[7] It was the general who gave in.

Reid and his thirty volunteers mounted their horses, leaving tents and wagons behind. Sandoval guided them, every day making smoke signals to proclaim their friendly intentions and every day promising that tomorrow they would meet the Navajos. At last the smoke signals took effect. Straggling horsemen began to meet them and to talk with Sandoval. Be sure that word was carried back across the mountains that strangers are coming! Even though they were few, they had muskets, while the Navajos had only bows. Better not to rush them was the

[6] *Ibid.*, 285–97.
[7] *Ibid.*, 224.

decision—let them come on and be looked over. So Reid was told of a great dance, being held in the Chuska Mountains. The Navajos would escort him there. The two strange groups of warriors eyed each other, each knowing that death might be around the corner. Then Reid said that meeting Navajos was what he had come for, and he would go. That kind of talk appealed to the Navajos, and they gave him a royal welcome. The Americans let the Indians swarm around their campfire and lead their horses out of sight to pasture. The Navajos were delighted—no one else in New Mexico treated them like this. They presented the half-starved soldiers with mutton ribs, roasted at the campfire. Then the Missourians, still armed with their muskets and revolvers, "danced all night among the Navajos to the music of drums and rattles."

Meantime runners had gone from the Navajos to the grassy valley beyond the mountains where the rich old man, Narbona, had his cornfields. What about these pleasant but unpredictable strangers? Should they be allowed to go in peace? Narbona, says tradition, answered that the corn was not yet harvested, and it would be better to keep the peace at least until they got in their winter supplies. The Navajos were behaving like any sovereign nation, faced with an international incident and stalling off trouble with some diplomatic "conversations."

The Americans must come farther, their hosts told them, and see Narbona himself. Captain Reid objected that they were out of food, and instantly the Navajos dragged in some sheep carcasses. The Missourians, who decided their affairs by ballot, voted to go on. So they crossed the Continental Divide, "each man leading his horse among the slabs and fragments of great rocks . . . fearful to behold" and seeming "to bid defiance to the puny efforts of man . . . ."[8]

[8] *Ibid.*, 288.

A day's march brought them to a grassy plateau on the western slope of the mountains, where a spring welled out from beneath a huge cottonwood tree. This was a great gathering ground of the Navajos, and here they kept their sheep, safe from enemy intrusion. There were thousands of them in view, said Private Moore, the black and the white kept separate.[9] His farmer's eye estimated five thousand black sheep in one flock. One of the great men of the Navajos had ridden out to meet the newcomers. He was Narbona, an old man of eighty and so crippled with rheumatism that he could hardly sit a horse. The Americans do not report his costume, but his fingernails, they say, were two or three inches long.

Narbona sent runners out in every direction to summon the Navajos, and thousands of them came on horseback. They met on the plateau, with huge pinnacles of rock towering above them. Narbona was carried in on a litter of willow rods and conducted the council lying on his back. His son stood near him to relay his orders, which were given and repeated in low, dignified voices. Captain Reid explained his mission and then Narbona's wife, a fiery little woman of fifty, rose to speak. She had oratorical qualities, says Private Moore, and she nearly persuaded the council that if they went to meet with the Americans they would all be killed. As the Navajos reached for their weapons, Narbona tapped three times on the mat with his long nails. His son stooped to hear his words, then spoke quietly to the man next to him. Instantly the little woman had her arms pinioned and was rushed from the council meadow. Not a Navajo turned his head or showed any expression. The council ended happily with the conclusion that the Navajos should come to Zuñi to conclude a peace.

[9] *Ibid.*, 294.

The Americans turned cheerfully homeward. Soon they were overtaken by a runner from Narbona who explained that the old man advised them to take good care of their horses, as some of the young fellows planned to steal them. When they arrived at Cebolleta, they found indeed that most of the stock had been driven off. Narbona had done what he could with his diplomatic conversations, but he was not a dictator. And thirty brave men were not enough to convince the Navajos that they should give up their means of livelihood.

The diplomatic conversations continued, much as they have in the past, on a larger scale, before other wars. Narbona, with other leading men and five hundred mounted Navajos, came to Bear Water (now Fort Wingate) to meet Colonel Doniphan in person. It was a bit hard for the colonel to explain why the New Mexicans, the ancient Navajo enemies, were now American citizens with a right to be protected. He was answered by a young Navajo, called Long Earrings, just rising to be a leader. Doniphan's aide translates his words in the elegant English thought proper to that day.

Americans! You have a strange cause of war against the Navajos. We have waged war against the New Mexicans for several years. We have plundered their villages and killed many of their people and made many prisoners. We had just cause for all this. *You* have lately commenced a war against the same people. You are powerful. You have great guns and many brave soldiers. You have therefore conquered them, the very thing we have been attempting to do for so many years. You now turn upon us for attempting to do what you have done yourselves. We cannot see why you have cause of quarrel with us for fighting the New Mexicans on the west while you do the same thing on the east. Look how matters stand. This is our war. We have more right to complain of you for interfering in our war than you have to quarrel with us for continuing a war we had begun long before you got here. If you will act justly, you will allow us to settle our own differences.[10]

Doubtless the Missourians agreed. However, they had orders to get a treaty signed and be on their way to Mexico. So, after much talk, a treaty was signed. Here we begin to get the names of Navajo leaders—at least their Spanish names, weirdly spelled by the American scribes. It is fascinating to puzzle out what their motives really were as they made this promise to give up their only means to wealth. There was Narbona, an old man rich in flocks and glad of protection. Doubtless he really meant the promise as far as he himself was concerned. Cabballada Mucha, or Big Horse Herd, the son of a Hopi, may have had the same motive. Then there was Sandoval, the Enemy Navajo, who had lived so long near the whites that he knew better than to fight them. There was Long Earrings, the young orator, who would soon grow to fame. He must have been rich, for all the various names the Navajos gave him refer to his silver ornaments. Perhaps he wanted protection but perhaps, too, he was better able to judge the strength of the newcomers and the wastefulness of opposing them. The ambitious young men who had not yet got their flocks were not asked to sign. The ambassadors from a democratic country had no idea how real was this other democracy in which no one man could dictate.

The Americans were now on fire to start for Mexico, but they still had to see that the Navajos made peace with the Zuñis so that everything could be left shipshape. Doniphan persuaded three Navajo leaders to ride to Zuñi with him, though they protested that they went in fear of their lives and must sleep in

[10] Ralph E. Twitchell, *The History of the Occupation of New Mexico,* 98–100.

the same house with him under guard. This making peace between two enemies who both had wrongs to right was a bitter
pill. The Navajos taunted the Zuñis (and how we wish we had
their actual words, instead of the stilted English of Lieutenant
Hughes):

The cause of your present dissatisfaction is just this. The war between
us has been waged for plunder. You kill and drive off our flocks and
herds and subsist your people upon them, and use them for your own
advantage. To resent this, we have plundered your villages, taken
your women and children captives and made slaves of them. Lately
you have been unsuccessful. We have out stolen you and therefore
you are mad and dissatisfied about it. But there is one thing you
cannot accuse the Navajos of doing and that is killing women and
children. You know, not many years past, when our women and children went into the mountains, to gather piñons, your warriors fell
upon and killed about forty of them. This cowardly act was per-
petrated when there were no Navajo warriors to afford them succor.[11]

The angry Zuñis, who really had generations of wrongs to
avenge, wanted to seize the three Navajos on the spot. With a
glance at the bluecoats, the Navajos replied calmly: "We have
not the slightest fear of any injury you may attempt to offer us,
for we trust ourselves with a more honorable people."

Would that that trust need never have been disappointed!
Yet Doniphan was no more able to make promises for the future
behavior of his countrymen than Narbona was for his. Each side
probably expected more of the other in the way of wisdom and
self control than any human beings could have given. Doniphan
departed for Chihuahua in a glow of goodwill, leaving New
Mexico at peace. But the feuds and anarchy of generations were
not to be put aside with a few words. The happy acquiescence of

[11] Connelly, *Doniphan's Expedition*, 310–311.

Navajos and New Mexicans evaporated soon after the papers were signed. Perhaps things might have been better had the army of occupation been sufficiently large and had its soldiers been well drilled, well supplied, and perfectly behaved. Also, had its officers been statesmen with a knowledge of Spanish, as well as economics, sociology, and anthropology. It soon became apparent that the bluecoats could not protect any of the warring New Mexico groups from each other. Some Indians began a little raiding, just to see what could be done, and the troopers never happened to be in the right place at the right time. Some New Mexicans began to reconsider their hasty surrender, to import arms from Mexico, and to see what opposition they could raise. They worked on the Taos Indians until a rebellion in that pueblo killed the appointed American governor. Then a series of governors and Indian agents were sent for from the east, and each reported that fantastic tales were being told the Indians as an inducement to revolt. The Indians found it best to go back to raiding.

By 1849, Congress felt that the war department should now be through conquering Indians and that their affairs should be turned over to the Interior. James S. Calhoun was the first agent for New Mexico, but he dared not move into Indian country without an escort (and horse feed) from the army. He had the hope of each new official that now a permanent treaty could be made with the Navajos. So he accompanied the military governor, Colonel Washington, out to the wild Chuska Mountains and the redoubtable Canyon de Chelley. Someone should unearth a Navajo account of the tragedy which occurred on that trip and which put an end to Navajo trust in the omniscience of white Americans.

Calhoun, the Indian agent, has told the story simply and tersely.[12] It was going to make his job harder for years to come.

A more dramatic version comes from eager young Lieutenant Simpson, interested in Pueblo ruins and appreciative of sunsets.[13] The party, he says, had with them fifty-four Pueblo Indians, some mounted New Mexico volunteers (who kept deserting), and two guides. One was a Mexican colonel and the other was Sandoval, chief of the Enemy Navajos and friend of the whites. Dragging their cannon up and down the steep ravines, the party marched from Jemez and past the ruins of Chaco Canyon and the Animas, which were first introduced to Americans in an enthusiastic description by Lieutenant Simpson.

Doubtless the Navajos were watching from behind every hill as they do today whenever strange creatures enter their land. Gradually they stole out to join the party, first the women as a sign of peace, then the men in bright blankets, their leather helmets topped with eagle feathers. Soon a horde of Navajos was galloping ahead in a cloud of dust with the Pueblo men. They led the way down the Tunicha Valley and across flat lands blooming with Navajo cornfields, the best Simpson had seen in that country. The troops were short of fodder for their mules, so they proceeded to cut the corn, but the Navajos did not resist. However, Simpson may have had forbodings of the sad affair to come. As they drew near the bristling hills which were the Indian stronghold, he describes "a dark, portentous cloud was hovering over the Tumecha (Tunicha) Mountains, the forked lightning ever and anon darting vividly athwart it."[14]

The Navajos, having fed at the army mess, were gaining confidence. Messengers must have galloped off for now some of their lesser leaders appeared. Yes, they agreed, they would

[12] James S. Calhoun, *Official Correspondence* (ed. by Annie H. Abel), 26–37.

[13] Lieut. J. H. Simpson, *Journal of a Military Reconnaissance from Santa Fe., N. M., to the Navajo Country.*

[14] *Ibid.,* 88.

send for the greater chiefs. Tomorrow at noon there should be a council. The great Narbona himself, the same who had welcomed Captain Reid, had his cornfields nearby. Now that things were going so well, he would meet with the whites, and all should be settled. It did not cross the mind of either Calhoun or Colonel Washington that Narbona was not the head of a well-organized nation, able to answer for the conduct of every Navajo. They decided that the "nation" was to be summoned to Canyon de Chelley, and the great and final treaty was to be signed.

Next day Narbona came. He was eighty years old but still riding his horse. The mask of his dead face, taken after the whites had shot him, has that grave composure which Simpson found "not unlike that of General George Washington—I hope the comparison will be pardoned." Narbona and the other leaders, Largo and Archuleta, delivered up 130 stolen sheep and several horses and mules. They regretted the raids, they said, and no wonder. Narbona, with his cornfields, was a rich man, who could not afford trouble. He could not keep his young men quiet, but he offered to make good their thefts out of his own flocks.[15]

Now, Colonel Washington rode forward. His words were translated by a Mr. Conkling of Santa Fé, who probably spoke in Spanish, Navajo being unknown to most of the white Americans of that day. Let us hope that some Spanish-speaking Indian understood the strange theorems presented and had words in which to explain them to his countrymen. I have taken the liberty of shortening the colonels ponderous phrases since we have them at best only from Simpson's memory. The simple, antiphonal responses of the Navajos are left as reported in the Senate document.[16]

[15] Calhoun, *Correspondence*, 38.
[16] Simpson, *Journal*, 90.

The old-fashioned cradleboard used to protect a baby while traveling.
(Courtesy American Museum of Natural History)

Manuelito, war chief of the Navajos.
(E. A. Burbank, Courtesy Ben Wittick Collection,
Laboratory of Anthropology, Santa Fé, New Mexico)

Colonel: "The Navajos are to assemble in Canyon de Chelley where a treaty will be made with the whole nation."

Interpreter: "They say they understand it."

Colonel: "Their friends are now those of the United States and their enemies its enemies. Instead of fighting with other Indians, they must apply to the United States for justice."

Interpreter: "They say they are willing."

Colonel: "When the treaty is made, all trade between themselves and other nations (this meant Mexico) will be under regulations prescribed by the United States. This is to prevent their being cheated."

Interpreter: "They understand it and are content."

Colonel: "If any wrong is done them by a citizen of the United States, the wrongdoer shall be punished as though he had harmed a white American."

Interpreter: "They say they understand it, and it is all right."

Colonel: "The people of the United States are to go in and out of Navajo country without molestation."

Interpreter: "They say very well."

Colonel: "The government of the United States has a right to put Military posts in their country—of course for the protection of the Navajos."

Interpreter: "They say they are very glad."

Colonel: "If the Navajos keep faithfully to the treaty, the government will make them presents of axes, hoes, farm tools, and blankets."

Interpreter: "They say it is all right."

If the Navajos had now galloped away from their powerful new friends, there would have been no crisis. They did not really need an explanation of the demands to which they had chorused assent so politely. Doubtless they did not intend to comply with them any more than convenient. However, Sandoval, the Enemy Navajo leader, took the matter seriously. Riding forward in his gorgeously colored blanket, he lined up three or four hundred horsemen, as gaily decked in red, blue, and white, with rifle erect in hand. Then he began to explain to them the "views and purposes of the United States government."[17]

Here trouble began. Looking along the line of mounted Navajos, one of the Mexican volunteers spied a horse which had been stolen from him months ago. He had been helpless against the vanishing raiders, but now he was under the aegis of a powerful government. He told Colonel Washington, and the colonel demanded the horse. To him, it seemed an unimportant item, and perhaps he expected another submissive chorus of assent. But the Navajos now were not talking about vague theories like the jurisdiction of the United States. Here was a subject which they understood, and they became voluble. Of course the horse had been stolen, they admitted, but that was long ago. Since then, it had changed hands many times and even been ridden back to its owner's village. Why had he not claimed it then? There must have been hidden smiles behind the grave faces as they implied that the owner would never have claimed it in this world had he not had a United States colonel beside him. After all, horse stealing was an honorable profession, practiced by the Mexicans as well as the Navajos. This sheltering behind a third party was not playing the game.

Colonel Washington's game, however, was played in a different way. To him, the protection of the United States was a sacred thing, even when offered unthinkingly in an Indian quarrel.

"Give back the horse," he ordered, "or we will fire."

Impossible! The colonel had struck a point where Navajo

[17] *Ibid.*, 91.

principles were as firm as his own. There could be no giving up
of "that by which men live."

"Seize the horse," commanded the colonel. "Seize any
horse."

Lieutenant Tores tried, but at his first move, the whole
blanketed horde whirled their horses and galloped away. The
guard fired. Only one man fell. Eighty-year-old Narbona, who
was nearest the whites and slow to move, was killed. Six others
were mortally injured. "Major Peck also threw among them,
very handsomely . . . a couple of round shot."[18]

Thus ended the brief honeymoon of friendship when white
soldiers were treated by the Navajos as "People" like themselves. The newcomers, it appeared, were simply an enemy
nuisance, like the Spaniards and the mountain lions. Their
actions were not rational and one could understand them only
as one understands a wild animal, by watching him, weapon
in hand. The Navajos established their policy with the Americans as with other foes—fight when convenient, otherwise use
any ruse to escape.

The rest of Colonel Washington's trip was anticlimactic.
True, he dragged his artillery and pushed his mules over the
Tunicha Mountains, just as planned, and his route is now known
as Washington Pass. (The mountains, he discovered, were not
high as the Alps and topped with eternal snow as they had
looked to the wornout Missouri volunteers.) He kept alert for
an attack, sending out Pueblo scouts under the valiant Captain
Dodge who will appear later in this narrative. The obedient
Pueblos expected death and rubbed medicine on their hearts to
make them brave, but of course the Navajos did not attack.
When an enemy was in force, it was the Navajo policy to let
him alone, waiting to leap on him at some defenseless mo-

[18] *Ibid.*

ment. This type of commando tactics was an old story with the Indians.

The troops came safely toward Canyon de Chelley, and "it was somewhat exciting to observe the huts of the enemy, one after another, springing up into smoke and flame and their owners scampering off in flight."[19] The soldiers camped among the cornfields and made short work of the ripe corn. There had been much coming and going of Navajos along the flanks of the party and much conferring with Sandoval. News of what had happened was common property throughout the Navajo country, and Mariano Martinez, the local chief, was prepared. To Washington's surprise, it appeared that on this side of the mountains, there were different leaders. The sombre faced Mariano had his bow and arrows slung over a blue American overcoat, perhaps from some caravan of the Santa Fé Trail. He and the youthful Chapeton, down from San Juan country, promised everything. Yes, the chiefs should be convened, stolen stock returned, and captives given up. (One Mexican captive of Chapeton, who was present, refused this privilege and did not even inquire of his family in Santa Fé.)

No promises were kept. After this, Navajos proceeded to raid the white Americans, as they had the Spaniards and the Pueblos. These were commando raids: a swift dash in the night, the clatter of horses' hooves, and—before the bugle could be blown—the thieves had vanished. It was decided that, for the first time, soldiers must actually be stationed in Navajo country. Toward its center, there was a meadow beside a flowing stream where the Navajos used to pasture their flocks. The Navajos called it Green Place in the Rocks. Here the whites built a little adobe fort and named it Fort Defiance.

[19] *Ibid.*, 100.

9: Little White Fathers

FIRST AGENTS

"WHAT ABOUT THE captives?" said the agent from the east.[1] It was the new agent's first meeting with the Navajos and a hard enough proposition since he had never seen an Indian before. He and three predecessors had been appointed "little white fathers" under the great white father at Washington, the secretary of the interior, and the governor of New Mexico. Already this particular incumbent had been exasperated beyond endurance. The military at Fort Defiance would hardly give him office room, let alone storage space for the gifts with which he was to pacify the Indians. He had been forced to move to Jemez, and now he had summoned the Navajos who were his charge. He wanted their chiefs to sign a permanent peace treaty.

"What about the captives? The people along the Río Grande complain that the Navajos have captured their children, stolen their stock, that their fields have to be idle for they cannot work them for fear of your people."

"My people are all crying in the same way," replied gray-haired Armijo who was speaking for the Navajos that day. "Three of our chiefs now sitting before you mourn for their

[1] Calhoun, *Correspondence*, 467–69.

children who have been taken from their homes by the Mexicans. More than 200 of our children have been carried off and we know not where they are . . . . Eleven times have we given up our captives. Only once have the Mexicans given up theirs. Is it American justice that we must give up everything and receive nothing?"

The agent was not ready with an answer. He would write to the Great White Father, he said. America always kept her promises. Mournfully, Armijo replied: "In the days of the Mexican government, our captains received staffs of office—and they were killed at the first opportunity. We do not know how it will be now."

The agent wrote to his superior, the governor of New Mexico Territory, who wrote to the Indian commissioner at Washington. In that year, 1852, it took three or four months for a letter to go across the plains and the same time for an answer. That is, supposing the commissioner did have an answer and the mail coach was not robbed. The Comanches were now rampaging through Texas, and once they even attacked a mail coach with several guards. After capturing a mail coach, they took pleasure in delivering letters over the desert at their own sweet will, an important proclamation from the president being left hanging from a pole in the breeze.

The little white fathers succeeded each other at the rate of about one a year. Rarely could they endure for longer than that the lack of instructions, the lack of funds, and the constant quarrels with the military. For the government had manned Fort Defiance with troops whose commander was in full charge in case of trouble. But the day of Indian troubles should really be over, thought the people at Washington. The civilian agent should now be able to get a peace treaty and start the Navajos on the road to civilization. No government at that time realized what was necessary for such a project, and perhaps we do not know even now. America, in the throes of the slavery question, had little time for planning and no Civil Service. Agents were sent out haphazardly, and one of them confessed:

... Indian agents ... are generally appointed for political services. Mr. Wingfield came here as agent because he was a friend of Mr. Dawson of Georgia; Mr. Wolley, an old man of seventy years of age, because he was the friend of Mr. Clay; Mr. Weightman because he wished to be returned as delegate and myself because I could sing a good political song. Neither of us was by habit or education better fitted to be an Indian agent than to follow any other business.[2]

The Navajos heard what their little white father said, translated from English to Spanish and from Spanish to Navajo. They went home and continued raiding. Grimly the fort commander sent out his small detachments of cavalry, on horses unaccustomed to mountainous country. No sooner were soldiers rushed to one scene of trouble than the Indians swooped down on another, miles away. The frantic citizens sent appeals to the government for help. Céran St. Vrain, the old plainsman, said that never in his experience had things been so bad. Then suddenly there came to the Navajos a white man who was a friend. They called him Red Shirt.

Captain Henry Dodge, who wore a red shirt with his cavalry trousers, was a veteran of the Rocky Mountain expedition and of the Santa Fé Trail. He had commanded a company of volunteers on the ill-fated expedition when Narbona was killed. Governor Calhoun, who knew well that Captain Dodge had a father and brother in the Senate, made official mention of his promptness and efficiency. Dodge liked Indians and really

[2] Edwin L. Sabin, *Kit Carson Days, 1809–1869*, 639.

planned something for the Navajos beside treaties. He built himself a house at Sheep Springs, near Fort Defiance, and proceeded to spend the $5,000 voted to his charges by Congress on useful gifts and on teaching.

His first distribution of gifts was planned at Red Lake near Fort Defiance, and two ox teams loaded with goods had come from Santa Fé. The Navajos, led by Long Earrings, refused to approach the lake, for they had heard rumblings there at night, they said, and knew it contained a water monster.

"I'll show you," said Red Shirt. He threw off his clothes and swam to the other shore and back. Old Navajos remember hearing the story of how he came wading back to them through the cattails and how the People meekly approached the lake at his bidding.

The ox teams drew up. The Navajos gathered, rank on rank, sitting on their horses, in their badger skin caps, and with their long knives held upright. They watched the unrolling of yard after yard of calico, a new luxury to them who were still dressing in buckskin and hand-woven wool. Then came copper wire for bracelets. The Navajos at this time were not working silver, but they loved the white man's copper wire which was so easily cut and twisted. It was the wire which set the wild young men to rioting. They dashed forward on their horses, grabbing an end and unrolling the coil over the prairie as they raced away. Then someone snatched a bolt of cloth and galloped off with that, while others hacked at it with their knives. What they did not seize was torn on the rocks and trampled under the horses' feet.

Red Shirt "jumped around and hollered," say the Navajos, quite understanding how he felt. Even Red Shirt Dodge may not have understood how the Indians felt, getting their first sight of calico by the bolt. And the senator's son had not been brought up in the tradition that the way to success for a brave youth is to rush and grab. But he could not stay angry at his friends. They respected him when he said quietly, "If you will leave me the wagons, I will send them back to Santa Fé for more goods."

Then Long Earrings rode forward and called for silence. This was the last speech he was to make before the people, and with the years it has come to have the ring of grim prophecy.

"My relatives," said Long Earrings, "if we go on behaving like this, soon all the trees and stones will fight against us. Soon you will all be dragging away on the white man's road and only the coyotes will be left here."

Then, say the Navajos, Long Earrings prophesied his own death. The people went away meekly, and Red Shirt sent four ox teams to Santa Fé for more goods. He had no further trouble. In the four pleasant years while he was agent at the fort, he brought an American blacksmith to teach the Navajos his art. Herrero, who later became a Navajo leader, began to make knife blades, bits, and bridle parts. Soon the Navajos would not have to steal these things. Red Shirt brought a Mexican silversmith to make the silver bridle ornaments, the belts, and pins which the Navajos now got from Mexicans and Utes. He brought a Mexican interpreter who knew Navajo, so that he could talk to his Indian visitors at all times. He married a Navajo wife, and now there was a friend and interpreter always at hand to explain what the People did.

Yes, the Navajos understood people like Red Shirt. But he was too much like a Navajo, and he met the fate of one. He was killed by the Apaches while out hunting. The Navajos went back to agents who held meetings and stern military men who gave them orders through subordinates.

They were not used to military etiquette, for they were a

democratic people. Each group of relatives decided its own affairs, and they followed their prominent men only because they seemed elderly and successful and therefore worth listening to. So they did not see why they might not stroll in and speak to the post commandant at any time they chose. If he would not speak to them, he was not their friend, so they proceeded to rob his supply trains, just as they would rob Utes or Mexicans. They had never been reconciled to having the fort built in one of the few grassy dells of their desert domain. It had been a favorite camping place because it contained a flowing spring where they could water their flocks. A little beyond was a grassy meadow which gave good pasturage, but now, they were told to keep their stock out of the meadow, on pain of having them shot. They did not obey, and the post commandant had sixty Navajo horses killed.

Horses were still the dearest thing to a Navajo's heart. Yet the people had learned that there was no gain whatever in making an attack on the bluecoats. One could only wait his chance and take some little vengeance on the sly. So months later, a Navajo lounging around the post suddenly shot an arrow into the back of the commandant's Negro slave.

It was little enough in return for sixty of "that by which men live." Long Earrings was called into consultation and tried to explain the Navajo viewpoint. He said he would pay for the slave which was a handsome offer, considering that no pay had been given for the horses. No, the commandant wanted the murderer and that within twenty days. The Navajo payment for murder involves either the payment of goods or the killing of one of the murderer's group who is of the same importance as the victim. The Navajos knew how the whites regarded a Negro slave, so they killed a Mexican slave of their own and dragged the body to the fort. To the whites it looked like an insult. Immediately six peaceful Navajos were killed, and a punitive expedition went out. All that summer, march after march was made, with scores of eager Indians as guides. They were the Enemy Navajos, from east of the mountains, who long since had decided on which side their interests lay, and there were the Zuñis, frantic for revenge and now carrying guns provided by the whites. For years they had begged to help in chasing the Navajos, and at last the army was admitting that their help was necessary.

Most unfortunate of all, the Utes, once considered the worst of culprits, were now accepted and employed on the winning side. Many of them were wearing the broad campaign hats of the United States scouts and were receiving pay from the government. Perhaps this was because the Utes—at least those bands nearest the Navajos—had had the luck to be given Kit Carson as their agent. Tipping his chair back against the adobe wall of his house in Taos, Father Kit could converse with his Indian visitors in sign language. He never reported any trouble. His Indians "stole some animals from the Mexicans and the Mexicans stole some from them. The Indians gave me the animals stolen by them and I made the Mexicans return the animals they had stolen, thus satisfying both parties." No agent had ever before talked about the two parties as though they had equal rights.

The Utes cheerfully guided the soldiers to the Navajo hideouts and picked up a few animals on their own account. All winter the soldiers shivered and starved and lost their mules over precipices, but no Navajos were found. Hidden in the canyons where even the Utes did not dare to pry, the Navajos were making their plans. Life was hard now, for they had to be always driving their herds from place to place. Every sentinal was alert to distinguish among the rocks the broad campaign hats of a skulking Ute. Old watchtowers were manned again.

On many a hill one can see ancient Pueblo buildings roughly repaired by the Navajos. Indians say that one of them near Wide Ruins used to have a grapevine rope attached to a bell in the valley. When enemies were sighted, the bell was rung and grazing horses were rushed to cover. As Edward Sapir's informant put it: "And then, you see, the Utes started killing us. The cornfields came not to be attended to. From different directions the Mexicans were doing likewise to us. (Navajos always spoke of the whites of New Mexico as Mexicans). And things became very bad."[3]

In fact, the Navajos were so desperate that they made up their minds to attack Fort Defiance. With the worst enemy demolished, the others might be frightened away. Never had the People organized such an attack, with assaulting and flanking parties and divisional commanders. Their years of hanging around the Fort had not gone for nothing. Indians who were children then remember hearing of the night-long arguments when the matter was discussed. The famous Navajo leaders began to assume their positions. Long Earrings was for peace, as always, and Ganado Mucho, or Many Cattle, stood with him, for obvious reasons. Barboncito, the Bearded, and Manuelito, the two leaders who had signed the treaty with Doniphan, took the other side. These were to grow more important in time to come. Perhaps the king pin of them all was Herrero, the blacksmith who lived inside the fort. It may well have been he who planned the strategy, but even Herrero was not expert enough to remember the cannon protecting the fort from the eastern hill slope. Nor did he consider that the Navajo watchman, inside the fort, might take the whites' side. The watchman gave the alarm, the cannon fired, and the attackers scattered. The only casualty was one soldier with a steel arrow through his heart.

[3] Sapir and Hoijer, *Navaho Texts,* 345.

The Navajos expected vengeance of a sweeping sort. Wildly they scattered, driving their sheep and horses into the deepest canyons. They watched from behind the rocks as General Canby marched across the land, and those whom he could find meekly made a truce. They expected years of hiding and then, perhaps, the vengeance which Long Earrings had prophesied. How could they know that the Navajos were only an incident in the history of a United States rolling into civil war? The Navajos watched incredulously while troops marched out of Fort Defiance in 1861. Then the Utes, the Zuñis, and Hopi were upon them. Again authority was gone, and New Mexico was a madhouse.

Only this time it was a madhouse where people had guns, where they were used to military maneuvers and exasperated to the point of carnage. It is fair to say that the Navajos were not the only raiders. The Apaches were out in full force. New Mexico had already had its influx of white outlaws, who were willing to steal whatever they could and blame it on the Indians. Laguna Pueblo told a pathetic tale of how some white horsemen arrived there one noon demanding cattle. The cattle were all out at pasture, said the governor. Whereupon they tied him up and went out to take everything they could find.

This was the opportunity for satisfying private grudges and filling private pocketbooks. This was when Long Earrings, the Navajo peace leader, met his end. Arthur Chester, the Navajo who seems to have been christened with a president's name, upside down, is the grandson who tells the story.

A party of whites came to Zuñi and said they were going on a Navajo hunt. They wanted help, for neither whites nor Zuñis dared to enter the Navajo country except in force. They rode north past Klagetoh, and there they saw a lone horseman coming toward them—Long Earrings, or Many Buttons, as he was sometimes called, with his silver ornaments shining in the sun. One Zuñi knew him for the great peace maker and called out a warning, but the others did not care. Then the Zuñi (so his descendants say) jumped off his horse and ran up and down, the scout's signal to announce an enemy approach. Long Earrings apparently did not see him. Still, one story says that he was tired of the struggle and thought the best way to die was by an enemy's hands. He came on.

A musket shot rang out. Now Long Earrings picked up his bow and shot four times, the magic number which appears in every Navajo story. He got one enemy in the breast, one in the throat, one in the mouth, and one in the ear, so say his grandchildren. He galloped away, firing over his shoulder, but the plunging horse rammed a tree and threw him. He crawled into a gully under a rain of bullets, and there he lay shooting until he had used up his arrows. Then the bullets killed him. The whites and the Zuñis came up and each threw a stone at him until his body was crushed, and then they scalped him.

Now the Navajos had no strong peace advocate for Many Cattle was occupied chiefly in his own affairs. The Navajos emerged from their hidden canyons, and they and the Apaches overran the country. They even entered the towns to drive off stock and murder citizens a few miles out of Santa Fé. They kept out of the way while, in 1862, a confederate army marched up the Río Grande to occupy Albuquerque and Santa Fé. After a few weeks, it was gone again, routed at the battle of Glorieta. To the Navajos, this only meant that now they could raid unhindered.

Yet now, when they least expected it, the government at Washington decided to clean the raiders out of New Mexico. General Carleton was put in charge, and he took the Apaches first. His orders were: All Indian men of that tribe are to be killed whenever and wherever you can find them. The women and children will not be harmed, but you will take them prisoners. The Indians are to be soundly whipped, without councils or parleys.

10: *Kit Carson Brings 'Em Back Alive*

THE ROUNDUP

Soon after Carleton took command, eighteen prominent Navajos waited upon him at Santa Fé. They wanted to make a treaty.

"Why a treaty?" asked Carleton.

"That we may hereafter have peace."

"Well then go home, stay there, attend to your own affairs, commit no more robberies and you have made peace at once, without the trouble of a treaty."[1]

If it had been so simple! But the Navajo affairs were raiding and fighting, and they were long past the point where an offer of friendship could turn them from their settled career. A peaceful and lowly subsistence did not interest them—at least not the young bloods. White Americans perhaps can sympathize with their desire to have big and ever bigger herds. They may realize that this does not make one either cruel or inhuman and that Navajo methods caused no more suffering than those of some unscrupulous factory owner who exploits his employees and ruins his business rivals. Still, those methods could not fit in with the development of New Mexico in the nineteenth century.

"You know you have always broken treaties," Carleton re-

[1] Ralph E. Twitchell, *The History of the Occupation of New Mexico*, 430n.

minded them. But of course—treaties were only a move in a chess game. They had broken six of them since the United States took over New Mexico and some before the Senate had time to ratify them. These "big talks" were a way of keeping strangers and enemies quiet, just as you would keep wild animals quiet by some ruse, while you got your weapons ready. The Navajos might have been amazed to know that Carleton regarded *them* as wild animals, "who can no more be trusted than the wolves that run through their mountains."

Of course, neither side could be "trusted" to hand over New Mexico to the other. The only solution was war. This time, said Carleton, it would be a war to end war, as far as the Navajos were concerned. The Indians must not only be whipped, but they must be removed, lock, stock, and barrel—or, rather, sheep, goats, and horses—to a point far away from the ravaged *haciendas* of New Mexico. There they were to be supported until they turned into respectable citizens. For "you can feed them cheaper than you can fight them."[2]

New Mexico enthusiastically agreed, but who was to do the whipping and removing? In this year of 1862, almost all the regular troops had been drawn to other battlefields. They had never been many. The brief, frantic blows required to hurl back the Confederates had taken all the strength of New Mexico's volunteers and others brought by hurried call from California and Colorado. Now the Coloradans had gone home again. The few regulars, who had not been paid for a year, were grumbling and ready to desert. The Californians were manning the southern forts, keeping the Apaches from the gold trail. Thus the fight against the Navajos was left to the New Mexicans.

These were citizens of all degrees who had volunteered at the governor's call, to save their country from the Confederates.

[2] Edwin L. Sabin, *Kit Carson Days,* 708.

Some were tough frontiersmen, like St. Vrain and Kit Carson who were now colonel and lieutenant colonel respectively. Some were old army men who had settled in the country, but most of the rank and file were Spanish shepherds and ranch hands. "They being gray Mexican soldiers" said the Navajos, who called all Spanish speaking people Mexicans and used "gray" as a term of scorn.[3] Perhaps they meant, also, that the volunteers had no uniforms. Soldiering was a new thing to these peaceful, farming people, some of whom had never handled a gun. They had not been drilled into fighting machines who would advance under fire, even when there seemed no sense in it. When the odds in a battle seemed too great, they walked away, Indian fashion, leaving their officers to command thin air.[4]

General Carleton, unused to such fighting material, called on the one man who could handle the awkward situation—Kit Carson. Carson was now colonel of the volunteer regiment assembled from his neighbors around Taos during the war. It looked forward to disbanding after the flight of the confederate army, when the orders came to dispose first of the Mescalero Apaches and make those raiders understand "that you are there to kill them wherever you can find them."[5] After only a few months of skirmishes, the Mescalero chief, the Ready, announced: "You are stronger than we are . . . . Do with us as may seem good to you but do not forget we are men and braves."[6] They were to be sent far from the mountains where they had been hiding and raiding.

There was empty land in the southeast corner of New Mexico which once had been claimed by Texas. There the barren expanse of the Staked Plains sweeps down to the little Pecos

[3] Sapir and Hoijer, *Navaho Texts,* 353.
[4] Twitchell, *Occupation of New Mexico,* 375–76, 378n.
[5] Sabin, *Kit Carson Days,* 702.
[6] *Ibid.,* 705.

River. On the river bank was a small fort with a row of one-story adobe barracks, a parade ground grubbed out of the sage brush, and a horse corral. A little grove of cottonwoods made a solitary patch of green, the Bosque Redondo, or Round Grove, which the Indians came to know so well. Otherwise there was no shelter anywhere—no hills, no canyons, and no hiding places. The Americans named it after a former territorial commander, Fort Sumner. Here the prisoners were to begin their new life. By March, 1863, there were four hundred Mescaleros at Fort Sumner, dazedly starting to till the soil under the eyes of American soldiers.

By June, Carson was ready for the Navajos. He had nine companies of volunteers, three of them without horses. The volunteers were designated as cavalry, but some of them never managed to get horses, any more than they got uniforms or pay. In all, there were 736 officers and men. They looked for a suitable fort in Navajo country and finally, so the records show, rebuilt old Fort Defiance. Three hundred more volunteers garrisoned Fort Wingate, the new fort built at Bear Spring to be used as a way station for the surrendered Indians on their way east. California volunteers manned the forts on the outskirts of Navajo country and kept the unconquered Apaches busy while Carson and his volunteers pursued the Navajos.

Colonel Carson never had more than six or seven hundred men who could be used in the field, and half the time these lacked horses, ammunition, and supplies. The orders were to corral and subdue some ten thousand Indians, owning huge herds of horses and familiar with every hiding place within several million acres! Carson, ignorant of military tactics, took the matter calmly. His campaign lasted six months, during which time only fifty Indians were killed. The surrenders, however took place by the thousand. By April, 1864, it was reported that the Navajo country was clear of hostiles. The Indians had either gone to Fort Sumner or fled to parts unknown.

In June, Carson started gathering the volunteers at Fort Defiance where there were supplies for a six months campaign. The fort issued a proclamation stating that the Navajos were given until July 20 to surrender and be moved to Fort Sumner. After that, the war was on. There was no surrender. How could the Navajos know that this new call for peace and good behavior was any different from the dozens of harmless and meaningless others? Then came other proclamations which might have made them tremble had they known and understood their significance. Prizes of twenty dollars for every horse or mule and one dollar for every sheep were offered for captured Navajo stock. A hundred Utes were engaged as government scouts, and Carson visited the Hopis and Zuñis to ask for guides and helpers.

How willingly all these tribes gave their aid! The Utes probably regarded the white soldiers as rather green allies in a war they had been prosecuting for centuries. To the Hopis and Zuñis, the new protectors, supplied with guns and food, were like the realization of a dream. Since 1849, the harassed Pueblos had been wanting to help the Americans whip the Navajos, and always they had been put off with military technicalities. Now they were being begged to do the thing their hearts desired. Said the Navajo: ". . . all of the different tribes spilled over on us."[7] The Pueblos and the Enemy Navajos joyfully guided the volunteers and armed New Mexican ranchers to the Navajos. "And so this Navajo tribe, of which we are, thus was entirely alone."[8] The Navajos were reaping the harvest of the years they had been Lords of the Soil. Colonel Kit Carson did not need a white

[7] Sapir and Hoijer, *Navaho Texts,* 345.
[8] *Ibid.*

army. He had what the military leaders had not perceived, a
reservoir of Navajo-haters ready to be let loose. Every Indian
and every white resident in New Mexico was eager to hunt
the Navajos.

It was these guerillas, ready to spring out from every ambush, who put despair into the hearts of the People. Utes and
Pueblos had always wanted Navajo livestock, and the Utes
wanted women who could make blankets and thus save the
purchase price. Now they could have all these. Carson inno-
cently told his commanding officer that it was too much to ask
the Utes to give up the captured women, believing that they
ought to receive something for their trouble.[9] He was sternly
rebuked, but there is no doubt that, unless the eye of the military was upon them, the Indians usually kept their spoils. Navajo stories are full of slave raids which occurred at just this time.
As the Navajos fled to hiding, says Charlie Mitchell's pathetic
tale, they sometimes abandoned their children, and then the
enemy swooped on them. "The Utes did so, the Mexicans did
so, the Pueblo Indians did so, the Hopi did so, the Oraibi did
so." As for the livestock, few Utes thought twenty dollars as
useful as a good horse. They kept what animals they took until
they had enough. Then they gave up government scouting and
went home.

"The corn fields came not to be attended to," say the Navajos. . . . "The sheep and the horses had become annihilated . . .
the several trails leading to the open flats had become impassable."[10] No wonder Kit Carson scarcely saw a Navajo as he took
his men out scouting methodically to the east, west, north, and
south of Fort Defiance. There was no chance for open battle.
Occasionally he might capture a woman or child left behind by

[9] Sabin, *Kit Carson Days,* 712.
[10] Sapir and Hoijer, *Navaho Texts,* 347.

the fugitives, or he might see Indians in the distance with a herd of animals. Like mountain goats, the Navajos scrambled off up the mountain trails with their sheep. It was unwise to follow them and lead worn-out horses and unskilled men into a trap. On one trip of twenty-seven days, Carson and his men captured one child and nineteen abandoned horses, killed one Navajo man and wounded one other. On another hunt, lasting three weeks, he captured a boy and a woman, destroyed two abandoned camps, and got 78 horses, 4 oxen, and 70 sheep and goats.[11]

Not a bloody campaign! Still, it did not need to be. In spite of Carleton's drastic orders, the aim was not to kill off the Navajos, but to convince them that peace with the United States was their only course. So Kit Carson killed crops not Navajos. He reports that once he camped for seven days and spent the whole time destroying Navajo fields of corn and wheat "as fine as the territory produced."[12] Once he got over 75,000 pounds of wheat for the starving army horses. The Navajos were really hit in a vital spot.

"There were no horses, there were no sheep . . . . Here on this country the starvation became terrible . . . and then plants of any kind at all became their means of subsistence." Cedar berries, piñon nuts, yucca fruit, wild potatoes, and other wild foods were all the fugitives could get. Peaches were ripe in Canyon de Chelley, but their owners did not dare pick them except at night. Then they would steal in, carrying bunches of weeds to erase their footprints. "In rock pockets, in places difficult of access they were squeezed in. Who would go out to where he could be seen? Smoke even was not. Fires were not."[13]

[11] Sabin, *Kit Carson Days*, 871–76.
[12] *Reports* of Commissioner of Indian Affairs, 1864, 85.
[13] Sapir and Hoijer, *Navaho Texts*, 347.

At last, the Navajos were really frightened. Those who still had sheep and horses began to collect them in some secret place and steal away, out of Navajoland. Southern Navajos joined the Gila Apaches; some western residents, led by the warrior Manuelito, crept down into Grand Canyon; others went to Havasupai or to the wild ravines along the Little Colorado; and some migrated to Navajo Mountain, a solitary dome of rock on the border of Utah. Legend says that one band magically found a rocky tunnel under the San Juan River and fled north. This time of fear was also a time of exploring and new settlement.

The eastern Navajos turned back to their friends, the Pueblos and especially to the Jemez, whom they had succored in the past. As Jemez women had once come to the Navajos, now Navajo women walked over the mountains in the night to seek shelter in the pueblo. They put on Jemez dress and took Jemez husbands, adding another item to the Navajo and Pueblo mixture. Kit Carson estimated that thousands of Navajos got away in one direction or another, although the guess in government reports was about one thousand.

In September the first band surrendered and was sent to Fort Sumner. They were Enemy Navajos, who had always trusted the whites, so their example did not do much good. In January came the real blow which broke Navajo resistance. The whites entered Canyon de Chelly. It was an intrepid venture for, by this time, most of Carson's horses were worn out and sent to the Río Grande for pasture. He and his four hundred men had to get along with officers' horses, a few army mules to carry rations, and some oxcarts for supplies. Twenty-seven of the oxen fell dead in the snow.

It snowed that January, even though the canyon had seen many snowless winters. Kit and his men marched to the west end of the canyon, where the Thunderbird trading post now takes out sight-seeing parties. There they camped while the commander sent parties along each rim, to see how dangerous this famous stronghold might be. Along the top of the towering cliffs, they marched without seeing an Indian or a way to get down. Not so Captain Pfeiffer—this doughty Swede, a graduate of the military institute of Stockholm, commanded a volunteer company in Carson's own regiment. He had been late joining his command because, while passing through Apache country, his wife and maid servant had been killed, and he himself had arrived at the fort naked and covered with arrow wounds.[14] Now he wanted to fight Indians, and he wanted little else.

Pfeiffer had been left at Fort Defiance, to come straight toward the canyon and operate at the eastern end. But why pause to "operate"? When he reached the canyon, he simply marched through, a feat that had never been performed by white men before. Most had gone in for a short distance and turned back, but Pfeiffer proceeded along the Del Muerto end of the Y through two feet of snow. His men slipped and fell under their heavy packs, and two had their feet frozen. The only path through the canyon is along the bed of the stream, and this was covered with thin ice, through which the mules' hoofs broke. The animals rolled and struggled, and one fell so hard that it was split open.

The men had little energy left to look for Navajos, but now and then they would see campfire smoke along the canyon walls. A few men would be sent to explore and, when they entered some dismal cave, would find a few starving women and children whom they took prisoner. The men gathered on the ledges above, high out of reach, rolling down rocks and yelling curses in Spanish. When the soldiers camped that night there was a large body of Indians on the rocks above them, so high that they

[14] *Ibid.,* 901.

looked "no larger than crows." The smoke of the army fires floated up toward them, but they were safely out of reach.

Safety was not of much use when they were starving, and those yells from the cliffs were a last gesture of defiance. As Pfeiffer's men moved stolidly on, the Indians followed them toward Carson's camp. Next day, three women approached the camp with a flag of truce. Might they bring in their families in safety? Yes, up to ten o'clock the next morning. Carson was not going to wait around for them to change their minds. By ten, sixty Indians had arrived, only anxious that they might have time to go to distant hiding places and rout out the others. "Come to Fort Defiance," said Kit. There they would be fed and sent in safety to Fort Sumner.

At last the Navajos believed that there was no hiding place for them. Next day Captain Carey went through Canyon de Chelly from west to east, methodically cutting down the peach trees. He came back bringing one hundred fifty Indians who had followed him and begged to surrender. They, too, wanted permission to go and bring their friends. Carson and his men marched away in various directions, escorting some of the prisoners and leaving the others only too eager to follow them to Fort Defiance. Total result of the expedition: 23 killed, 34 forcibly captured, and 200 came to surrender.[15]

After this winter march through the canyon, Kit Carson no longer needed to hunt the Navajos. They came to him. Sitting in his adobe shack at Fort Defiance, he spent the rest of the winter receiving delegations and explaining the advantages of surrender. Yes, they would be fed. No, they would not be killed or even badly treated. All they need do was to promise to stop raiding and go peacefully to Fort Sumner. They surrendered by droves, a score of families riding in together, with all the married daughters, their offspring, and such animals as they had left.

[15] Sabin, *Kit Carson Days*, 878–88.

Even surrender was not easy for the hounded Navajos. They swear that captives who gave themselves up to Hopi or Ute scouts never saw Fort Defiance. They were herded to the Hopi mesas where the men had their heads bashed in with war clubs, and the women were turned over to Mexican slave traders. The Hopis deny this, but they admit that, since they had centuries of wrongs to avenge, the act would have been justified. Pete of Pete's Spring, which is located in a canyon near Hopi country, told the author of his mother's capture by the Hopis some months before his birth. Pete's family—Pete's father and his two wives and several young men of the clan—had decided to surrender and was riding toward Fort Defiance. Pete's mother, the younger wife, had a little girl of five on the horse behind her, and the baby was in its cradleboard hanging from the saddle. As they came near where Holbrook, Arizona now is, a group of Hopis, Zuñis, and Mexicans came galloping toward them. There were no uniformed soldiers with them, and that meant one could expect the worst. Even as they approached, Pete's father was killed by a rifle shot. The young clansmen grabbed such of the women and children as were near and made off at a gallop.

Pete's mother and her two children were left. The captors, when they could take time from rounding up the Navajo animals, tied the captives on horses and proceeded to the Hopi village of Polacca. There they were met by some Mexicans who made regular trips to the place to buy slaves. The woman and little girl were sold and started off with their captors, but not the baby in his cradleboard! He was too young to be useful and was simply thrown over a cliff. However, that happened later. That night when they camped, the woman and her children were placed under a canvas, in the usual way, with their captors sleeping on its edges. The woman crawled out. It was horrible to leave her two children, but she could not have escaped with them. Led by the calls of night birds who answered her prayer for guidance, she felt her way out of the camp. Hiding by day and travelling by night, living on shoots and berries, she made her way to Fort Defiance. No use in telling the soldiers there what had happened, even if she could have found an interpreter! They had no time to chase Mexicans and Pueblos. Years later, she met her daughter, returned from slavery. And she heard how the baby had been thrown over a cliff.

Even with such horrors before them, the Navajos had no choice. It is true that some die-hards were still raiding. On April 9th, 1864, when the governor proclaimed a day of Thanksgiving because the Navajo war was over, they swooped on Laguna Pueblo and stole forty head of cattle. But forty head could not feed them for long. In the secret hide-outs where the fugitives gathered for the Blessing Rites that would banish fear and disease, there was talk about the "Fuerte," or strong place (*hwelte*, said the Navajo, whose language has no r and no f). There, its native ambassadors had told them, rations were given out every day. "They were walking about in food, it being in such large quantities." The starving Navajos, with their blankets in rags and their feet protected from the snow with moccasins of cedar bark, began to tell each other: "We shall go. We shall all go over there. Let us hope that it is really true."[16]

By March, there were 2,400 Navajos at Fort Defiance. They had no shelter except their own blankets and such walls of earth as they could erect, but there were rations. Every evening, when the bugle blew, the Indians lined up to receive "something white," which was flour, and "something black," which was coffee beans. Sometimes there was a tough-rinded slab of bacon. They returned to their shelterless camps where now and then the sentries passed, speaking only to each other. There was no one

[16] Sapir and Hoijer, *Navaho Texts,* 351.

to tell them what to do with the peculiar food. They tried eating the flour raw and licking it off their hands, or mixing it with ashes, like a Mexican tortilla. Sometimes they threw bacon, coffee beans, and flour into the pot together and boiled them as stew. The hardness of those coffee beans was beyond their understanding. The women boiled and boiled them, throwing out the dirty water each time, as they did with Mexican beans. Still they were hard to chew. It was a long time before some soldier made them understand that the beans were to be ground, and the dark water drunk as coffee.

On March 6, 1864, the first caravan started for Fort Sumner. There were twenty-four hundred Navajos, thirty ox teams piled with rations, four hundred horses, and three thousand sheep and goats. On March 14th, seven hundred more Navajos made the trip. The weary ox teams shuttled back and forth until, on April 24th, twelve hundred Navajos departed with their twelve hundred ponies and six thousand sheep and goats. New Mexico had already held a day of Thanksgiving, and the governor had begged the unofficial Navajo hunters to cease their activities and go home. The war was over.

The Navajos will never forget that journey to *hwelte,* known in their traditions as the Long Walk. Only the old, the sick, and the infants rode in the carts, along with the piles of supplies. The able bodied walked, and boys of ten were proud to take every step of the three hundred miles. Three hundred miles, at fifteen miles a day! No wonder the Navajos felt they were marching to the ends of the earth. The way led gradually out of the fierce, red rocks and high plateaus of their own country, past Bear Springs, their old stamping ground, where Fort Wingate now stood menacingly ready to push them on their way, and then past the long flow of lava which is the life blood of *Yeitso,* the monster slain by the war gods. Beyond rose the long slopes of Mount Taylor, the southern sacred mountain. When they left it behind, they were out of Navajoland, entering un-hallowed ground where no ceremonies would be effective. They say they held no ceremonies at Sumner except the War Dance which nullifies the evil effects of contact with strangers and enemies.

The country flattened out toward the Río Grande, the land of the Mexicans and the Pueblos. They forded at Isleta Pueblo home of the Enemies by the River. Once the Navajos had de-lighted in raiding this rich village, escaping through the Sandia Mountains. Now the Isletans watched with stolid faces as the wagons and the pedestrians plunged into the muddy stream. They had lent the United States sixty thousand dollars of their savings, so that the soldiers might have their back pay and might stay to defend New Mexico from the Indians. Now they were getting their reward. The Navajos tell wild tales of how the wagon beds were sometimes flooded in crossing and the babies floated out. Older children, holding to the wagon as they were dragged through the water, were swept away and washed down-stream. The way led along the river bank to Albuquerque, where the Navajos camped in a corral with two bells hanging from posts. They called it the Place of Bells. Here bread was bought from the Mexican ovens. The soldiers warned the Navajos to stay together, as their detachment was too small to guard against possible kidnappings. Still, some of the women wandered away into the magically strange city and were pounced on by the slave traders. Before the caravan started next morning, their men stole out with all the silver ornaments they could collect, but, even so, the ransom offer might not be enough. Often, says Navajo unwritten history, some beloved daughter had to be left behind.

Beyond Albuquerque, they traveled straight east across the

plains, and here began country which was foreign to all but a few buffalo hunters. This was almost the same route that Coronado had followed when he set forth into the unknown over a country "rolling like the sea." It is a completely barren land, tufted only with coarse clumps of gray grass or, now and then, with dry spikes of yucca stuck like pins into an endless flat cushion. It was from these that the Spaniards named that desolate flat expanse the *Llano Estacado,* or Staked Plains. Most of the Navajos had never seen a land completely without rocks and trees. As day after day passed, the flatness was never broken by even a tiny hill. Every morning the bugle called them to line up for coffee, bacon, and flour. At sunset it called again, and then they lay down in their blankets, the babies crying and the old people murmuring against this dreadful emptiness. Next morning another bugle. Then they set forward, over a shadowless land, toward a horizon which was perfectly flat. Thus began the new life.

II: The Army Worm

GENERAL CARLETON WAS an idealist among conquerors. His plan to remove the Navajos far from the scene of mischief was not new, but few had thought of it in his high-minded terms: "there to be kind to them; there teach their children how to read and write; teach them the arts of peace . . . . Soon they will acquire new habits, new ideas, new modes of life . . . . Little by little they will become a happy, contented people."[1]

The trouble was that neither Carleton nor any one else had thought out the details. Consider what is done for Indians today, when some still require help in adjusting to modern conditions. A group of only four or five hundred have grade schools and a high school up to the white man's standard, with teachers specially qualified for Indian work. They have a hospital, doctor, nurses, and sometimes home teaching in baby care. Extension workers teach the same women canning and dressmaking. Hundreds of thousands of dollars are spent on roads, dams, and

---

[1] *Reports* of Commissioner of Indian Affairs, 1863, 112. The narrative of events at Fort Sumner is taken from this and succeeding reports for 1864, 65, 66, and 67. Frank Reeve, "The Government and the Navajo," *New Mexico Historical Review,* Vol. XIV (1939). Other authorities are mentioned as quoted. Many traditions of that time were recounted by the Indians.

fencing to improve the land. There may be skilled farmers and stockmen or perhaps foresters and irrigation experts to advise the Indians in handling their property, and they can get cattle and machinery on loan from the government. Good houses may be built for them to rent or buy on very easy terms.

In 1864, no one had dreamed of such an establishment. Some seven thousand Navajos were dumped on forty square miles of land, which was mostly flat and grassy. The Pecos River ran through the tract, and on its bank sat the small adobe fort with four hundred soldiers. The only provision for the Navajos was a corral which they walked into to be counted. There were no teachers and no helpers, and there was only one man who could even tell the Indians what the white officers wished them to do. That was Jesus (the Americans wrote it Assus) Arviso, a Mexican who had been captured in childhood by the Utes. He had been sold to the Navajos, grown up among them, and taken two Navajo wives. He surrendered with the others and now served as interpreter, translating from Navajo into Spanish and from Spanish into Navajo. Some Spanish-speaking soldiers took care of the rest.

The dazed, tired, and guarded travelers were herded into the "Navajo Corral," counted, and given their first week's rations of bacon, flour, and coffee. How these meat eaters hated the eternal white flour which the white men seemed to prize! How glad they would have been to exchange the bitter coffee beans for some piñon nuts or good, oily sunflower seeds! There were old army tents for a few of them, but the others were turned loose on the land to make their homes. There were no trees for the construction of their old, conical dwellings—not unless they traveled twenty-five miles upstream and floated the logs down. Most did not venture such an expedition in the new land. The old people say they dug a shallow pit, large enough for the family to sleep in side by side, then roofed it with slender boughs. Some day they hoped to be lucky enough to steal a cow and use the hide for a waterproof covering. The women made their fireplaces outside, and those who had sheep urged their men to get logs and set up a loom. At least they could make clothing.

As for the men, they were to farm. So the word was passed around from headquarters, where a Spanish-speaking soldier had told it to Jesus Arviso. They were to dig an irrigation ditch from the Pecos River. The army had shovels to lend them, and sergeants and corporals were to stand around and see that they worked. Yes, but the Mescalero Apaches already had a ditch and were using all the best land beside the river! Well, the Mescaleros must make room. There was grunting and black looks while this was accomplished, the soldiers walking unconcernedly about and issuing commands in their incomprehensible language. The one interpreter could not be everywhere at once, so most Navajos never knew what was being said.

They got a ditch—seven miles of it. The Mescaleros were pushed into a corner so that the Navajos could have planting room. That very spring the Mescaleros began to talk about decamping from the reservation, and one night forty of them did. Next year, they all went. Now the Navajos had the land to themselves, but of what use was it when nothing would grow?

Carleton had not counted on the vicissitudes of nature. That year after six thousand acres had been planted to corn, wheat, beans, and pumpkins, a caterpillar destroyed almost everything. Ironically, this was the caterpillar which fills vegetation with white webs, like tents, and is known as the "army worm." The next year the trouble was floods, then hail, then drought and wind. Each catastrophe seemed to the Navajos to be a direct visitation from the spirits. Most singers would not hold ceremonies to banish the ill luck since they were out of sanctified ground.

True, the early reports picture them as dancing and singing for that was the way they always spent their leisure.[2] Still, they hated the alkaline water which, they said, made them sick and the poison weeds of the mesas which killed their sheep, who were unaccustomed to the new vegetation. As winter came on, they were already feeling the scarcity of fuel. The cottonwoods along the Pecos had been cut down immediately, all except those around the fort, the Round Grove, or *Bosque Redondo,* which gave the place its name. Soon the Navajos were going ten, fifteen, or twenty miles to haul logs. Or they grubbed for mesquite roots on the barren uplands, but soon even the mesquite would be gone.

"God knows what they will do for fuel!" wrote the Indian superintendent. For letters of complaint and argument were already posting back and forth between Washington, Santa Fé, and the new reservation, known to jibing newspapers as "Sweet Carletonia." The United States had no machinery geared to take care of a helpless minority group. At this date, the country still seemed to be a small nucleus of energetic people in the midst of almost boundless resources. Their creed was "every man for himself, and those who cannot make a fortune must be either lazy or stupid." This left little room for social planning, and in spite of Carleton's fine words, no one had considered who was to feed and teach the Indians.

So the military and the Bureau of Indian Affairs shared the job—the military feeding and guarding the prisoners and the Indian agent providing clothing and tools, if he could get them. The Navajos, who thought their bosses were merely four hun-

[2] G. Gwyther, "An Indian Reservation," *Overland Monthly,* Vol. X, No. 2 (1873).

dred blue-coated soldiers, had no idea of the double line of authority which stretched all the way to Washington. At the fort were the military commandant and the Indian agent, each jealous of the other's authority and watching for mistakes. At the desks in Santa Fé were their superiors, General Carleton and the superintendent of Indian Affairs for New Mexico, and in Washington were their superiors, the United States Department of War and Bureau of Indian Affairs. Above them all was Congress, which appropriated the money. Even the president might take a hand now and then by sending out a special investigator.

The chances for a concerted plan were slim. Already it was an honored tradition that the civilian officials and the military should not co-operate. The files of the Indian Bureau at Washington were full of complaints about inflexible army men. Now the letters from New Mexico blazed with arguments about what an absurd choice Fort Sumner was. The agent there was instructed not to feed the Indians. Let the Army do it. Indians were their baby, or, as the superintendent formally put it, their prisoners of war. Carleton had not foreseen this expense, but he accepted it manfully. That spring the soldiers at the Fort went on half rations.

Then came the civilians' turn for trouble. They were to distribute food and clothing, but they had almost none in stock. So, in that first summer of 1864, Congress appropriated $100,000 and gave carte blanche authority to two commissioners. It is a sad story. In those lusty days of make-your-fortune-no-matter-how, the diverting of government funds was no uncommon thing. Later investigators said that out of $100,000 appropriated, only about $30,000 got to the Indians. Shoddy blankets worth about $4.50 were appraised at $22.50, and even so there were too few to go around. The Navajos patiently untwisted the threads

131

and tried to weave them better. They needed more wool, and soon they were back at the one expedient they knew—stealing sheep. However, that came later. First, the Navajos gave the new life a fair trial.

The skimpy and shoddy goods arrived about Christmas time, and, said the camp doctor, "If those who had grabbed no inconsiderable portion of the fund had witnessed it, I sincerely believe that conscience would have twinged them right sharply."[3] By February the graft situation blazed up in a scandal. The quartermaster of the post was court-martialed for selling government cattle, and the Indian agent was sent from the fort for receiving them. Both were exonerated and quietly dismissed. Others took their places who may or may not have been more honest, and Carleton went eagerly on with his plans.

"Tell them not to be discouraged," he had written, "to work hard, every man and woman, to put in large fields next year when, if God smiles on our efforts, they will, at one bound, be forever placed beyond want and independent."[4] Human aspirations for this sort of change are still running centuries ahead of any workable plans for bringing it about, but Carleton tried. This year, he planned, there was to be school. An adobe schoolhouse had finally been built by Navajo labor, and the bishop at Santa Fé had sent some young priests as instructors. The Navajos did not understand this new system by which their children were taken away for hours every day and forced to sit on benches in a house. They thought all parents and children involved should have extra bread rations.

Then there was to be a responsible native government. It was hard to build up such a thing from the Navajo local bands,

[3] Frank Reeve, "The Federal Indian Policy in New Mexico," *New Mexico Historical Review,* Vol. XII, No. 2 (1937), 262.
[4] *Ibid.,* 263.

each clustering around some rich or influential man. "A man that can think, a man that can talk," say the Navajos, "that's who got to be leader." There were a score of such men at the camp, and their names were signed to the ultimate peace treaty in English, Navajo, or Spanish, weirdly spelled by the clerk. The whites selected twelve of the most prominent men, and divided the tribe into twelve bands, each to be under the charge of one of these army-made chiefs. For the next fifty years, Navajo chiefs would receive their final authority from the whites.

This description of the Sumner chiefs comes from Henry Chee Dodge, the revered mixed-blood leader who died in 1948. As a boy at the fort, he saw these "big men" walking among the people, urging them to work. In young manhood, Dodge interpreted for those chiefs still living. He knew their families, their clans, and their homes as only a tribesman could.

Foremost of the leaders was Barboncito, or Little Beard as the Navajos called a moustache. His real name or "war" name was "He-Is-Anxious-To-Step-Forward." He came from Canyon de Chelley and was of the Jemez clan, a descendant of those valiant women who had come to get Navajo husbands and keep their strain from dying out. Old Navajos remember the moustached one as a short, quiet man, always on the side of peace. The whites put great trust in Barboncito and, say the Navajos, gave him a commanding position much greater than would have been allowed by tribal custom. This, by the way, was a familiar development wherever whites began to rule Indians. They always looked for responsible leaders with whom they could deal, so they tried to make the chiefs into little kings. Usually the chiefs had no objection, and so Indian government changed before anyone realized it.

Then there was Herrero the smith and Ganado Mucho, or Many Cattle, the big livestock owner. Ganado was another famous Navajo of mixed descent. For his father had been a Hopi captured by the Navajos. The Hopis are known in the Southwest for their excellent business ability, and Ganado's father was no exception. He proceeded to accumulate cattle, and his son followed in his footsteps, getting his herds by raiding, like any other Navajo. Before the captivity, Ganado was already a *rico,* well established and ready for peace. He had brought his cattle with him to Fort Sumner, and, later, he took them home again. Old Ganado never lost the right to be called Many Cattle. There was one skinny old man whom the Navajos nicknamed Muerto de Hambre, or Dead of Hunger, and there were Hombro and Largo, both medicine men, and Chiquito, a handsome and active little fellow, whose female ancestors were from the Río Grande Pueblos. Even these few give a glimpse of the mixed nature of Navajo descent with all its hybrid vigor.

One leader was all Navajo and all fighter. This was Manuelito, the handsome warrior of the powerful voice whose life from early boyhood had been spent at war with Utes, Mexicans, and, finally, the white Americans. His photograph, taken at the fort, shows his broad chest marked with a bullet wound, acquired when he galloped his horse past some ambushed Mexicans. He had a following of eager warriors, and often he had led them against the whites, even in the attack on Fort Defiance. He had refused to sign treaty after treaty. He and his band had been among the last to come in to Fort Sumner, and several times they left again, unable to stand the restraint. Hunger always drove them back.

In 1865, while a certain Major Cremony was visiting the fort, there was a gala day of footraces between Navajos and Mescalero Apaches. Manuelito was one of the runners, and since the race was not open for men over forty, he must have been just under that age. "He was," says Cremony, "the finest looking

Indian man I ever saw. He was over six feet in height and of the most symmetrical figure, combining ease, grace and power and activity in a wonderful degree."[5] Manuelito never had time to collect cattle, but he dressed gorgeously, as a great warrior should. While most Navajo men at the fort wore ragged muslin pantaloons, this handsome war chief was clothed from head to foot in well-fitting buckskin. His head was adorned with a bunch of many-colored plumes, and he wore a blanket which, even in those days, was worth $100.00.

General Carleton hoped that each leader would encourage his band to construct an adobe village, where, like their Pueblo neighbors, they would settle down to a life of contented farming. It did not happen. The Navajos, who were quick to learn when they chose, were immovable when they did not choose. A smaller acreage was planted in this summer of 1865, so there was less disappointment when the crop failed. Also, less was needed, for nine hundred Navajos had quietly escaped since the arrival last spring. Many had died, perhaps from the poor food and water or perhaps from sheer discouragement. Poor General Carleton from his office desk wrote: "Tell them to be too proud to murmur about what cannot be helped," but the Navajos were murmuring. "Oh our beloved Chinle, they would say, that in the springtime used to be so pleasant: Chinle, they would say. Oh beloved Black Mountain! Would that one were at these so-named places." It sounds like the Hebrews by the waters of Babylon, but the Navajos were not repentant. The wails ended by the rich and peaceful ones scolding the raiders. "Oh, you wicked people! You did not finish what you started. The Mexicans that you killed, the Americans that you killed, you did not defeat them!"[6]

[5] John C. Cremony, *Life Among the Apaches,* 305.
[6] Sapir and Hoijer, *Navaho Texts,* 359.

So far, the Navajos had got almost no food from their crops. For a second summer, the military had to feed them, and the cost for these eighteen months was over one million dollars. It began to be a question whether you could feed them cheaper than you could fight them. The Navajos, who felt themselves starving unless they had meat every day, had found various means to increase their rations. The system of distribution required each Indian to walk, one by one, through a gate into the square enclosure marked on the fort plan as the "Navajo corral." Each person, as he passed through the gate, received a cardboard ration ticket. If he had sick relatives at home, he might speak for them also. Old pictures show a soldier, with a fixed bayonet, guarding the unkept and wild-eyed Indians, huddled in their striped blankets. None were allowed out of the corral until all had passed in, for thus, thought the management, no person could get more than his rightful share of tickets.

However, the Navajos could master a new art when they chose. They were soon forging ration tickets and presenting them blandly on behalf of sick relatives. The army substituted stamped metal tickets, but these were forged also. No one knows just how the Navajos procured the metal, made dies, and stamped the counterfeit tickets. When we look for the origin of Navajo silverwork, perhaps this craft, developed under stress of hunger, may point to an early inspiration. The army finally had to send to Washington for elaborate metal disks which could not be copied.

This skill in metal work was one of the few things the Navajos learned at the fort. It may be worth while to point out that it was the only project undertaken on their own initiative and without the white man's teaching. These people who had been so outstanding as learners and adapters seemed to close their minds in sullen resolution when learning was forced on them. At the fort they used plows for the first time and saw large-scale irrigation. Yet they did not go home to irrigate, and they did not use plows unless they received them from the government as gifts. Under Pueblo inspiration, they had made farming an essential in their lives. Under American command, they lost interest in it.

The women were equally slow to learn new ways. True, they had to change some food habits because of necessity. Probably the Navajo addiction to *cah-whay* (coffee) dates from the distribution of coffee beans at the fort. Also, they finally became reconciled to wheat flour. Few Navajo women, since the captivity, have cared to grind maize on a stone in the old painstaking manner learned from their Pueblo sisters. Still, they continued to think that meat, stewed, broiled, or sun dried, is the only food. So they do today, although poverty often keeps their wishes from fulfillment.

As for sewing, the women did almost none. It has been suggested that the picturesque full skirts which they now wear were copied from those of the officers' ladies. However, there were almost no officers' ladies at this small post. Even had there been, a woman who had never used a needle could not learn to make a skirt by merely seeing one swishing by. Old Navajos tell how calico was distributed to them, and how they had not the least idea what to do with it. They took a length of this material, cut a hole in the middle for the head, then tied it around the waist with a sash, like the old blanket dress. In fact, this blanket dress, borrowed from the Pueblos, was to be their wear for another thirty years.

Carleton's proposal to "teach them the arts of peace" resulted for the Navajos in two practical skills. They learned to make metal dies and to swim in the Pecos. For the rest, their years of tribulation had only one sure result. They became very sure they must not fight the whites. It may be that this one piece of wisdom was worth the ordeal. When we compare the energetic Navajos of today with the despairing Sioux, we may feel that the drastic about-face was a blessing.

The learning of the lesson, however, was as painful as a surgical operation. A second winter came on without fuel and with the new supplies voted by Congress stalled in Kansas City. The Navajos hunted rats and rabbits, dug wild roots, traded with the near-by Mexicans, and they stole. "But no more than the Mexicans stole from us," the old men declare. There were slave raids to steal girls, even under the noses of the military. Hair-raising tales are told of how some girls escaped and came plodding back to prison at Fort Sumner.

The real raids were between Navajos and the buffalo hunting Comanches and other plains tribes. The Comanches were horsemen and horse stealers like the Navajos, and in the beginning the two tribes had had the same history. Both had been humble seed gatherers, the Comanches in Colorado with their relatives the Utes, and the Navajos in New Mexico. Both had acquired new animals which changed their way of life. A geographic accident, however, had brought the Navajos into Pueblo country and started them at agriculture and sheep raising. Comanche rovings did not bring them among the village people except for occasional raids. They never had corn or sheep, but they were among the very first Indians to get horses from the Spaniards. For them, horses were enough. They spread out into the plains, where they became buffalo hunters and fighters, roving all the way from Oklahoma to Mexico. They had been the scourge of the Spanish settlements and then of the Santa Fé Trail. Now they were stealing cattle in Mexico or Texas and selling them to the traders who swarmed along the Río Grande. The Fort Sumner reservation was directly in their path and located on land they once considered their own. Four hundred soldiers could not keep them from swooping down on the Navajo horses—nor could they prevent the Navajos from giving chase.

The Navajos say that the Comanches began stealing their animals, one by one, from the time they first came to the fort. Things did not come to a head until the third summer, when these wild riders, whom the Navajos called Many Enemies, ran off two hundred horses and killed four people. Navajos and soldiers went after them, and there was a fight within fifteen miles of the fort. After that, the Navajos felt at liberty to steal over to Comanche territory and drive off all the animals they could. Arthur Chester tells how four Navajos sneaked into a Comanche camp and lay all day in the long grass, watching the horses graze under guard. When darkness came, the horses were picketed and the guard slept. The Navajos cut the picket lines and drove off the herd, galloping first on one horse, then on another, as their mounts grew tired. They knew the Comanches were following and dared not stop for food, water, or sleep.

Finally, thinking they had eluded the pursuers when they were in the open plains where some buffalo were grazing, they killed a calf, cut it up without taking time to skin it, then made a fire, and began to roast chunks of meat. No one had yet had a bite when they saw dust in the distance. The pursuers were coming. They leaped on the best horses, abandoning the rest, and reached Fort Sumner without being caught. Another time the pursuing Comanches were stopped by a thunder storm and had to hold a ceremony before they dared proceed. Sometimes the Navajos were stopped by the sight of a mirage, for the appearance of that plains country was new to them. They were terrified by the pathless, flat land and the Many Enemies with their terrible war yell, yet they ventured forth on foot, time after time, hoping to find a horse to ride home.

The third summer had come, and the third crop failed. The Mescaleros had all sneaked away. Poor Navajos were stealing out to get work as sheep herders for the Mexicans. Women were earning money as prostitutes in the near-by towns. So many Navajos were leaving the fort that they were now required to have passes, and the fort commandants of New Mexico were instructed to kill any found without these—if they could catch them. They did kill a few. Over the heads of the despairing Indians still raged the controversy between Carleton and the Superintendent of Indian Affairs. Fort Sumner was an ideal place, insisted Carleton, with six thousand acres of irrigable land, good grazing, and as much fuel as could be found anywhere in New Mexico.

"What," jeered the superintendent, "big enough for 8,000 Indians? Why it would just about accommodate the 400 Mescalero." Those Indians had been doing nicely before the Navajos arrived, but now they had been driven out and another good project was spoiled. As for the Navajos, they were sick, discouraged, and without fuel. And here was something more to the point. Ranchers around Fort Sumner did not want these thieving Indians in their midst.

Carleton stuck to his pet idea like Barbara Frietchie to her flag. New Mexicans wanted the Navajos moved back, he said, so that there would be a longer freight route for government supplies and bigger earnings for freighters. Also, if the Indians were returned to their old home, they would have to be surrounded by forts, and these would bring business to the local residents. These economic arguments have never been absent from projects proposed for the Indians. Always there have been white men who hoped to make money out of any plan for Indian betterment.

Washington, as usual, heard the rumblings from a distance

and tried to get information. Three separate investigations were made by special agent Woolson, special agent Graves, and a senate investigating committee. They reported things as good as could be expected. Meanwhile, the usual turnover in government offices went on. The superintendent was changed again and again, the Indian agent was changed, and the fort commandant was changed. In September, 1866, Carleton himself was relieved of his command. Three months later, care of the Navajos was transferred to the Department of the Interior.

The Department, through its Indian agent, took one look at the appalling cost of caring for the Navajos and began to make plans. The Indians were no more self-supporting than when they had first reached Fort Sumner and had cost the military over one million dollars in eighteen months, without counting what Congress had appropriated for clothing, tools, and general help.[7] "Better send the Indians to the Fifth Avenue Hotel to board," said General Sherman.[8] The civilians decided to ask Congress for $600,000 for the year and got one third of it. Obviously the Indians must be moved to a place where they could do something for themselves. It was the question of expense, rather than the desperate pleas of the Navajos, which sealed the fate of "Sweet Carletonia." Officials began discussing where the most economic place would be—Oklahoma, Arkansas, Northern Arizona? While special investigators were drawing up plans, and letters were surging back and forth, the Navajos killed five soldiers. That summer, 1867, they had refused to plant. The next winter, several hundred deserted, and the following spring they were all planning to go.

That May, 1868, General Sherman and Colonel Francis Tappan were sent as special commissioners to the Navajos. They

[7] A. E. Shiras to Doolittle, December 28, 1865, Bureau of Archives, 181/66.
[8] Stanton to Browing, October 12, 1866, Files of Office of Indian Affairs.

were to make a new peace treaty and get the Indians moved. Oklahoma was their choice, but they changed their minds on hearing the desperate Navajo pleas. The Indians would sign anything—anything just so they might go back to the land of mesa and canyon. The two commissioners drew up a treaty by which the Navajos promised never again to fight with whites, Mexicans, or other Indians.[9] Eighteen leaders put their crosses on the document, including Barboncito of the moustache, Herrero the smith, the wealthy Many Cattle, and the warlike Manuelito.

The Navajos, however, have already raised this event to the rank of myth, as magical as the tale of how the first horses came. Arthur Chester told me his version of how He-Who-Runs-Forward made his eloquent plea to the white chiefs. "You must understand," Chester explained, through an interpreter, "that when a Navajo wishes to speak beautifully, he must hold under his tongue a turquoise anointed with 'live pollen.' That means pollen which has been sprinkled on a live, moving animal, then brushed off. Best of all, for diplomatic purposes, is the sagacious coyote. So the men went out on horseback and rounded up a coyote. Someone produced a turquoise given him by the chanter after a ceremony in the homeland. This was put under the tongue of He-Who-Runs-Forward, whom others call Barboncito. He stuck a knife into his moccasin, and then he went to speak to the white chiefs, while all of the Navajos gathered around the door."

He-Who-Runs-Forward took that knife from his moccasin and threw it on the floor. "If you wish to send my people away from their home," he said, "first take this knife and kill me."

[9] Treaty with Navajos, 15 Stat. L 667. Ratified July 25, 1868; Proclaimed August 12, 1868.

This made the white chiefs think. They said: "If we let you go home, will you promise never to fight again?"

The Navajos around the door shouted with one voice their word for yes, *"Hao, hao!"*

"Will you work and irrigate the soil, as you have seen the soldiers do?"

"Hao, hao!"

"Will you send your children to school every day that they may learn paper?"

"Hao, hao!"

"Very well, your past behavior is now taken from you." Thus it was said. "The oxcarts are ready. Start now."

Government records show that the treaty was signed on June 1, 1868. On June 18, the Navajos started home.

12: Third Beginning

THE NAVAJOS WERE to make a third beginning. Almost as poor and naked as when they first reached the Southwest, they were to enter the land again and by work become self-supporting. This time, the cause was different. When they had taken over agriculture from the Pueblos and sheepherding from the Spaniards, they had been in the position of conquerors, learning because they chose to do so. Now, at the behest of a foreign power, they were to adopt new ways, with no choice open. That part hardly weighed with them as they collected their old army coats, their gray issue blankets, and their remaining sheep, goats, cattle, and horses.

" 'Would that it might be today! Would that it might be tomorrow,' it was said as the confused bustle started to kill them."[1]

The chiefs had signed a treaty, or, rather, they had placed their crosses on it. Probably they themselves scarcely understood the carefully numbered paragraphs with their talk of dollars and acres. Their agent, Colonel Dodd, tried to explain it to them, and the chiefs explained to the people—such as would

[1]Sapir and Hoijer, *Navaho Texts*, 369.

take the time to listen. This treaty of 1868 was to be their charter of liberties.[2]

They were to give up banditry. Yes, to that they had agreed. "All that was washed away," say the old people. "All our past behavior was taken from us."[3] They were to be educated. No one had any idea what this meant, and, in fact, they would not give it a thought for many years to come. They were to settle upon the land, and within ten years they would be self-supporting farmers. So the government arrangements seemed to imply, and surely the assumption was no less magical than the Navajo belief that ceremonies would make the grass grow. Treaties of the same general type were being made with a score of Indian tribes in the last years of the nineteenth century. The limit of years varied, but there was the innocent belief that rovers and fighters could tear apart their fabric of custom, as closely related as a system of blood vessels, and settle down to land ownership as eagerly as any New Englander.

The government would help. There would be rations for all until the harvest of the first crops. (After that, it was assumed, the Navajos could feed themselves.) There would be five dollars worth of clothing for every man, woman, and child each year, during the ten years of the treaty period. Also, there would be ten dollars worth of supplies for every farmer or mechanic among the People. They were to select farming land (160 acres for a family head, 80 acres for others), and each farmer would have $100 for the first year and $25 for the two succeeding years if he kept at it.

If the Navajos had understood what an acre was, they might have objected to this stipulation, since in their barren mesa country it takes several acres to feed one goat. Moreover, each

[2] See Chapter 11, note 9.
[3] Sapir and Hoijer, *Navaho Texts*, 369.

sheep owner has to make long treks between mountain and plain in the wet and dry seasons. The task of explaining to a white man is more than most Indians care to attempt, and doubtless even the chiefs never opened their mouths on the subject. What they really understood was that they were to have sheep. The government would spend thirty thousand dollars to replace the animals Kit Carson had killed. They could start again.

In fact, they had really begun starting from Fort Sumner even before the treaty was signed, and the military were only too glad to relax supervision and let them go. Down toward Mexico, up over the pass between the Manzana and Los Pinos ranges, and over the old war trail toward Jemez—what joy to travel without the watching soldiers and to camp when and where they chose! In April, when the first groups left, the Río Grande was in flood from the melting snows. There were no wagons to ferry them over, so, they say, the men made rafts and boys swam, as the soldiers had taught them. On the slopes of Mount Taylor, the rivulets were washing prairie dogs out of their holes, as always happens in spring. What bliss to camp for days, feasting on the fat little animals, with no bugle to urge them on.

Word had gone out that all Navajos must gather at Fort Wingate while arrangements were made to establish them on their reservation. Who cared about that! Even those who had nothing but their bare hands made straight for the old homeland of mesa and canyon. They would live like the rabbits and prairie dogs rather than go back under military rule.

The majority, with the old and crippled and those who had flocks to guard, waited for Major Whiting, the spectacled fort commandant, known to the Indians as Owl Man. There were some seven thousand of them, and with oxcarts, sheep, horses, goats, and a regiment of soldiers as guard, they made a procession ten miles long. They were thirty-five days on the march, and it cost the government $50,000.[4] Even so, there was not enough to eat. Or, perhaps, the Navajos were so tired of beans and coffee that they did not bother with them. At every camp, they were off into the hills and gullies, foraging for desert rats, rabbits, or yucca stalks. "Yet," insisted Major Whiting, "they stole and destroyed less than would a column of soldiers of the same size."[5] There were many who did not come back from those foraging expeditions, for the first taste of freedom was too intoxicating. At Albuquerque, at Cañoncito, at Mount Taylor, they dropped away, and the old people report: "There were many who married Mexicans that year."

At last Fort Wingate was reached. This was a new fort, built at Shushbito (Bear Spring), where the very first treaty had been made between Navajos and white Americans. The lovely, round pool, with its sheltering foliage, had been a Navajo gathering place since the adventurous days when the People first spread out from old Navajoland. It was the only perennial water for miles around, and when the government first began to establish forts to keep the Indians in check, of course Bear Spring was one site chosen. Now it was just outside the limits of what was to be the Navajo reservation. Here Major Whiting handed them over to their agent, Colonel Dodd, the active and alert little man known to the Navajos as Gopher. Their traditions tell how the Gopher warned them over and over again: "You are at peace now. At peace with the Mexicans and the other Indians, as well as the United States. That means no more raiding, no more slaves."

The Navajos agreed. That promise, which paid for their freedom, they meant to keep with their last breath. True, it was

[4] Frank Reeve, "The Federal Indian Policy in New Mexico," *New Mexico Historical Review,* Vol. XIII (1938), 35.
[5] *Reports* of Commissioner of Indian Affairs, 1868, 159.

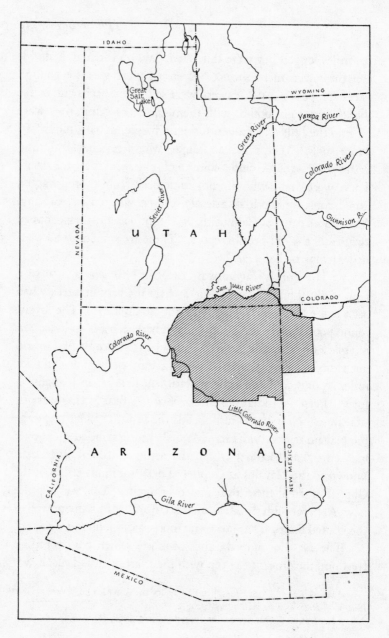

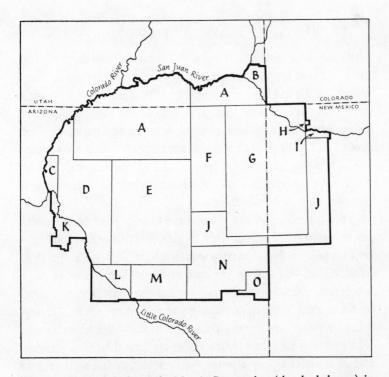

The map on the left shows the Navajo Reservation (the shaded area) in relation to surrounding states. The ancestors of the Navajos, as part of the Athapascan group from British Columbia, may have arrived in the Southwest by migrating southward across the northwestern states through Nevada or Utah and into New Mexico and Arizona. For the location of early settlement of the Navajos, see Escalante's Map. The early Navajos ranged over an extensive area, including northern New Mexico and Arizona and southern Utah and Colorado. The map above shows the reservation in more detail, indicating the successive additions and their dates.

A–Ex. Ord. May 17, 1884
B–Ex. Ord. May 15, 1905,
   Act of Mar. 1, 1933
C–Act of May 23, 1930
D–Ex. Ord. Jan. 8, 1900
E–Ex. Ord. Dec. 16, 1882
F–Ex. Ord. Oct. 29, 1878

G–Treaty of June 1, 1868
H–Ex. Ord. Dec. 1, 1913
I–Ex. Ord. Apr. 24, 1886
J–Ex. Ord. Jan. 6, 1880
K–Ex. Ord. Jan. 19, 1918,
   Ex. Ord. May 23, 1930,
   and Act of June 14, 1934

L–Ex. Ord. Nov. 14, 1901
M–Act of June 14, 1934
N–Ex. Ord. Nov. 9, 1907,
   Ex. Ord. Jan. 28, 1908
O–Act of June 14, 1934

hard to see how they would live without raiding and slave taking, their means of support for the past hundred and fifty years. They waited for the mighty being known as "Washington" to arrange their lives with a wise and powerful hand. How could they know that Father Washington actually comprised a score of groups and individuals, mostly at sword points with each other. Up to this day, after many trips to the nation's capital, and at much expense, they do not understand why Washington is so complex and changeable.

Washington had not yet surveyed their reservation. It had not expected that seven or eight thousand wards would suddenly be dumped in New Mexico rather than Oklahoma. In fact, Washington was new to the role of Great White Father on a wholesale scale. So the Navajos spent five months on tenterhooks at Fort Wingate, camping and receiving rations. "It was a hard winter," say the old people, with the quiet remote smile which they wear when telling about the past. I have never seen one of these old people bitter. They speak of the slim rations as they do of ruinous storms or the death of sheep. These things are life, and one moves quietly through them, armed with prayers, secure in the affection of clan and family which bulwarks a Navajo against emotional storms.

Poor Gopher Dodd was already worrying about the dwindling ration money, as many an agent would do after him. Congress never could believe that the needed sums would be quite so large as they turned out to be. There was little use in writing anxious letters to Washington, when part of their transportation must still be on horseback. Ultimately, the military usually came to the rescue grumbling that this would be the last time. So they did on this occasion, but that was not until the April after Colonel Dodd had died at his post. He had had five months as Navajo agent, but some of his successors would have even less.

There was a new agent when the People moved to the reservation in January, 1869. The red rocks, the gray plains, and the deep, abrupt canyons were still there, but they did not all belong to the Navajos. No longer could the People roam at will between the four mountains, considering that Hopis, Zuñis, and Mexicans had no rights as compared with themselves. Now their allotted space was a long, narrow rectangle of three and one-half million acres straddling the border between Arizona and New Mexico. At the east, the canyons and mesas of old Navajo-land had been sliced away; and at the west, another great stretch as big as the Navajo reservation itself was left for the Hopis. At the south, a bite had been taken off for the Zuñis and for white homesteaders. The railroad, which was to revolutionize the Southwest, was to have every alternate section along a strip of fifty miles which had once been some of the best grazing land. At the north, there was another slice for the Paiutes and Utes. The Navajos were no longer Lords of the Soil.

No one had considered how they were to make a living in this restricted area without banditry. In fact, that question has never been answered. In the meantime, until the harvest came in, Uncle Sam was to feed them. The agent's office and, more important, the sutler's store, where the rations would be given out, were at Fort Defiance. It was the same little group of log and adobe houses from which Kit Carson had sent the Navajos into exile. "A collection of old, dilapidated mud pig sties and sheep pens and nothing more," said a later visitor.[6] The roofs had been mended and the walls patched, but still, as Captain Bennett, the fort commandant admitted, there were holes where snakes crawled in and out.[7] Yes, there was a military commandant with

[6] L. B. Bloom (ed.), "Bourke on the Southwest," *New Mexico Historical Review,* Vol. XI (1936), 81.

[7] *Reports* of Commissioner of Indian Afairs, 1880, 132.

his detachment of cavalry. The Navajos were no longer prisoners of war, but they were not to be trusted to a civilian agent without some defense for "emergencies."

Rations were to be given out once a week. Every Saturday herds of beef were driven in from the Texas plains and oxcarts came creaking from Albuquerque loaded with corn or wheat. At the fort, a high-walled corral or stockpen had been built, with a little door at one side. The Navajos walked one by one through the door, receiving tickets, and then waited in the pen until all were in, so that no one would be counted twice. Then they might take their tickets to the sutler's store. The ration was a pound of beef and a pound of wheat or corn for every day in the week. If they were lucky, there might be salt and tobacco thrown in. While they congregated, Barboncito, sixty years old but still "Anxious to Step Forward" sat on the adobe wall and lectured them in chiefly fashion. "My kinsmen," the old Navajos repeat his words, "we lost everything and we promised peace. Tell that to your children. See that they do not fight. See that they work!" It is said that once he asked the government for an old ram, so that he might tie it to a tree in front of this very corral and say to the Indians: "See how it breaks its horns and bruises its head. That is what will happen to you if you fight the white man's government. So go home and be at peace."

Many of the Navajos had gone home as soon as they got their first week's rations—those whose homes were still included in the reservation. They found ruin. Earth-covered huts had fallen down. Peach trees were stumps. Corn, which does not seed itself and cannot grow wild, had vanished from the lumpy red earth. The People camped as they could in makeshift shelters. Some made the weekly tramp to Fort Defiance, perhaps as much as thirty miles, to get rations. For some it was not worthwhile. They lived on birds, rats, or any wild food they could find. Others camped at the fort, in dugouts or old army tents. "We housed ourselves like animals," they say, "for we never knew what would happen next." Some found themselves homeless. During those years of the third beginning, the Navajos redistributed themselves. As in the migration after the Pueblo revolt, there were some who stayed near the village dwellers, some who raised crops in the fertile canyons, and some who roamed widely with their sheep; so now the People drifted into different groups, each with its slightly different way of life. No true history should speak of them as "the Navajos," an undifferentiated mass. In time they came to differ, even in pronunciation."

There was no thought of dividing their narrowed country into the 160 acre plots mentioned in the treaty. That idea was so foreign to the Navajos that no agent ever suggested it. The People had their own system of "squatter's rights" established when they first spread out to occupy the land. Then, much as the whites did later, each family pre-empted such planting and grazing grounds as it found, and no one interfered. The next comers passed on and found more land. In time, as the families grew, there were clusters of huts in all the desirable spots. Now the owners of the huts went back to Canyon du Chelly, to "Little Water" or the stream-fed valley stretching north from Fort Defiance.

Some, uncomplainingly went to less fertile places, with no hope of roving to increase their pasture, and some found that their old homes were entirely off the reservation. They made no move to seek asylum with people who were not their relatives. As self-reliant as their white brothers, these Navajos collected their families and moved. Some went to Ramah, among the Mormons, and some to the lonesome canyons around Navajo Mountain. Others roamed through the public domain or the railroad property. They could not believe that they were trespassers on the grasslands where they used to pasture, and for years there were fights between these Navajos and the whites.[8] Brawls, rather than "fights," for the People kept their word never again to fight the whites officially.

In the spring the fort commandant, Captain Bennett, now temporary agent, distributed seeds. The Navajos soon came to know the big, kindly captain, who substituted when their civilian agents were whisked away by death, removal, or resignation. They called him Big Belly, not in derision but as a statement of fact. They liked him, as they did most military men for "you always knew what they were going to do." The People took the seeds and everybody planted. Then one of those storms of snow and sleet which visit Navajo country as late as June destroyed the crop. "I think," reported Bennett, " . . they were the most sorrowful, downhearted, discouraged set of people that could well be imagined."[9] He gave out the few seeds he could procure, but they only supplied a fraction of the People. The rest looked out for themselves. Some, they recount, had providently saved the corn spilled around Wingate cavalry stables. Some went to the forts, at Wingate and Defiance, begging for more. Some made the long trip to Hopi or Zuñi, trading their clothing, their blankets, their cherished Mexican silver—anything to get seed. They planted with digging sticks as of old and hoped for some corn before the early frosts of mesaland. But that summer was droughty, and grasshoppers ate the crop. It would hardly have consoled the Navajos to know that this same misfortune was happening to other Indians. Drought and grasshoppers, grasshoppers and drought! It almost looked as though Nature was persecuting those who planned to make the Red

[8] *Ibid.*, 1886, 204.
[9] *Ibid.*, 1870.

Men into farmers. Or was it that the lands given them were so often droughty and grasshopper-ridden?

Rations continued through the spring, supplied by the grumbling military. It was plain that there was no sense in hailing the Navajos in from all parts of the reservation every Saturday, for this meant a death blow to steady work. Soon the local headmen were allowed to take consignments, each for his whole group. Manuelito, Mariano, and others would drive off small herds of beef and government wagons loaded with grain, while detachments of soldiers went along as guards.

So far, the promised tools had not arrived. The young Congress, for surely such a body can be called young when it is only eighty years old, had its hands full with reconstruction after the war between the States. The treasury was exhausted, the country was expanding with almost magical speed, and here were some twenty or thirty tribes of Indians, all to be fed and supported while they learned a new way of life. To the harassed legislators, it looked as though the Indians simply slumped, without learning anything. Yet the bills for beef and flour came pouring in. Congress grew bewildered, irritated, and balky. That winter, 1869–70, it refused to pass the Indian appropriations bill at all, and President Grant got it through only by a political ruse.

However, the Navajo sheep had been bought, and in the fall of 1869 they arrived, fifteen months after the signing of the treaty. Word went out through all the reservation, and Navajos appeared from hidden places where, perhaps, they had evaded Kit Carson. There were 8,121 altogether, say the government reports, and they owned some 1,965 sheep and goats. Now 14,000 sheep and 1,000 goats were being driven across the mesas from the Mexican ranch at Las Cuevas, near Fort Union. They were the real little Spanish *churros,* slim-legged and long-haired and now adjusted to the plains of New Mexico as though it were their native home.[10]

The excited Navajos in their ragged blankets walked one by one through the little western gate in the corral while Big Belly Bennett stood on the wall to count them. There were two animals for every man, woman, and child, and Bennett wrote afterward: "I have never seen such anxiety and gratitude."[11]

So the Navajos started a sheep industry which in later years would be valued at millions of dollars. They had reason to be thankful to the Spaniards who had brought the little *churros* to the Southwest, to the Pueblo Indians who had taught the care of them, and to their own century and a half of herding with its ingrained habits of industry. In these very years, there were other Indians newly settled on reservations who sat down to mourn that life held nothing worth doing and some who seemed likely to become permanent pensioners of the government. Of all American Indians, only the Navajos had an established livestock industry. A job was waiting for them, and without repining they went into it.

Sheep were often the property of the women who tended them "like babies," brought them home at night, hacked off the wool with any bit of metal they could get, and spun it into yarn for blankets. These blankets were not for home use in this time of poverty, but for trade. While men kept the families alive by hunting and planting, it was the women who produced new wealth. They saved every shred of wool that was not traded for food, even though the *churro* sheep only gave a pound and a half at a clipping. Dressed in flour sacks, living on rats and wild plants, the women sat down doggedly to weave—not the brilliant, intricate patterns of their great period before Fort Sumner,

[10] Personal information from Mr. Sam Day.
[11] *Reports* of Commissioner of Indian Affairs, 1870, 148.

and not their own handsome blanket dresses in red and black! These wore out gradually and were never replaced. All weaving now was for trade. Experts have pronounced it the worst in all Navajo history, and no wonder. Working against starvation, they wove what would bring quickest results. The Mormons, at Salt Lake City, would take plain saddle blankets and so would their new settlement at Tuba City, beyond the Hopis. Utes and Comanches wanted strong, rainproof camping blankets in blue and white stripes, and the Mexicans liked brighter colors. The Navajo woman put the work through her loom as fast as she could. When two or three articles were ready, her man loaded them on his scrawny horse and was off on a trip of hundreds of miles. What he brought back were horses, always horses, for the Navajos had to build up their self respect again. If they could not raid, if they could not wander, they must still have the one sign of a lordly people. When young men had their horse herds and brides could be properly purchased, then the Navajo could be himself again.

Men went off to wage work when they could find it, hauling wood and water, making adobes, or herding sheep. "They work for us faithfully" said Commissioner Burke "at any kind of labor they can perform and we find them a very orderly and agreeable people."[12] The American silver dollars they earned were sewed on clothing or melted to make jewelry.

The famous Navajo silverwork began in these hard years of reconstruction. It was a move made on the Indians' own initiative and, at first, without help from school or agent. For fifty years or so the Navajos had been wearing silver jewelry and bridle ornaments stolen or traded in Mexico. Why should they bother to make such things themselves? They were too busy with war and sheep raising. However, one medicine man called Etsidi

[12] W. S. Burke to Kirkwood, Files of Office of Indian Affairs, 5015.

Sani, or Old Smith, had at least been interested in ironwork.[13] He had got a "Mexican" friend, which means New Mexican, to teach him how to make iron ornaments for bridles. Some have said he made silver as well as iron, but Old Smith's descendants are sure that the Navajos knew nothing about silverwork before going to Fort Sumner.

At the fort, Old Smith had no chance to practice his art—unless, indeed, it was he who counterfeited those identification tags. "How could the Navajo work silver at Fort Sumner!" exclaimed their late chairman Chee Dodge. "They were locked up there just like sheep in a corral!" But when they returned to a poverty-stricken land, that was a different matter. Old Smith went back to his Mexican friend and, say his descendants, learned how to forge and hammer silver. He taught his four sons, using a forge made of baked mud, a bellows of goat skin, and tools out of any pieces of scrap iron begged or filched from the whites. Eagerly the Navajos seized this new means of trade and livelihood. The Zuñis still tell how Ugly Smith, one of Old Smith's sons, came to their village in 1872. He came as a poor man, with nothing but his tools and the horse he rode. He stayed a year, teaching the Zuñis to make bridle ornaments, belts, and bow guards. When he left, he was driving a herd of horses and sheep ahead of him.[14]

That was a bit later in Navajo history. In those early days, silver was not yet a source of Navajo livelihood—nor was farming. The confident hope that the People would soon be living on their own produce had been evolved by lawmakers who never saw the gravelly plains of the reservation nor heard of its unseasonable frosts and droughts. There was no division into farm plots. The People planted where they could, near the hollows

[13] John Adair, *The Navajo and Pueblo Silversmiths,* 4–5.
[14] *Ibid.,* 124.

and water holes, but there was no assurance of a crop. In their first summer on the reservation, in 1869, the crops were delayed by spring snow and then destroyed by frost. In 1870, there was sleet; in 1876, grasshoppers; in 1878 and 79, drought; in 1880, wind and rain; and in 1881, drought, followed by floods. In fact, it was the usual reservation climate.

Congress was swamped with expenses after the Civil War and was not sending even clothing to the destitute Navajos, who wore white men's castoffs and flour sacks saved from government issues. Old women now recall that they knew no other costume in childhood but a flour sack, split up the sides and with PILLSBURY in a circle on the back.

It did not seem worth while to build the solid, earth-covered houses of ancient days, and the new reservation often could not supply the poles. Some families lived for years in caves and brush shelters; others hastily constructed the "four-legged" house, which dates from this period. One can still see these flimsy structures on the reservation; made with poles, with four corners, and the flat roof of Mexican style, they were covered sometimes with brush and sometimes with earth. Such shelter was good enough for people who did not know where their next meal was coming from, but it was not adequate for a Navajo ceremony, which requires the old-style circular house. It is impossible, said the People, to hold a ceremony in a square house.

The Navajos kept their promise not to war on the United States. But as the restraints of reservation life began to irk them, there was nervousness and ill temper. This trying situation is evident in the stories of fights between Navajo and white, and Navajo and Navajo. It is evident in the constant complaints of Indian agents who charged that the traders were bringing in whiskey and that drink was the curse of the tribe. Doctors are telling us now that drunkenness is not a cause of nervous instability but a symptom. When young men could not raid and acquire horses, when they had no sheep and their corn patches were ruined by drought, why should they not drink? That was the one kind of luxury they could share on even terms with the white man, who could get no drunker than a Navajo or have grander visions. And if the Navajo was useless for work afterward, well, what work was there to do?

The unrest bubbled in anger between the People themselves. They had always believed, like their Pueblo neighbors, that many of the unexpected misfortunes of life are due to witchcraft. Perhaps that was a necessary relief in the close little groups where everyone had to be friendly and helpful, sharing with clan and family whether they did their part or not. It was against Navajo ethics to say that a certain relative was lazy or selfish, but custom allowed one to whisper that he might be a sorcerer. In these ten years after Sumner, sorcery seemed rife on the reservation. The Navajos tell with bated breath how a terrible sorcerers' society came into power, how its members were hunted down, and eight, ten, or twenty were killed.[15] The authorities once found two men bound and ready for execution, and they arrived after two others had been lynched in the territory of old Many Cattle.[16] His descendants still boast about what a just man he was. One of the medicine men thus accused was his own uncle, yet Many Cattle had him clubbed to death. The misfortunes of the Navajos were getting beyond their control.

Chiefs like Many Cattle had never been able to calm the People, nor could they now, even though they had official authority from Washington. After the return from Sumner, it had been decided that there must be some machinery of organi-

[15] Clyde Kluckhohn, *Navajo Witchcraft*, 77.
[16] Frank Reeve, "The Government and the Navajo," *New Mexico Historical Review*, Vol. XVI (1941), 279.

zation among the Navajos themselves, so three chiefs had been appointed. Barboncito, "who is anxious to step forward," was made head chief. "He was nothing but a tool of the agency," say some of the old Navajos now. Yet what else could the poor man be? It became his duty to urge his tribesmen not to quarrel and not to steal, but to work hard and take care of their sheep. Every Saturday, when rations were given out, he sat on the corral wall and harangued them in the good old-fashioned way, throwing in bits of news to sweeten the pill. Ganado Mucho, rich old Many Cattle, was appointed subchief for the western side of the reservation. The sagacious old Hopi had kept his cattle all through Sumner days and now was settled at the Fertile Spot, called Ganado, and quietly engaged in collecting more. When irate Navajos visited him, his only response was: "Remember, my children, we promised peace."

The warrior Manuelito was subchief for the eastern side. The People remember how he lived with his two wives at the Place Dark with Plants, which is now called Manuelito Springs. His hogan was always thronged with visitors, and he could have gathered a little army to raid the fort whenever he wished, but Manuelito, too, was on the side of peace—at least to begin with. The Navajos remember his powerful voice ringing out in the intervals at the ceremonies, the immemorial time for speeches: "Now my brothers, work. Be peaceful." Every cluster of huts also had its local leader, and these met frequently with the three officials. They were constantly begging the agent for more food and more land. Once the fiery Manuelito requested impatiently that a new agent be appointed, "one who could furnish more rations."

In 1870, two years after the return from Sumner, Barboncito died. The peaceful Ganado took his place, even though he was now aging and suffering from eczema. Manuelito was second in command. There was an opportunity here, had the government known how to use this sturdy warrior, still in the prime of life, and for a few months it looked as though the opportunity would be taken. General Howard, commandant for New Mexico, suggested that a corps of Navajo police be appointed to guard the reservation and retrieve stolen cattle. One thousand men were enlisted at five dollars a month with Manuelito at their head at eight dollars. Now that was a job for a warrior! The new corps proceeded to comb the reservation, and in three months they had got back sixty head of cattle. "Very good," said Congress. "In fact, so good that the force is no longer needed and shall be disbanded."[17] It is true that on the pleas of agents, the force was finally reestablished and did good service for many years. Still this was done without Manuelito.

Perhaps it was after this fiasco that Manuelito began to drink. In 1873, the agent had to reprove him for getting drunk and permitting his people to trade sheep for whiskey. What matter that the government presented both him and Ganado with windmills, the only two on the reservation beside the one at Fort Defiance? The windmills were never put up, and ultimately they were carted off to the Hopis. What if they were each given a wagon brought all the way from the east! Manuelito's, according to Fort Defiance records, was an old ambulance. It was pleasant to bump in state over the desert hillocks with all the people cheering, but that could not take the sting away from Manuelito's position as a poor man and a mouthpiece of the whites.

There is a pathetic picture taken of him in the 1880's, seated in half-naked splendor and wearing a tall, silk hat which some white man had given him. He probably looked no more ridiculous to his people than a white politician looks to his, when his

[17] *Reports* of Commissioner of Indian Affairs, 1873, 273.

pale spectacled face is decked in a Sioux war bonnet. But in former days, the great war chief would have had no time to accept garments from the whites and to sit around being photographed in them. The story of Manuelito goes on diminuendo, to end in drunken sprees and the guard house.[18]

We should be wrong, however, if we thought the despairing chief was typical of the average Navajo. The indomitable energy of the tribe was not so easily killed. True, they did not make the transition from nomadism to civilization in the ten years planned by Congress. They have not made it yet, in the white man's sense, for a people's emotions and traditions are not so easily uprooted and sown anew. The Navajo did not learn what the agent meant him to learn. He did not go to school. Yet, through those desperate ten years, he kept himself and his family alive, and his numbers increased from 8,181 to 11,850. By 1880, the year of first reliable report, Navajo flocks numbered 700,000. The Navajos had acquired horses. The tribe had, in fact, made a lusty third beginning. All this was accomplished with the minimum of help and advice from the government. What was occupying Father Washington?

[18] *Ibid.*, 1884, 135.

13: Father Washington

AT A BOARD table in his hut at Fort Defiance, the agent was at his usual job of writing reports and accounts, all to be copied by letterpress in purple ink. Such reports boil with complaints about how the roofs at the fort were falling in, the sides giving way,[1] and the sand outside drifting up two feet higher than the floors inside.[2] He was, perhaps, in no mood to sympathize with the blanketed beings who stood before him, emitting sounds unknown to the English language. When the agent found himself held responsible for rations and clothing which had not come, he could give but one answer: "Washington."

The Navajos had no idea of the varied and changing entities responsible for their welfare. For them, the President, Congress, Secretary of the Interior, and the Commissioner of Indian Affairs and all his subofficials were subsumed under the one potent word—Washington. Such an attitude is not unknown among white citizens today. As for the fact that Washington's component parts might not agree and might even be opposing each other, that was far beyond an Indian's ken.

[1] *Reports* of Commissioner of Indian Affairs, 1872, 303.
[2] *Ibid.*, 1877, 159.

The chief arbiter of the Indian's fate was, and still is, Congress. Congress was a changing body, representing a changing country, where it was fitting that every group should have its chance at the national purse. This suited the eager whites, who were now spreading and building all over the land. The Indians, however, if they were to be wards, needed an informed and consistent guardian with long-term plans for their adjustment. Such plans were made eighty years later, and we wonder how different Indian history might have been if the world in the 1860's had possessed the knowledge of sociology and the fervid interest in minorities which it has today.

One early visitor to the Southwest fervently described the difficulty as he saw it. Cremony wrote, in 1868:

"One of the most serious obstacles in the way of a settled and satisfactory arrangement with our Indian tribes results from our own form of government which requires a change of the whole working department of the Indian Bureau whenever a change of administration takes place . . . . Nor can this evil be remedied as long as the Indian Bureau continues to be a political machine. The savages cannot comprehend why it is that every few years imposes upon their acceptance new and untried agents to regulate matters between them and their Great Father at Washington nor why the new agents should institute a policy different from that of their predecessors."[3]

The agents as well as the savages were bewildered when successive congresses issued orders which were constructive according to their lights but varied from year to year. In 1870, judging that the tribes were now pacified, the legislators ruled that army men should no longer be eligible as Indian agents. (That meant that Big Belly Bennett, friend of the Navajos, had suddenly to leave.) But in 1892, army men were again per-

[3] John C. Cremony, *Life Among the Apaches,* 313.

mitted to hold this office. In 1886, the order was that no Indian children should be sent to school without their parents' consent. In 1887, schooling was made compulsory. These decisions might be issued as separate laws or, more often, be carried along by that potent weapon, the Indian Appropriation Act. The money promised to Indians by treaty was never automatically forthcoming. Every year, it had to be voted in such amounts as Congress thought advisable or could afford. Naturally—it seemed at the time—the largest sums went to hostile groups like the Utes and Apaches who might thereby be induced to stop fighting. In fact, these former enemies were urging the Navajos to go out and fight, then be paid to quit. "If they were not the best natured Indians in the country" sputtered one agent, "they would do it."[4]

The agent could do nothing about the shortage of funds but write irate reports, but even the commissioner began to encounter financial problems. The commissioner presented to Congress his report of what was owed to the Indians and what was needed. Pressure groups for other interests appeared with their demands and arguments. All parties soon learned to request far more than they needed, in view of the cuts sure to be made. Even so, the sums with which Congress was willing to part were always too little. By 1886, the commissioner estimated that $792,-000 was still owing to the Navajos.[5]

The commissioner had to request not only treaty money but rations, for the promised day of self-support stretched far beyond the ten year "treaty period." Some blame could be laid on the land, which, said one agent, "is about as valuable for stock grazing as that many acres of blue sky."[6] More blame goes to the weather. A record of thirty-two years shows that the story of drought, frost, and grasshoppers went on as usual.[7]

<hr />

[4] *Reports* of Commissioner of Indian Affairs, 1884, 133.
[5] *Ibid.*, 1886, LXXIX.

1870: Crops insufficient. Bad Navajos will steal, good ones starve.

1871: No crop.

1873: Grain gone by December. Then six months with no food.

1876: Wheat destroyed by grasshoppers.

1879: Drought.

1880: Drought.

1881: Drought, then floods.

1882: Good crop, but early frost spoiled much.

1893: Drought. Animals dying, people starving.

1894: Bad crops and price of wool down. Help needed.

1895: Great suffering. Animals killed for food.

1900: Poor crops.

1901: Poor crops, rations issued.

1902: Same. Rations issued winter and spring.

These constant rations nibbled remorselessly into the treaty money. When the latter was paid, it was in the form of goods, since the Indians still had no use for cash. Goods were provided by eastern contractors among whom, for a time, exploitation was rampant. They made their own choice of how many overcoats, hats, and suspenders should be sent to the blanket-wearing Navajos, and this proved an excellent way of getting rid of surpluses. There was a period when Indians all over the country received crates of high-buttoned shoes. These could, perhaps, be worn, if the heels were knocked off, but what could the Navajos do with their 1881 shipment of sixty-four dozen lead furniture castors neatly packed in barrels.[8] They used the barrels.

The next step down from Congress was the Secretary of the Interior who, in those days of western settlement, was chiefly interested in homesteading. He appointed a Commissioner of

[6] See note 4.

[7] *Reports* of Commissioner of Indian Affairs, 1868–1902.

[8] L. B. Bloom (ed.), "Bourke on the Southwest," *New Mexico Historical Review*, Vol. XI (1936), 91.

Indian Affairs, from his own political party, of course, for this was the period of the "spoils" system. The commissioner was rarely in office more than two years.[9] Hardly one of them visited Indian country, and certainly not the Navajo reservation. Some were more interested in feathering their own nests than in any problem of the Indian. One Commissioner was reprimanded by the House Appropriations Committee for irregularities, neglect, and incompetency.[10] Another resigned after being accused of lax accounting for Indian funds,[11] and a third was at least criticized for carelessness.[12] President Grant, in 1869, tried to deal with the difficulty by appointing a Board of Indian Commissioners to inspect records and agencies and to advise on procedure. They were unpaid, but had an appropriation for travel. Although this travel budget was reduced as time went on, this board did yeoman's duty for half a century. However, in these early days they did not get around to the Navajos.

The only representative of Washington whom the Indians saw in the flesh was the agent. On him devolved all decisions of how rations should be distributed, who should have special favors, and the general rules for behavior on the reservation. His staff consisted of a clerk and sometimes an interpreter, while school teachers came and went, as a later chapter will show. There might be some Indian laborers, and later there were farmers and matrons, but these were slow in appearing. Meanwhile, the agent was expected not only to keep the Indians at peace, but to keep accounts, distribute "issue," and send in reports on Indian population and progress. A difficult matter, when any Indian hogan looked merely like one sandhill among other sand-

[9] Edward E. Dale, *The Indians of the Southwest*, 124.
[10] Loring B. Priest, *Uncle Sam's Stepchildren: The Reformation of United States Indian Policy, 1865–1887*, 67.
[11] *Ibid.*, 71.
[12] *Ibid.*, 67.

hills, and the occupants disappeared quietly into the brush at a stranger's approach! Rarely did he venture out over the rocky or muddy trails (Miller, who did, was killed.). The agent viewed what he could from buckboard or horseback, and most of the early agents confess that their estimates and reports were guesswork.

The agent was appointed by the secretary of the Department of Interior and generally as a political favor. However, it was none too easy to find a man, in or out of the party, who was willing to live in a "hovel" among "savages" for $1200 a year. Military men, of course, were used to the conditions, but their behavior was often routine and arbitrary. Local men were likely to have ranching interests and inherited quarrels. As for appointees fresh from the East, they were appalled at the conditions at the fort, "fit only for vermin," and usually departed or were dismissed within a year or two.[13]

In the thirty-one years between 1869, when the Navajos came to the reservation, and the end of the nineteenth century, when their economic comeback was practically complete, they had some fifteen agents, with long interims when the military took charge.[14] The period began with a spurt of hopefulness and idealism. President Grant, concerned about the Indian situation, took a suggestion from the Quakers. He asked the churches of the United States to nominate men fit to serve as agents. At first glance, the plan looks ideal, considering the times, but it was not so easy to find competent church members willing and free to live in the wilds. Moreover, they sometimes felt that securing members for their denomination was a more pressing duty than taking care of the Indians' business.

[13] *Reports* of Commissioner of Indian Affairs, 1878, 109.
[14] For a list of all Navajo agents, with dates, see Ruth Underhill, *Here Come the Navaho*, 275–77.

Each sect, after much discussion, decided on an area, and the Navajos fell to the Presbyterians. This denomination has done magnificent work, with school, church, and hospital, but in the 1870's, they had no trained men for the work. Four came to the Navajos, with intervals filled by the military and local men.[15] The first was killed (by the Utes, the Navajos said). The next found the salary too small and retired. Then came an invalid, who took leave of absence and was not returned. The last, known to the Indians as the Tarantula, quarrelled with white ranchers, military, and Indians. Finally they all joined in demanding his removal.

Yet the Tarantula had been a righteous man who, from his own point of view, was fighting evil. He wanted to prohibit liquor in the Southwest, to stop all activity on Sunday, and to outlaw "squaw men" from the reservation. It is true that some white settlers were mating with Indian women as an easy way to get land and a living. Sometimes, rumor said, even officials had Indian "wives." Regardless of what is said about the squaw men, they were sometimes a godsend to the Navajos. The Indian woman acted, to her people, as a privileged interpreter, not only of the white man's words but of his feelings and the reasons for them. More than that, she turned the remote official into a relative. To most Indians, including the Navajos, there can be no real friendship with anyone but a relative, real or symbolic. Even today, they react successfully only in intimate, face-to-face relationships—the last thing officialdom can usually give them.

The frustrated Tarantula left after two vituperative years. It had become apparent that church membership and zeal was no substitute for executive training and human experience.

---

[15] *Reports* of Commissioner of Indian Affairs, 1870–1883; Richard Van Valkenburgh, *A Short History of the Navajo People;* Frank Reeve, "The Government and the Navajo," *New Mexico Historical Review,* Vol. XVI (1941).

Grant's administration was long over, and with Chester A. Arthur the spoils system came back to its own. The next appointee was a Republican who "put up his money like a man."[16] Hardheaded politician though he was, Denis M. Riordan showed what could be done with the Navajos by intimate, friendly relationship. They talk yet about his trips among them, when the white man in his fur cap sat down and talked things over "like a relative." Some of these trips resulted in the People giving up stolen cattle, and once they had to deliver a murderer. Still, Riordan was equally keen on bringing white offenders to justice. As one of the few early agents who really saw the Indians and thought about them, Riordan objected to having the little sawmill left to rust in the winter storms. He offered to repair it at his own expense so that it could make $500 a year for the Indians. He was told to await the decision of Congress—which never came. "The indifference, the neglect, of the legislative branch of the government in regard to this important work," he commented, with what must have been almost agonizing self-control, "is not conducive to serenity of disposition."[17]

To give some picture of the Navajo problem from an agent's point of view, we can do no better than quote further from the highly articulate Riordan:

The labor demanded of an agent here is such as to prevent his performing any of his duties in a satisfactory manner. The reservation embraces about 10,000 square miles of the most worthless land that ever laid out doors . . . . The country is almost entirely rock. An Illinois or Iowa or Kansas farmer would laugh to scorn the assertion that you could raise anything there. However, 17,000 Indians manage to extract their living from it without government aid. If they were not the best Indians on the continent, they would not do it.

[16] Reeve, "The Government and the Navajo," *New Mexico Historical Review*, Vol. XVIII (1943), 17.

[17] *Reports* of Commissioner of Indian Affairs, 1883, 129.

No help is given to the indigent and helpless Indians, the agent being compelled to see them suffer under his eyes or else to supply the much needed articles at his own expense .... Knowing the failure of the government to fulfill its obligations to them, I for a time did my best to supply their needs. I spent some $800 in that way but the money was not repaid and the expenditure stopped. The United States has never fulfilled its promise made to them by treaty. It is safe to assume that it never will ....[18]

When Riordan resigned because the leaky houses at the fort made his family ill, the Navajos offered to add $1,000 a year to his salary out of their treaty money if he would stay. Later accusations of sullenness and lack of co-operation look unreal in the light of that offer. Somehow in such cases, the touchstone which would elicit the People's goodwill was being missed.

This touchstone was not used too often in succeeding years. To read the report of one agent after another is like watching some very sensitive indicator of blood pressure or electric voltage. One incumbent, even when honest and well meaning, finds the Indians "conservative" and "unteachable." Then, without apparent explanation, comes a report full of hope and vitality. Between the lines, we can read that here was agent, teacher, or military man who behaved "like a relative."

It is amazing how quickly the Navajos responded to such treatment, even after years of apparent sullenness. It is equally amazing to see the avenues of communication close again before a white man who is intelligent and conscientious but impersonal.

No touchstone was used by Riordan's immediate successors. The first was "an eminently qualified Republican" dismissed because of a sex scandal.[19] Then, in 1889, came "a fine lawyer and

[18] *Ibid.*, 119–20.
[19] Reeve, "The Government and the Navajo," *New Mexico Historical Review*, Vol. XVIII (1943), 31.

a Democrat"[20] whose fault was embezzlement;[21] and with him ends the story of the early fumbling years before the government and the Navajos had any real connection. These early agents were men catapulted into a job for which they had no training and almost no supervision. In their own eyes, doubtless, they were no worse than others in other walks of life, for that was a corrupt age in the nation's history. Nor was the situation worse than that of many colonies all over the world, where conquerors were ruling the conquered.

Even during this trial-and-error period, the chaos of postwar years was slowly subsiding. The Board of Indian Commissioners had begun tours of inspection. The Indian Rights Association was bombarding Congress with demands of justice for the Red Man. By 1884, almost fifteen years after the Navajos had come to the reservation, some of the promised tools and wagons began to arrive. Not that Congress had yet any real comprehension of the situation. Urged to greater activity they proposed to send farmers to teach the Navajos, and agent Patterson sputtered: "No farmers needed. The Indians have no plows and they know all about hoeing!"[22] Once there came a consignment of corn cultivators which could not be used on the Indians' hilly patches. One hundred of them were turned back to the agency.[23] Wagons proved equally useless on the bumpy, trackless ground, but the Indians had learned better than to turn them back and wait, perhaps a year, for the next consignment. They tell how they used them for hardware and firewood.

It became ever plainer that rations, seeds, and tools could not overcome all the difficulties of sterile land and unreliable weather. The agents, whatever their faults, could at least see

[20] *Ibid.,* 44.
[21] *Ibid.,* 31.
[22] *Reports* of Commissioner of Indian Affairs, 1888, 91.
[23] *Ibid.,* 1886, 203.

this and write to their superiors about it. They had no expert knowledge of what could be done, nor had the legislators. So fumbling attempts were made at windmills, dams, and ditches, never suited to desert conditions and always ineffective.[24] The Tarantula must be given credit for some fifty pumps which brought up underground water in the desolate stretches where no springs were to be found.[25]

Little by little, a water supply was developed in a few fertile spots.[26] Finally there was an appropriation for a big irrigation system. The job was given to army engineers who were unfamiliar with the torrential summer rains that cut the ground into gullies thirty or forty feet deep and carry tons of silt down the Colorado River.[27] The ditches washed out again, but it was long before this lesson bore fruit in the form of an efficient irrigation system.

All this looked bad for agriculture. The picture of prosperous little farms, envisioned by the eastern planners, faded away. However, it had never been a dream of the Navajos. Useful as they found their corn and, later, their peaches, wheat, and watermelons, these had never meant wealth and family pride as did their flocks and herds. During the worst years, when crops failed, most of the Navajos still managed to keep some sheep and even horses. The latter, in fact, could be eaten when there was no mutton. So, though animals were sometimes lost from drought or cold, their total number increased from year to year. Often there was not enough grass for them on the poorer lands, and then their owners quietly moved off the reservation for the summer. Agent Bowman said the People consider that this right

[24] *Reports* of Commissioner of Indian Affairs, 1880, 131; 1887, 175; Valkenburgh, *A Short History of the Navajo People*.
[25] *Reports* of Commissioner of Indian Affairs, 1881, 138.
[26] *Ibid.*, 1886, 205.
[27] *Ibid.*, 1883, 121.

was given to them by treaty, and he estimated that one-half of them were off bounds.[28]

It was obvious that the Navajos needed more land. In fact, they and the agents had been clamoring for this since 1880. By degrees small slices were added at one side or another, and by 1884, these amounted to eight million acres (see map). This may sound opulent on paper, but by the time each new grant was legally available, it had already been occupied by Navajos and their flocks for many years, and hundreds more were clamoring for homes and pasturage. True, they were eligible to homestead like the whites. But a Navajo did not understand that an adobe hut and a brush corral did not constitute the improvements demanded by law, and, naturally, no rancher was anxious to tell him. So land that had been occupied outside the reservation was soon lost.

To the credit of the Navajos is the fact that, during this period of stress, they had never ceased to do their part in working toward self-support. In 1871, the commissioner's report stated: "The Navajo are a hard working people and but for their unfortunate location, they might have been self-sustaining by this time."[29] In 1872, the report affirmed that: "they are peaceful, well disposed, energetic, hardworking and industrious."[30] In 1878: "they have grown from a band of paupers to a nation of prosperous, industrious, shrewd and (for barbarians) intelligent people.[31] In 1884: "The Navajo are the best behaved Indians in America."[32] In 1886: "the Navajo is by nature inclined to habits of industry and an independent desire to acquire property and to

[28] *Ibid.,* 1885, 155.
[29] *Ibid.,* 1871, 367.
[30] *Ibid.,* 1872, 53, 302.
[31] *Ibid.,* 1878, 108.
[32] *Ibid.,* 1884, 134.

maintain himself . . . (with proper government assistance). His future improved condition is assured."[33]

The "proper government assistance" had so far been lacking. Yet the industrious and hardheaded Navajos were approaching self-support according to their own standards and by their own chosen means. They were adopting such white man's ways as appealed to them. If the government agent had little part in this, the Navajos, nevertheless, had found another friend and teacher—a friend whom they could meet intimately, whose interests were close to their own, and who was not replaced with every administration. This was the trader.

[33] *Ibid.*, 1886, 203.

Navajo weaver. Note basket canteens, used for desert travel.
(Courtesy American Museum of Natural History)

Aged commercial weaver.
(Photograph by Milton Snow, Courtesy U. S. Indian Service)

Three Navajo leaders during early reservation days (left to right):
Ganado Mucho, Tiene-su-se, Mariano.
(Courtesy Museum of New Mexico)

14: Navajo Shoguns

THE TRADERS

". . . The Indian crier had set up a fearful gabbling, yelling and screaming at the top of his voice to let all know that it was time to draw rations . . . . The column surged along, a steady stream of whinnying ponies, each with its cargo of humanity; some bore only a painted and jewelled warrior; others only a squaw with a papoose slung in its cradle to her back and others again had two or three youngsters perched from withers to croup, all jabbering, laughing and calling out in their own language . . . . I am certain that at least a dozen of the children I saw riding by could not have been four years old and one little toddler, scarcely able to keep on his own pins was unconcernedly lead- ing a gentle old pony through the mass of Indians, dogs, burros and horses, crowding about him. The scene was essentially bar- baric, the dresses of the riders gorgeous and fantastic, and the trappings of the ponies jingling with silver . . . . The display of coral and turquoise beads was something to excite astonishment while those who were not fortunate enough to possess such heir- looms, contented themselves with strands of silver hemispheres and balls of copper."[1]

[1] L. B. Bloom (ed.), "Bourke on the Southwest," *New Mexico Historical Review,* Vol. XI (1936), 83.

These were the Navajos in 1881. True, they were still receiving rations, even though the ten-year treaty period was past. And it is true that the government storekeeper had said that there was not enough flour on hand to feed them for three months. But it is evident that they were no longer a starving and beaten people. Most of them had ridden to Fort Defiance with sacks of wool tied on their ponies, for exchange at the government store. They were dressed in handsome blankets and decked with silver jewelry, and so were their horses. For the Navajos, twelve years after their return to the reservation, were again supplied with "that by which men live." They were ready to move on toward prosperity, as they had done before.

There is a special reason for viewing them in this year, 1881, for it marks the arrival of a momentous influence in their lives. The railroad had come to the Southwest. The Santa Fe Railroad, crawling year by year from Topeka, Kansas, over the Raton Pass, and down through Las Vegas and Lamy, had at last reached Albuquerque. From there Lieutenant Bourke, who wrote this description, had traveled in a caboose as far as the desert outpost of Fort Wingate. Trains went no farther, but as he took horse for the "Hellgate" known as Fort Defiance, he could see the partially laid tracks of the new Atlantic and Pacific Railroad which would connect Albuquerque with California. The Navajos, who had earned some silver dollars carrying wood and water for the track layers, had no idea what the "iron horse" would mean to them. They were still living comfortably in conditions comparable to those of the Middle Ages, as were most of the people in New Mexico, in their various ways. Earth-floored houses, water carried by hand, hand-loomed clothing, hand-coiled pots, hand-hammered jewelry, transportation on horseback over roadless country, and wealth measured by the size of flocks and herds—this was the situation for almost everyone, and the difference between Indian and white was that the Red Men simply had a little less of some things.

There was regular train service to the little station west of Gallup, first called Ferry and later named Manuelito. From here, oxcarts brought the first big consignment of wagons, harness, plows, hoes, scrapers, wheelbarrows, cookstoves, overcoats, and boots. The Navajos, coming in from their earth-covered hogans, miles out in the desert, were totally unprepared to handle such unfamiliar objects. Now, however, the day of handmade equipment was ending. Soon the railroads would be bringing the Navajos bales of cheap cloth, boxes of nails and metal tools, and even wagons, pumps, and windmills. Steam sawmills would arrive to saw up lumber for modern-style houses. There would be wagons for travel and roads built to accommodate them. More than that, there would be new people—floods of them. Eating houses, saloons, and gambling places were springing up along the railroad. "Congregations of desperados and outlaws," growled the Indian superintendent. Homesteaders were crowding into the public domain which bordered the Navajo reservation. And the traders were coming.

The influence of the traders can hardly be overestimated in this next period of Navajo history. They were the bearers of a new way of life, even as the Pueblos had been three hundred years ago. When the half-naked Navajos came prowling into the Southwest, they needed teachers to show them how and why corn should be planted and what a people could do with this new possession. The Navajos had not wanted lectures or commands. They needed and often took Pueblo neighbors and spouses who hoed the fields, shared the corn, and personally taught them the new way of life. The same sort of help was needed now, as calico, string, colored yarns and dyes, hammers, axes, wagons, and harness began changing the way of life of the people of New Mexico. The government had no means of providing the Navajos with a friend who spoke their own language and was ready day after day to talk things over with them. After making the long journey to Fort Defiance, the Indian was lucky if he got a curt word of direction from the agent and perhaps a paper from the clerk entitling him to some government issue. There was no time for questions, even had there been an interpreter to ask them.

But the trader's very life on the reservation depended on his ability to please the Navajos. So he set himself to learn as much of the language as his white tongue could manage. And if he could not talk, he could at least lean over the counter with a friendly smile, waiting patiently while the Indian inspected every article in the store. He could give little gifts of coffee and candy. He could let people sleep on his floor overnight, when they were belated. That, thought the Navajo, was normal human behavior. Little by little, as traders penetrated the reservation, the Indians turned to them as interpreters of the new life. Too much blame should not be placed on the transient agents, who were so busy with papers and accounts that they had not a moment for talk with the Indians. They scarcely had time to grasp the main problems of their mandate and write to Washington about them when poor health, poverty, or a change of administration would send them east again. So the agent was little more to the Navajos than a name. Sometimes it was a derogatory name, like "Old Man Who Smells His Moustache," a name they repeated later for Hitler.

Real contact with the white man came through the trader. We are reminded of the ancient situation in Japan, when the emperor was too sacred to have any contact with his people. It was his prime minister, the shogun, who guided the nation while the sovereign remained in godlike isolation. The trader was the

Navajos' shogun, and it is no exaggeration to say that he guided the People's development for some thirty or forty years.

This came about so gradually that neither government, traders, nor Indians realized what was happening. A government agent had even been the one who encouraged the Navajos to sell their wool directly from the reservation instead of peddling it. Willy Arny, one of the transient agents in pre-railroad days, was a New Mexican and sheep-minded. In 1871, he persuaded some Navajos to bring their wool to the sutler at Fort Defiance for trade in goods. He engaged ox teams to take it to Albuquerque, and then it was shipped east to carpet manufacturers. The Navajos took up the idea. True, their scrawny sheep gave no more than a pound or two of wool, which was hacked off with a homemade knife shaped from a tin can. But when the Navajos saw an economic advantage they took it. By 1886, they had a million pounds of wool to trade,[2] and by 1890, two million.[3] Even the skins from the slaughtered sheep and goats were not being wasted. Sheep pelts were selling for six to ten cents, and goat from twenty to fifty. The Navajos had found a steady source of income which partly took the place of raiding.

The army sutler at the fort soon ceased to be their only trader. As soon as freight trains began to arrive with carloads of goods, adventurous and enterprising pioneers moved on the reservation. They needed courage and a gambling spirit, for this land was almost unknown to whites, American or Spanish. There were still Ute and Apache raiding parties abroad, and, some whispered, Navajo parties, too. No one knew just where there was a good center to catch the roaming Indians nor what they would want to buy. It was necessary to get a license from the Indian Commissioner at Washington, and this might be

[2] *Reports* of Commissioner of Indian Affairs, 1886, 203.
[3] *Ibid.,* 1889–90, 256.

revoked any time the trader made some false step or, more likely, there was a change of administration. No wonder the tents and cabins of those early adventurers appeared and disappeared like so many mushrooms as the owners moved, changed partners, or bought each other out. By 1890, there were nine traders on the reservation and thirty more surrounding it at different points. In spite of all their difficulties, they were making money. A ruling of 1886 had put a ceiling on their profits, which were not to be more than 25 per cent of the cost of an article, plus freight charges.[4] Nevertheless, Sweetland, at Tse-hili, up toward Chinle, grossed $10,000 in one year, and the trader at Defiance, $4,000.[5]

No wonder the adventurers pulled wires with their senators to get the coveted licenses. They crowded into Navajoland, packing their goods by mule back or ox team from the distant railway. They were ready to live like the Indians while a fortune was being made. The Navajos, who never need urging to look at something new, came crowding around the tent with its counter made of a board across two barrels. When once they had made the journey from home, they were willing to camp for a day or two, fingering the newcomer's clothing and staring at every can and bolt of cloth on the shelves.

No money was used in those early days. The Navajo would bring his sacks of wool—or, rather, hers, for often the sheep were women's property—loaded on horseback. The trader weighed the sacks, first poking into them for the stones which the Indians soon learned to insert to make the wool heavier. Then he gave the Navajo a written statement of how much credit was due. This could be taken out in goods which the Navajo might

---

[4] *Reports* of Commissioner of Indian Affairs, House Exec. Doc. 1, Pt. 5, 115.

[5] Reeve, "The Government and the Navajo," *New Mexico Historical Review,* Vol. XVIII (1943), 40–43.

touch and select with his own hands. Naturally, the Indians had no way of knowing whether the trader had been fair about the weight or the amount of credit. So the Navajos found ways to protect themselves from this unknown power in their lives. "We fooled him," one of them proudly told Mr. Van Valkenburgh. "We traced that paper and made more, so we could get paid for the same wool over and over again." This was the sort of treatment one would give a Ute or any other enemy, outsmarting him, if possible, before he could attack. Realizing this trickery, the traders finally had to use stamped metal or pay in money.

Many of these traders made their fortunes and departed. Some stayed to grow up with the country, and their names are famous in the annals of the Southwest. One was Thomas Keam, an Englishman, a United States army captain, and, for a time, Navajo agent. He took a Navajo wife and finally settled in the canyon which bears his name. Another was John Lorenzo Hubbell, known to the Spaniards as Don Lorenzo and to the Navajos as Old Mexican. His father was a Connecticut Yankee who came to seek his fortune in New Mexico soon after it became part of the United States. He married the daughter of a proud old Spanish family who had come over with a land grant of twenty square miles or more from the king of Spain. Don Lorenzo had lived in the homes of the Paiutes and the Hopis until he knew their customs and could speak a little of their languages. This was the sort of man the Navajos could understand. When he settled at Ganado, where Old Many Cattle had held sway before reservation days, they flocked to his store. The land was now off the reservation, so that Don Lorenzo could homestead a tract, and part of it is Hubbell property to the present day. Since 1876, the Navajos have flocked there, not only to trade but also to ask advice, to get their letters written, and to make contact with the incomprehensible Washington. As one Hubbell put it:

183

"Out here in this country, the trader is everything from merchant to father confessor, justice of the peace, judge, jury, court of appeals, chief medicine man and *de facto* czar of the domain over which he presides."[6] Why not? He had the touchstone of friendly personal contact which opened the hearts of the Navajos. While the government was striving to civilize the Navajos by issuing orders that they should cut their hair and cease their heathen dances, and while the missionary was trying to convince them of their errors, the trader simply laid before them the possibilities of the new life.[7] It was Don Lorenzo who presented buggies to the two chiefs, Manuelito and Many Cattle, even when Manuelito was turning into a discouraged drunkard. It was Don Lorenzo who sent to Mexico for a silversmith to instruct the Navajos of his neighborhood in the new way to earn a living. His adobe-barracks store was like a feudal castle, always crowded with retainers whose economic life revolved around him. He might well have called himself, as his son did later, the "king of northern Arizona." And, appended a white editor, "his influence and power through five decades have been greater than that obtaining with the governors of many of these United States."[8]

That old adobe barracks, reeking with the smell of sheep wool and stacked with bags of flour and sugar, was to the Navajo what a world's fair might be to a modern American. Here they were able to choose, unhurried and unadvised, from the products of the white man's world. Coffee and sugar came first on the list, say the old traders, for the Navajos had learned to like these at Fort Sumner. Next were canned peaches, like the traditional

---

[6] Juan Lorenzo Hubbell, "Fifty Years an Indian Trader," *Touring Topics,* Vol. XXII, No. 12 (December, 1939).

[7] *Reports* of Commissioner of Indian Affairs, 1902, 157.

[8] *Ibid.*

fruit of Canyon de Chelly, but larger and sweeter. A liking for canned milk came more slowly, and traders lost many dollars by stocking a brand with the picture of a large carnation on the label. The Indians were sure it was made of vegetable matter and not milk at all. Often they bought a can without regard to the contents but merely for its size, for it made a container far better than breakable pottery. Or one could split it apart with an ax, then use the precious metal to make knives.

Pocket knives could be found at the store, and they were a cherished luxury. More necessary was cotton cloth, for now the Navajos could spare no wool to make clothes for themselves and the men got few deerskins. Men used unbleached muslin for the loose, white pantaloons which they usually sewed for themselves, just as they had once sewed their deerskin garments. In time they changed to the bright, flowered calico seen in many of the old pictures. Women also bought cotton goods, but slowly. Both sexes wanted blankets, and those on the trader's shelves were usually blue or gray with a red border. The Navajos were not making blankets for themselves any more, but they still peddled them throughout the Southwest. And the weavers wanted red. So they unravelled the borders from the white man's blankets and got enough red to weave a touch here and there in their Indian blankets.

Some time around 1890, the traders began to realize the possibilities of the Navajo blanket. Amsden says that the man who first got this idea should have his bust, crowned with a laurel, above every trader's door. In the Southwest, the blanket already was in demand by cowboys, army officers, Mormon settlers, and other Indians. But it took a woman months to save wool enough for one blanket, to make her vegetable dyes, and to unravel old cloth. She could hardly bring more than one or two blankets a year to the trading post. But suppose that yarn could be imported in quantity, already spun and colored! Then, if the Navajos could get some cotton string for the warp threads, which do not show, they would not have to use their wool clips at all. If the Navajo women could work fast and turn out plenty of blankets, then the next thing would be to get a market in the East. Or why should she weave blankets? What easterners buy more often are heavy floor rugs, of the texture of a Navajo saddle blanket. The idea was a "natural." Yarn and string were ordered. Trader Cotton, in 1894, sold out his share in the Ganado post and went to Gallup, to advertise, notify the eastern merchants, and start a booming wholesale business.

In the history of Navajo weaving, 1890 is a date which stands out as do those of the steam engine or the spinning jenny in the history of other crafts. That date—or thereabouts—marks the time when the Navajos ceased to make blankets of hand-spun, hand-dyed wool and began to make rugs from commercial yarn. The prostituting of an art? Yes, for in the next ten years there were turned out some of the weirdest and ugliest products ever made by Indians. Yet we could hardly ask that the Navajo woman continue to make her product by slow and difficult methods any more than we would force the white woman to continue with her homespun coverlets or her patchwork quilts. When the necessity for such things passes, so passes the urge for making them. Thereafter, the old craft was practiced only to make a quality product, made only by a few, for a few.

The Navajos had a necessity, but of a new kind. They wanted wealth. Strong in their hearts was the ambition to get back to their old place as Lords of the Soil. If they could not be raiders, they would use some other means to regain the flocks and herds which had once been theirs. Miraculously, it seemed, the white man's money opened the path.

Here again it was the women who saved the day. It was

often they who owned the sheep and decided how many the family might eat and how many must be saved for the wool clip. And it was they who wove the rugs that brought in real money. Navajo men had a right to be discouraged with the constant crop failures and the never ending delay in getting more land and more tools. Men in many other Indian tribes were discouraged by the same failures and never found a means of financial independence, but they had no army of earning women like the Navajos. With this new way to wealth open to them, the Navajo women sat down to their looms and, with tireless, brown fingers, pulled the tribe past its misfortunes and into prosperity.

The trader was their guide and teacher, the spokesman for necessity. He sent for a new kind of yarn now being made in Germantown, Pennsylvania. It was not so fine or so beautifully colored as the Saxony yarn of the great Navajo period. Still, there was plenty of it and in shades impossible to vegetable dye—purple, crimson, orange, and bright green! These colors had never appeared in Navajo weaving but not because the women did not like them, as some would have you believe. It was because the juices of bark and berry could not produce intense bright shades. Now that these colors were available, the women for a time reveled in using all they could get. And they found it even cheaper to buy a small package of aniline dye and color some of their own wool.

This phase might almost be considered as a new beginning in weaving, and indeed it had the crudity of a beginning. The women became careless with their new materials, weaving literally fast and loose. Three or four rugs could now be made in the time once required for one. And there were many new ideas for design. When the Navajos began to weave, they used mostly stripes. Stripes were the choice of their Pueblo teachers and also the most feasible pattern when there were only two or three colors. In the great period of Saxony yarns, the Navajos had used geometric patterns like those popular in Mexico. But now there was a brand new clientele, and the old patterns were discarded. At the same time, the women saw fascinating new shapes around them—the brilliant picture on a tomato can, the gay colored American flag, and even the railroad train! The fine, soft, Germantown yarn with its brilliant colors could be manipulated to form any of these designs, and Navajo textile skill was equal to the task. This skill was, in fact, the one legacy from the former days of weaving. Everything else was new, an adventurous plunge into the unknown.

It would be interesting to know what style the women would have developed had they gone their own way at this point. The gaudy rugs picturing trains, tin-can art, and letters of the alphabet might in time have been toned down and refined.

This was almost the Navajos' first attempt at weaving curved figures, yet the technique used was the same as that found in the famous European tapestries. If white women of the Middle Ages could weave figures as complex as those of an oil painting, why could not the Navajo weavers manage at least a tree or a bird? Given time, they might have worked out interesting conventionalized versions of the native scene, but there was no time. The People were as anxious to regain their flocks and herds as the trader was for success in business. They made what the market demanded.

The trader was their interpreter. It was he who had to find a market for the rugs in the wealthy East, since the West could not furnish demand enough. Eastern housewives wanted durable products in fine, close weaving and this the Navajos could understand. But these same customers would not buy rugs with pictures of railroad trains or tomato cans upside down. Nor could the bold stripes of the ancient rugs in black, white, and blue be fitted into their softly shaded interiors. What these eastern customers bought were oriental rugs crowded with tiny crosses, forks, and hooked figures, or else carpets copied from these.

The trader obliged. One who feels that the designs produced by the Navajos—or, indeed, of any group of craftsmen— are an indigenous development, welling unaided from the maker's soul, would be interested to see the catalogue of J. B. Moore, trader at Crystal, New Mexico, from 1896 to 1916. Moore wanted fine, durable weaving, and for this he picked his craftswomen. He supplied the designs, which he copied from rug and carpet patterns. These were designs of disciplined ranks of crosses, forks, hooks, zigzags, and swastikas, all caged within one or even two or three borders. He had some trouble, he says, with the "stubborn and conservative women," but finally their "senseless opposition" was overcome.[9] These rugs sold, and rugs in the same tradition are selling at Two Gray Hills to the present day.

Nor was Moore alone in his venture. In his office at Ganado, Don Lorenzo Hubbell had scores of blanket designs painted in oil, after patterns found to be pleasing to purchasers. When an order for a blanket came in, a weaver would be summoned, given the proper materials (the Hubbells were addicted to crimson), and told to memorize the design. In time, she came back with a replica "with such slight variations" says George Wharton James "as she is sure to introduce."[10] The Navajo creative urge was not completely killed, although it had very little scope in those days. One can still visit old traders and see their sketchbooks of designs, standardized for the eastern trade. Each trader has his specialty in forms and colors—the latter, perhaps, de-

[9] J. B. Moore, *The Navajo*, 3.
[10] George Wharton James, *Indian Blankets and their Makers*, 125.

pending on what yarn he could get cheaply. Modifications of these designs still hold their place in different parts of the reservation.

So the Navajo rug is, in a certain sense, a product of the trader. This is no criticism on the People's originality. How many art forms have developed directly from the artist's soul, without benefit of suggestion. Consider Chippendale furniture from China and Empire from Rome, via France, and even some modern art takes its inspiration directly from Africa. The Navajo woman, with practical intent, took over the trader's ideas and slowly adapted them, just as she had done with Pueblo stripes and the giddy diamonds of the "slave" blanket. Proof of her efficiency is that Navajo rugs are selling today, while the striped blankets of the Hopis are of interest only to collectors.

It was the traders themselves who began to see new possibilities. Cheap cotton warp was discarded, and there was a hunt for softer colors to replace orange and purple. In 1896, the Hyde Exploring Expedition started its own stores, for rugs free from those "leprous discolorations."[11] By 1900, Fred Harvey, the great hotel man of the Santa Fe line, began his campaign of buying up tasteful and well-made Navajo rugs and paying higher prices for them. The traders and the Navajos were in a successful business.

For the Navajos, this did not mean merely a short call at the store, when they took their goods. Navajos traveled in families, and once they arrived, they stayed all day. They watched with interest the building of the trader's cabin, which was often of logs if trees were near. In the old days, the Navajos had never been able to get logs except by the painful process of burning through a tree trunk, then hacking out the charred part with a

[11] George Pepper, "Native Navajo Dyes," *The Papoose*, Vol. I, No. 3 (1903), 1–11.

stone ax. Therefore, the old hogan had only three tall poles with a mixture of smaller ones and bark leaned against them. Now the trader could sell axes and saws, and the government was even talking of importing a steam sawmill. Some Navajos proceeded to build log cabins.

It is from the coming of the railroad and the traders in the eighties that the Navajos date the hexagonal house now so common on the reservation. It is made of strong, even-sized logs which could never have been cut without steel tools. Its floor shape is somewhere near circular, partly because that was the shape of the earthen hut and required for ceremonies, but also for another reason. Many Navajos worked on the railroad as it crawled slowly from Fort Wingate toward the coast, and they had plenty of chances to get the ties which were always being discarded because of some imperfection. Those who could drag them to their homes behind horses, did so. The ties were just the right length to make a good, six-sided house. If other logs were available, the house might have five, seven, or eight sides. Its roof was no white man's gable, but the old cribbing with short logs, learned from the sunken, circular rooms of the Pueblos.

The traders and the railroad did their part to change the Navajo dress. One Navajo told how his cherished long hair, a ceremonial necessity, was given up because of the railroad. He caught it in the door of a box car and was dragged. Thereafter, he went short haired, with no need of a government edict. The government had promised $40,000 worth of clothing, and by the end of the eighties, it had given out many bolts of calico and unbleached muslin and dozens of gray or blue blankets. This might not have influenced the Navajos had they not seen that the trader had these very things on his shelves, a proof of what was current in the white man's world. They did not care for the plain blankets, and soon a mill in Oregon was making fine, soft ones in their own most gorgeous style. As the women's woolen dresses wore out, they could buy calico and soon learned which type was the smoothest and strongest. Old Navajo traders say that when they saw an Indian woman coming they knew there was only one pattern they could show, a strong blue cotton with white stripes. From this, the women made a full skirt and a loose sack, falling from a yoke, and once known to white women as a dressing sack. Apache women wear such a costume still.

How had the Navajo women learned to sew? None of them can tell how they emerged from those puzzled days of the flour sack or the strip of calico tied around the waist, but photographs taken in the eighties show full calico skirts. Perhaps the Navajo wives of traders had something to do with it, for this was long before schools, missions, or field matrons had appeared. For myself, I am inclined to give much credit to the returned slaves, two or three hundred strong, who filtered back to the reservation in the seventies and eighties.

For many a Navajo, slavery was the introduction to the arts of civilization. Spanish ladies could not tolerate the Navajo dress, open down the sides and without underwear, as the Spaniards conceived it. They must have taught their slaves to sew and insisted on their wearing the long, full skirts proper to females of the day. Perhaps they also taught the Indians how to make the velvet blouse which now tops the skirt. Certainly the Navajo woman's "native" costume today, with its colorful, flounced skirt, tight velvet basque, and silver jewelry, has a decidedly Spanish flavor. Men at first did not wear the blouse. Their costume was the Spanish gentleman's underwear: loose white cotton pantaloons with a shirt hanging over them. The same con-

Navajo weaver passing the woof.
(Courtesy American Museum of Natural History)

Navajo hogan and sheep.
(Photograph by Milton Snow, Courtesy U. S. Indian Service)

Navajos at Fort Sumner. Note old-style striped blankets.
(Courtesy National Archives)

venient clothing was adopted by Pueblo and Mexican Indians and may sometimes be seen in Mexico to this day.

Long after the Emancipation Proclamation of 1863, the Navajo slaves remained with their Spanish masters. Graves, a special investigator while the Navajos were at Fort Sumner, was shocked at the fact and recommended that Congress take action. In that case, said New Mexico's Spanish governor, Congress should pay for the slaves, since the owners could hardly be expected to lose their value.[12] They told their slaves nothing of their new privileges, and the Indian agents after many a futile protest still had no time or money to get anything done. In 1872, one hundred women were finally returned from the Mexican settlements.[13] Slowly the news of freedom spread. Frantic relatives began to implore the agent for help and even to set out themselves for a search of the Mexican towns. One father told how he found his little daughter, captured as a baby during the Sumner roundup. She was afraid of the strange man and hid behind her Mexican master, swearing that she was his daughter. Years later, she at last came home, complete with husband and children. A man of Lukachukai told how he sought his wife for months, taking four male relatives with him. They carried sacred cornmeal and every day on the journey held ceremonies and prayed. They had to kidnap the woman and her three children from her Mexican master.

These house-trained women from the towns must have exerted some influence on Navajo customs. Surely they taught their daughters and probably other female relatives, too, how to sew. Such slow, intimate sharing is the chosen Navajo way of dis-

[12] Hubert H. Bancroft, *History of Arizona and New Mexico, 1530–1888*, 681.

[13] *Reports* of Commissioner of Indian Affairs, 1872, 304.

seminating information. Although the estimate is based on such Navajo dating methods as "after I had my second child" or "just after they dug the new irrigation ditch on the San Juan," it is probable that the present fashion of the velveteen blouse started about 1890. "A woman from near the railroad came to visit," say the women of Chinle, "and she had such a blouse. So we all wanted one. We told the trader to get us that fine, soft material, so he did. Then the men wanted them, too." It seems very likely that the "woman from near the railroad" was a returned slave. Thus, the Navajo dress, as we know it today, was started in the late nineteenth century. This date coincides more or less with that when plush "basques" went out of style in the East. Can it be that the Navajo liking for such soft material was fostered by traders who had a surplus to dump?

Since 1900, the life of the Navajo has remained remarkably constant, with a combination of Middle Ages living conditions, ancient Navajo and Pueblo customs, and a dash of modern American influence. In spite of bad years, the Navajo flocks and herds increased until they were as large as in ancient raiding days. They were well supplied with "that by which men live"— a hundred horses being only a moderate herd. In 1897, the tribe owned over 100,000 horses. For a population of 20,500, this meant almost five horses for every man, woman, and child. Their clothing was as gorgeous as in the old days of velvet trousers and silver buttons though now it was velvet blouse and homemade jewelry. Their blankets, made by the mills in Pendleton, Oregon, were in imitation of the classic Navajo style. Some still used the pointed earthen huts, though now the reservation was dotted with the hexagonal log dwellings thought of by many today as typically Navajo. In fact, this picture of the Navajo after 1900 is the one found in most accepted descriptions.

It had its bad side. Not everyone was a *rico,* with flocks and herds. Some ate their sheep, and in the years when their little corn patches failed, the agent reported them starving. Still, there had always been rich and poor among the Navajos, but the difference was that now the poor could not go raiding to alleviate their condition. By and large, however, it can be said that the People had made their comeback. By their own sturdy efforts, they had moved back to a position as great livestock owners. It was the same goal they had sought a hundred and even two hundred years ago, and, so far, the white man's influence had done no more than show them new ways to attain it. Sales to the trader had taken the place of raiding, but the People were still proud and content to be illiterate nomads. Except for a few trader's materials which, at any time they could have given up, they were living in the Middle Ages and willing to go on so forever. Yet the world around them was no longer that of the seventeenth century. New Mexico had changed. Surrounded by railroads and homesteaders, the Navajos were now hopelessly restricted. Soon they would have to come to grips with the question: could the life of their choice be lived on the land available to them?

15: Learning Paper

SCHOOL

"Your children shall learn paper," General Sherman had told the Navajos at Fort Sumner. *Hao! Hao!* they had assented, as joyously as they did to every other demand which preluded their return to their beloved country. Then their chiefs had placed crosses after the treaty which stated, in words as simple as the white men could manage: the Navajos pledge themselves "to compel their children, male and female, between the ages of six and sixteen years to attend school . . . and the United States agrees that, for every thirty children between said ages *who can be induced or compelled* to attend school, a house shall be provided and a teacher competent to teach the elementary branches of an English education shall be furnished . ."[1]

One wonders what was in the minds of the contracting parties as they made these two equally fantastic promises. Perhaps the framers of the treaty pictured a reservation blossoming with little red schoolhouses and children, trotting with their lunch boxes the two or three miles between school and their cozy farms, just as hundreds of white children were doing at that moment. None of these officials had ever seen a Navajo and

[1] Navajo Treaty, 15 Stats. L., 667–71, article 6.

had no idea of the vast, roadless expanse of the reservation, where one cluster of two or three huts might be ten miles from the next. To find one spot within walking or riding distance of thirty children would be a problem. Even the powerful busses of later days could not collect their quota without subjecting some sleepy youngsters to a trip of several hours.

If this first problem could have been solved, there was the fact that no Navajo family was stationary. Each group moved with its sheep just as Berber and Spanish shepherds had done before them. A likely place for a schoolhouse in autumn might be utterly deserted by winter. The treaty makers, who had never heard of sheep being handled in this way, were quite unaware of the real situation. Who can blame them when, some sixty years later, thousands of dollars were spent for useless schools because of this same ignorance. As for the Navajos, how could they know what was involved in "learning paper?" Perhaps they thought that a few incantations spoken over the children would generate this magic power. It could scarcely have entered their heads that learning meant sitting in a room five or six hours a day for three, four, five, and even ten years. Nor did their activities require any such preparation.

This chapter must take the reader back past the picture of progress presented by Navajo-trader relations, to the earlier picture showing the People's relations with the government. To read the reports of the hard-working and usually desperate agents, one would gather that the Navajos were unteachable louts, utterly unfit for schooling. So had been all the peasantry of Europe only a few centuries earlier. Picture a group of eager benefactors descending on the cheerful English peasant of the twelfth century. Would it have occurred to any of them that activities, divided between small field and small hut, would be helped by reading and writing? The English peasant was left to find his way toward education through long centuries, while the England around him slowly changed from a land of farmers to one of traders and manufacturers. Not until an industrial revolution drove him and his like to the cities did the English peasant and those who would benefit him begin to think about education. The Navajo was living in a world quite as primitive as rural England in the twelfth century. He was content in it and, after the return from Sumner, even blissfully content. His picture of the future meant the building of a new hogan, the enlarging of his fields and flocks, and then a peaceful life in the open, much like the life before Sumner days. His children, of course, would be with him, doing their needful share of work and learning the ways of the People.

No one gave a thought to the clause about "inducing or compelling" children to leave home at this crucial time. Nor did the agent force them, although the treaty had made it his duty to see that the stipulation was "strictly complied with." The government, in 1868, had no facilities for teaching Indians. Indian agents, so far, had been under the War Department, with duties merely of handing out presents and keeping the peace. Now the War Department was winding up its duties with peace treaties all over Indian country. The Interior Department, heretofore concerned only with the management of land, was to take over the Indian Office and carry out the treaties. It possessed no schools, no teachers, and very few funds for such a project. The start must be made from scratch.

The department turned to the churches and their mission boards. To devoted young church members, the teaching of Indians in the unknown west seemed no less adventurous than a trip to the African jungles. The Department of Interior agreed to furnish a schoolhouse and pay the missionary teacher $600 a year. So, Miss Charity Gaston was sent by the Presbyterian

Home Mission Board to Fort Defiance. The young eastern lady, in her white shirtwaist and long woolen skirt, may not have felt so adventurous when, after a six weeks' wait, she finally saw the dark, mud-walled room where she was to teach. True, it was no worse than the other buildings at the fort, and Indians, used to sitting on the earthen floor, even found its rough wooden benches too civilized.

It was a day school, for the few tumbledown buildings at the fort could not possibly provide accommodations for boarding pupils. However, the fort, in 1869, was the center of quite a Navajo village. Some hundreds of families were camping there, in tents and dugouts, hesitating to tackle their ravaged farms and waiting for rations. These, having little work for their children to do, did send a few to school. Old people say they were careful to pick only slaves or, at most, sickly children, so that if any were killed by the white man's magic, there would be a minimum of loss. Even such undesirables rarely risked the strange place for more than a day or two each month. Sometimes a young man would drop in, lazily curious. Or parents would come to stare for an hour or so, then eat the school dinner. On some days Miss Gaston had three students; on some, thirty-three, but rarely the same ones. She soon married the local missionary and finally left with him for the more civilized Pueblos. All we hear about the school is the report in 1872 that it was useless. Attendance was too irregular.[2]

From that time the reports for the treaty period proceed in zigzag pattern, with high hopes one year and utter discouragement the next. Or there may be a discreet silence which tells more than words. In 1873, Agent Arny thought that in four years he could turn out two hundred native teachers who would educate the whole reservation. The next year, Arny was driven

[2] *Reports* of Commissioner of Indian Affairs, 1872, 296.

away, with his three teachers. The modern-style looms which they hoped would speed up Navajo weaving were never used again. Teachers from the Home Mission Board came and went, taking vacations, complained one agent, whenever they chose and without consulting anyone.[3] Once they quarreled and all left together.[4] Pupils went, but very few came. In 1879, the average attendance was eleven.

During this time, American sentiment about Indians had been slowly changing, although it would be long before any effects of the change reached the Navajos. Those who wanted the Indian treated as a useful human being were gaining ground, even with Congress. A much larger appropriation was made for Indian education in 1880 and in the years following. Few indeed did much to analyze the meaning of that magic word education, which to the white man was as miraculous as a Blessing Chant to the Navajo. The Indian was expected to gain enlightenment and inspiration from reading, writing, and arithmetic, taught by any normal school graduate in the same way used in New Hampshire or Pennsylvania. The money spent on the Navajo reservation was used to build a boarding school where young Indians could get more of these subjects for a longer time.

The dormitory was in the usual adobe style of New Mexico, with bunks for eighteen boarding pupils (the agent said sixty), and with iron shutters to keep them in.[5] Major Bourke, who saw it in 1881, commented acridly: "It consisted of one miserable, squalid, dark and musty adobe dungeon, not much more capacious than the cubbyhole of an oyster schooner: it was about 12 x 10 x 7. No light ever penetrated, but one window let dark-

---

[3] *Ibid.*, 1882, 128.
[4] *Ibid.*, 1888, 195.
[5] *Ibid.*, 1892, 577.

ness out from this den and one small door gave exit to some of the mustiness."[6] This was not very different from the windowless Navajo house of that day, yet the expected sixty pupils did not come. It is true that exuberant reports by a new agent or a new teacher from the Presbyterian Board of Home Missions sometimes mention eighty at the beginning of a year. On the situation at the end of the year, reports are discreetly silent, and the next one may grunt briefly: "School not a success."

If they could have heard the children's comments, they would have realized how terrifying was this new experience, substituted for the loving companionship of home. The youngsters coming from their earth-floored huts in nearly waterless country, were dirty. In the desert, where the whole day was spent in purifying sunlight, this had not mattered greatly. Now, as they sat for hours in the schoolroom and slept three in a bunk at night, conditions horrified the teachers. They made new calico clothes; established a Friday night bathing session with two tubs, to which water had to be carried in buckets by hand; and cut the children's hair to get rid of lice.

"I was awful scared when they cut my hair," an old man remembered, "because hair means rain. You can't dance in the ceremonies unless you have long hair." The girls shuddered at the loud voices of the teachers, which echoed through the flimsy partitions, and the frightening brown beard of the agent stamping into the school room in his frock coat. They disliked the white man's food, which somehow had to be placed in their mouths with forks, from tin dishes. They said it made them ill, but more likely the trouble was measles. In fact, there was frequently a report of illness at the school. Once the agent com-

[6] L. B. Bloom (ed.), "Bourke on the Southwest," *New Mexico Historical Review*, Vol. II (1936), 85.

plained of the doctor who had given the sick children too little attention (four died). Another doctor was called by the Navajos Tarantula Number 2, the agent being Number 1.[7]

More sinister than any outward appearance was the terrifying impersonality of the whites. A Navajo was used to living from birth to death in a warm circle of family and clan mates. Never had he needed to go out among strangers and make his way by charm or aggression. Strangers, in fact, were shunned as possible sorcerers. It was in this light that young Navajos had been taught to look on Utes, Comanches, whites, and even other Navajos not of their own clan. True, a boy expected to marry and to leave his own relatives for another group. But this was done only after long discussion by both the families concerned so that, when he settled in his new home, his wife's kin were ready to treat him as one of themselves. Whether he was ugly or attractive, talkative or silent, his place in the group was assured. Even if he sinned against his own group by laziness or bad temper, the punishment would be only an admonition: "Do you wish to shame your family?"

At school, he found no one but strangers. It is hard to imagine the horror of a child who found himself thus helpless in the midst of probable sorcery. His refuge was the usual Navajo expedient in time of doubt: be silent and make no move. I can remember, as late as the 1940's, visiting a school where three orphan girls had been brought in from a remote part of the reservation. The kindly teachers who had washed and clothed them came to me in despair. Since their arrival three days ago, the children had not spoken a word. Older and younger girls had spoken to them in Navajo, and the teachers had caressed them and offered food. Were the children dumb? Were they

[7] *Reports* of Commissioner of Indian Affairs, 1887, 175.

not Navajo? I advised no caresses and no touching, only kindly waiting. In the end, the children's fear lessened and they joined the others.

How much more heart-rending must this situation have been in the first days of the schools. It is granted that it was quite enough to turn people away—unless they had a profound ambition to be educated. At this same time, white boys were leaving the farm to spend icy New England winters at Normal schools, sleeping three in a room, cooking their meals on a wood stove, and, when funds got low, living on oatmeal and occasional boxes of food from home. These boys saw reason in the sacrifices they were making to become white-collar men. Ahead, they saw a steady income as teachers and, more than that, a rise in social status. Their parents had been dirt farmers, but they would be dignified professionals, and their children might go much farther. Even if they made no money, these white boys had a tradition of book learning, ensuring the respect of family and community.

No such tradition encouraged the Navajo. In spite of a few rations and tools, his life was still what it had been in the 1700's—or, if not, he hoped to make it so. What use had he for English, especially written English, when he could trade blankets for horses by a gesture and the trader supplied his needs in the same way? Said one agent, who had taken more time than most to study the Navajos: "... the girls usually marry ... as soon as they become ten or twelve years old, until which time they are kept busy herding sheep. The boys also rush into matrimony early in life, generally becoming heads of families before they are eighteen. Until this time, they must herd horses. This does not leave them much time to acquire an education. It seems impossible to awaken any interest in regard to education among any of them. I have worked hard to build up the school here, have argued, coaxed, begged, bribed and threatened, but it has been of little avail. . . . I believe some arbitrary means to compel attendance should be resorted to."[8]

That arbitrary means was finally resorted to, and with disastrous results. By 1887, Congress had decided that it was futile to spend money for Indian schools which Indians would not attend, so education for Indians was made compulsory. There was little use in enforcing the law on the Navajo reservation with its one school, but others, financed by the new money, were going up outside the reservation. Many of these sturdy, old buildings are still standing, at Albuquerque, at Phoenix, and in Oklahoma. Navajos balked at going to school, but it was hoped they would really enjoy the one at the old army camp of Fort Lewis in the "salubrious climate of Colorado." Here, with a trained principal, a matron, and a staff of teachers, it was hoped that some professional work would be done. A special agent went through the tribes of New Mexico and Arizona to coax the Indians to send their children, but he had no success. Apaches, Utes, and even the civilized Pueblos replied that they were afraid to send their children so far away. The poor principal, who was to get his appropriation in proportion to the number of children cared for, was in despair. He had to let part of his staff go, including the doctor.[9] Most of the Navajos likewise refused. "One who is my son, one who is my daughter . . . I am stingy with them. They will not go to school, I think."[10]

The agents, told to go out and collect children under the compulsory education rule, did their best. The Navajos say that they simply drove about in their buckboards and collected children wherever they found them. The terrified children were

[8] *Ibid.*, 1885, 151–55.
[9] *Ibid.*, 1893–94, 409.
[10] Sapir and Hoijer, *Navaho Texts,* 389.

taken to Fort Defiance and from there shipped to Fort Lewis or its successor, Grand Junction. The agent did not know who the children's parents were, nor did the children know how to notify them. Old men now tell how they were in school three years, and their families thought them dead. Again and again boys escaped and made their way back through the snow-covered mountains to their home in Navajoland. An old Navajo police-man has told how, when word was received that some child had "escaped," he would take his horse and search through the snowy mountains. He once found a boy dead and several times found boys starving and with fingers and feet frozen.

Once in 1892, Agent Shipley, obedient to orders, had taken his buckboard and gone out to collect children. He sent his Navajo policeman in one direction while he himself made head-quarters at the little trading store kept by Charlie Hubbell, "the Bat," in Navajo parlance. There the unfortunate agent met Black Horse, the local headman. "He being asked in vain for children," and, so Charlie Mitchell, the policeman, tells the story, "on that account he and his friends were angry."[11] Mitchell him-self was cheerfully negotiating with some Navajos at a wedding feast when two women rode up on horseback, calling: "There is great trouble, my children. The agent has sprinkled his mouth-blood inside the house."

The policeman and some friends hurried to the store where they found the agent inside, the door barricaded with sacks of flour and sugar. "On the outside, what a terrific noise was heard! What shouting took place! And then a man from over there car-ried an ax, for the purpose of chopping this up, the door . . . that Black Horse was riding along on horseback carrying a gun . . . 'Good! Good! Good!' he said. What a dreadful uproar was heard outside! What terrible sounds of fighting were heard. And in this

[11] *Ibid.,* 375.

way that agent, holding a gun the wrong way round, with the hole out, was trotting about stooping. He was afraid, he was afraid of the Indians."[12]

There was a night of yelling and recriminations, and by morning two ranks of Navajos, the friendly and unfriendly, were facing each other on horseback. It looked like war.

Then the military rode up. Lieutenant Plummer, who knew the Navajos, rode toward them, throwing away his pistol. As the Navajos tell it: "Come on," he called. "That which you have done to each other you shall not do again. All of you get off your horses . . . . Every one of you shake hands with each other."[13] They did. The Navajos liked a firm man, and they appreciated his feeding them crackers and coffee after the night of excitement. They obeyed when he told them, "You must move home. With what you have done, right now you go over the crest of the mountain with it. Else I shall write a paper about what you have done to Fort Wingate. In that case, dust will be flying."[14]

The Navajos knew how dust could fly, and there were no more rebellions. In 1893, when Lieutenant Plummer took charge of them, as military men so often did, a whole party of chiefs went docilely with him to the Chicago World's Fair to see how the white men lived. They came home asking for sawed lumber and glass windows for the building of new houses. But they did not want school. Especially did they not want it after the heroic example set by Manuelito had ended in tragedy. The old chief, still the most revered man among the people, even though he was far gone in drink, had been urged to send his sons east to school. The school was Carlisle, the famous institution that achieved such a spectacular success with Indians in the late

12 *Ibid.,* 375.
13 *Ibid.,* 393.
14 *Ibid.,* 393.

nineteenth century. Anyone interested in Indians knows the story of its founder, Colonel Pratt, "the Red Man's Moses."

In 1875, the young army officer, then a captain, found himself saddled with a number of Indian prisoners from the plains. He decided that their period of incarceration should be spent in learning, and thus was evolved the famous school at Carlisle, which functioned until World War I. It occupied an old army camp in Pennsylvania, a thousand miles or more from the homes of the pupils who were sent in at government expense from twenty-four western tribes. The purpose of the school was "To civilize the Indian," Pratt had said, and "put him in the midst of civilization. To keep him civilized, keep him there."[15] The long-haired Indian boys who were shipped in from the west, clad in miscellaneous government issue, were kept for years under steady and kindly tutelage. In the summers, they went out to work as members of the family in Pennsylvania farming homes, often those of Quakers. The graduates of this school can be picked out to this day on Indian reservations by their fluent English and their easy white man's manners. But are many of them on reservations? Often, they found the life there no more possible than did other "civilized" people. Many are living among whites or in a halfway world which does not involve the full confidence of their fellow Indians. Many died.

Among the last were Manuelito's two eldest sons. The old chief had consented to their going perhaps because he understood that his influence was still the one thing that might lead the Navajos to school. Or, perhaps, he had begun to realize that no hope lay in the direction he had taken. He knew nothing about the ravages of tuberculosis among Indians with no immunity to the disease. Nor had the white enthusiasts realized it in those early days. In 1885, there were six Navajos at Carlisle.[16]

[15] Flora Warren Seymour, *The Story of the Red Man,* 355.
[16] Loring B. Priest, *Uncle Sam's Stepchildren,* 83.

Only one returned, and, said the report of 1885, "He will be no credit to the community." Perhaps the Navajos cannot be blamed for feeling that, in those years, school was not their solution. As one superintendent of schools for the Indian Service summed up the situation: "During the twenty-four years since then (1868), there has been some kind of school but the results have been extremely meagre, in the tribe at large, in the number and quality of returned students and in the condition and scholarship of the present school, which ranks among the very lowest of the Indian schools . . . with an enrollment of 75 in a tribe of more than 16,000."[17]

We might pause here to ask what kind of school would really have suited the Navajos. Perhaps the ideal, as suggested by a later commissioner, would have been some approach to the old, family teaching method. Suppose there had been an English-speaking Navajo or a kindly, pioneer type of white person quartered in each cluster of Navajo dwellings. Suppose he had lived and worked exactly like the people, moving with the flocks as they moved and giving a little instruction in the evenings just as grandfather used to do with his myths. We will grant that no one in the nineteenth century thought of such a thing. But if they had, where would they have got the teachers? Hundreds of them would have been needed, and no white person would have followed this moneyless life for very long. As for the Navajos, there were none who spoke English. The few who did learn, preferred to use the hard-earned knowledge to make money, as interpreters or in business.

One man on the reservation exemplified the kind of education which would really have been effective. Chee Dodge, whose picture and whose life history have appeared in many a national publication, might almost stand as a symbol of the Navajos and

[17] *Reports* of Commissioner of Indian Affairs, 1892, 577.

their way of learning. He was of mixed descent, like many of the Navajos. His father was a Mexican, captured as a boy by the People in their days of raiding and brought up with the tribe. His mother was a Navajo woman. In the wild days before Navajo captivity, one was killed and the other captured by the Hopis. Their son, called Chee, the Red, was taken to Fort Sumner by an aunt when he was five years old.

Perhaps it was then that his education began, for the toddler, with no strong family ties, made friends with the soldiers. He never hated the bluecoats as other Navajos did, and as he grew older he did errands for them, sharing their food and hearing them talk. The vital part of his education, however, came after the return to Fort Defiance. His aunt married a white man, Perry Williams, the supply clerk at the Fort, who took Chee into his home. There he learned to speak English, to dress as a white man to sit at table, to read and write, and to tell time. More than all, he learned to handle money, to spend and save, and to plan for the future. He used to boast that he never went to school more than two months in his life, but he did not need to. Daily tutelage, with a kindly Navajo to make explanations, produced in him the psychology of a white man. It is no wonder that in later years Chee, renamed Henry Dodge, after the beloved Red Shirt, became rich and a leader.[18]

By the time of the Black Horse trouble, Chee was already serving the Navajos as an interpreter, not only of the white man's words but also of his ideas. He helped persuade the angry people that they would gain nothing by fighting the government. For the next fifty years of a successful life, he preached the advantages of school to the People and set an example by sending his own children. They saw what modern methods could do, and they gave Chee the kind of awed respect which whites accorded

[18] Personal information from Henry Chee Dodge and his son, Tom Dodge.

to their Morgan or Rockefeller. But they did not imitate him. People whose childhood training had been that of the hogan and the open mesa could not make the mental switch to the attitude of the calculating businessman.

The life of the People still held no use for school. However, as the nineteenth century drew to a close, new influences had begun eating their way in at a few vulnerable spots. The year 1900 may very roughly be considered as the close of an era of Navajo isolation. During most of this time, there was no railroad connection and, later, little efficient service or constant travel. Indian officials were chosen haphazardly and had little supervision. Washington was almost completely without understanding of Navajo needs, and the plans and money which came from the government were utterly inadequate. After the turn of the century, travel to the West became easy. Homesteaders, students, and tourists began to visit the country. Navajo rugs and silver were popularized. The government, more conscious of Indian problems, chose better officials and gave them longer terms of service. The quarter century after 1900 marks a new era in Navajo history.

Naturally this division is an arbitrary one for there were signs of change years before 1900. In 1891, the Indian schools were under the control of the Civil Service, and Agent Plummer, in 1894, reported the teaching much improved. There were actually 206 students at Fort Defiance that year, and in 1896 there were 113 who "came without urging and remained throughout the year." A day school was finally (1895) started at Tohachi, which the whites translated as Little Water, with a kindly woman in charge. In 1898, school was opened in a western stretch of territory recently bought from the Mormons. Unfortunately the youngsters who came had to be sent home again, since the government had not yet sent clothing that was satisfactory for school attendance. It came by spring, when school closing time had almost arrived, and twenty-two children were collected. That school continued and was the first of the new boarding schools to be started on the reservation. A day school at Keams Canyon on the Hopi reservation had fifteen Navajo pupils.[19]

The oldest generation of die-hard opponents to education were gone. The ancient school at Fort Defiance was repaired and improved. For two years running it was full, and already there were plans for more schools.[20] The first faint stir in the school world was apparent, yet it was faint indeed. As late as 1901, the agent had to report "the feeling and disposition of camp Indians toward school is not very encouraging." Why should it have been? The matter-of-fact Navajos were not very likely to want school until their life had become such that school could be useful. "In fact," complained the agent, "parents seem to think they are conferring a great favor on the whites by bringing their children to school and they ought to be compensated."[21]

[19] *Reports* of Commissioner of Indian Affairs, 1899, 159.
[20] *Ibid.*, 1898, 124; 1899, 160.
[21] *Ibid.*, 1901, 181.

16: New Summit

In beauty (happily) I walk.
With beauty before me I walk.
With beauty behind me I walk.
With beauty below me I walk.
With beauty above me I walk.
With beauty all around me I walk.
It is finished (again) in beauty.
It is finished in beauty.[1]

THIS POETIC TRANSLATION from *The Night Chant* by Dr. Washington Matthews drew the attention of students in the early 1900's to the existence of an Indian tribe which was not vanishing or despairing but apparently in the prime of primitive vigor. The railroads were now running efficiently. Homesteaders and even tourists were coming to the Southwest in quantity. Scientists had been studying the Indians of the Southwest for at least a decade. And all were loud in the praise of the Navajos who seemed to be still a happy and integrated group, their arts and ceremonies not a nostalgic memory but a functioning reality.

Anyone privileged to witness the great public spectacle on the last night of the Night Chant could see Navajo costume, craft, and ceremony at their peak. In some clearing in the hills,

[1] Washington Matthews, *The Night Chant*, 145.

against a background of shadowy cliffs and cold November stars, stood the ceremonial hogan, round and earth-floored as in ancient days but now constructed with iron tools. The open space before it was lighted by a row of blazing fires by which one could see the figures of the men, hair in buns and turquoise earrings dangling, although here and there appeared a short-haired schoolboy in a cowboy hat. Around the open space, a huge oval, were Conestoga wagons, the same type in which the whites had traveled the overland trail half a century ago. They suited the rough trails of the Navajo reservation, and families which could not get them from the government had bought them for themselves. The little cooking fire before each wagon revealed the women's bronze faces and glistening, black hair, set off by silver jewelry and velvet blouses in green, orange, and purple. On the fire was the metal coffee pot, and here, in the pauses of the ceremony, the women entertained relatives with roasted goat ribs and "fry bread," a kind of hollow, wheaten doughnut learned from the Mexicans. If the son-in-law had wandered off with the men, the matriarch of the family might be doing the cooking. Otherwise she was in the wagon, concealed behind a blanket which was hung up for her special benefit. The mother-in-law taboo was still in full force.

A weird cry in the distance! The huge fires down the center of the oval had been re-stoked, and by their light the *yei,* the beneficent spirits, entered stamping, in single file. Red firelight and deep shadows pointed up buckskin masks, short kilts, and rattles resembling those of the Pueblo spirit dancers. Yet this ceremony with gaunt, striding figures and a wild chant which ranged from base to falsetto was unlike the schooled performance of the villagers. The blanketed patient, sitting with the medicine man outside the hogan, was a sign that the ceremony, no matter what its overtones, was still given in hunter fashion for the health

213

and power of one individual. Perhaps he was rich. But it is more likely that a whole family, with many distant clan members, had pooled their resources for the benefit of one who was ill or unfortunate. The process might be called a faith cure, for it consisted in bringing to memory, by songs and sand paintings, the adventures of some early hero who had had the same trouble. The hero's story was a compound of myths from the north and sacred beings from the south arranged in a saga of almost Wagnerian grandeur. It ended with the cure of the hero by supernatural beings and the gift of songs and sand paintings which would cure others. The patient, whether ill or merely depressed, had merely to follow the story through a nine-day series of symbolic acts and, in the end, to repeat with the hero some such comforting formula as

> *Happily my head becomes cool*
> *Happily my limbs regain their power*
> *Impervious to pain I walk*[2]

Many have testified that they *were* healed, and modern doctors, aware of psychosomatic influences, sometimes agree with them. Not only the patient benefited from the ceremony. The onlookers, perhaps numbering in the hundreds, shared in the blessing. Moreover, they were fed for as long as they stayed—a contribution of the "patient" to community welfare.

In view of the social and economic functions of the "sing," it is hard to accept Agent Shipley's statement in 1891 that "heathenish ceremonies are diminishing."[3] Fortunately we need not believe him, for the Navajos were not likely to report the incidence of ceremonies at the agency. It is easier to believe the figures which show an increase in the number of Navajos and

[2] *Ibid.*, 81.

[3] *Reports* of Commissioner of Indian Affairs, 1891, 310.

their flocks. In spite of some bad years, the People, toward the end of the nineteenth century, had reached a new summit of prosperity. In 1899, thirty years after they had come to the reservation, their population was quoted at 20,000, more than twice the original number. Their sheep were numbered at 1,000,000, goats at 250,000, and horses at 100,500. They had traded 1,000,000 pounds of wool and 210 pounds of skins and sold $50,000 worth of blankets.[4]

This period of the nineties, when the Navajos were first examined by American scholars, was a new summit in their history. As a tribe, they owned at least as much wealth as they had before Sumner days and far more than they had had when they entered the Southwest. All the arts and ceremonies for which they are now famous had been achieved, largely by learning from association with other people. They learned agriculture from the Pueblos, sheepherding from the Spaniards, weaving from the Pueblos and traders, silverwork from the Mexicans, and new costumes from the Spaniards and Americans. Each of these, though suggested by others, had been given new character as the People made it their own. Even the art of sand painting was perhaps an imaginative enlargement of a Pueblo custom.[5] Throughout this period of assimilation, the Navajos had kept the customs which gave tribal coherence, such as the mother-in-law taboo, the maiden's rite, and the intense family and clan loyalty.

This is a general picture of the Navajos at their new summit. It does not apply to every individual of the tribe or even to every segment. Long before Sumner days, the People had been divided not only into rich and poor, as we have frequently

---

[4] *Ibid.,* 1899, 156, 562, 582.
[5] Underhill, *Ceremonial Patterns in the Greater Southwest,* 41–46. Also see Stevenson, *Ceremonial of Hasjelti Dailjis,* 236.

noticed, but also into local groups, with different inheritance, traditions, and, to some extent, livelihood. Enforced contact during the captivity perhaps had induced some amalgamation, but on returning to the reservation they had scattered to their old haunts. When we read statements about "the Navajos" of this period, by agents or even scientists, we should consider what group was under observation. Was it the civilized people around Fort Defiance, who lived in frame houses with windows and doors and who sent their children to school? Was it the people in the permanent agricultural settlements, like San Juan or Little Water, who also gladdened the hearts of agents by asking for beds and cookstoves? Was it the isolated dwellers in Canyon de Chelly with their solid, hexagonal dwellings, their peach trees, and their apparent indifference to the agency? Or was it the half savage people of the barren, western lands, who lived in the ancient, conical hut and whose children fled into hiding at the sight of a stranger, as they had done in Kit Carson's day? There were other variations on the Navajo life of farming and sheepherding, including people who had taken up claims off the reservation and who lived among Mormons or Mexicans. These different aspects of Navajo life will become more important as we follow the Navajos through the changes which now began to gather momentum.

Washington also had changed. The early days of disorganization and inefficiency were passing. The Board of Indian Commissioners, the Indian Rights Association, and the missionaries were making themselves heard, so that scandals in contracts and agents' behavior were being eliminated. Agents now were selected carefully and stayed longer. In 1902, Civil Service was adopted for a few employees and slowly spread to encompass more and more government workers. In 1904, Commissioner Jones was able to state that political and personal favoritism had largely disappeared;[6] and in 1906, Leupp, the next commissioner, voiced the understanding of the Indian which was now permeating government policy: "The truth is that the Indian has as distinct an individuality as any type of man who ever lived and he will never be judged aright till we learn to measure him by his own standards, as we whites would wish to be measured if some more powerful race were to usurp dominion over us."[7]

If every agent and every succeeding commissioner had adopted this attitude and maintained it, the outlook for the Navajos would have been heartening. However, the gradual cleansing from financial dishonesty which went on in the Indian Bureau laid bare a deeper fault which few had had leisure to consider. This was the trouble once so clearly seen by Cremony, the constant change of policy with each administration. There was no stable, high-ranking officer to keep plans consistent and advancing toward a known goal. The Commissioner was a political appointee, as he still is, and many of his important executives came in and went out with him. Each new incumbent felt it necessary to make at least some small changes, like the rule of Congress and Commissioner Jones that all Indians had to cut their hair before they could receive wagons. Or the change of attitude might go very deep, as when the same Commissioner Jones assumed that: "the entire educational system ... is therefore predicated upon the final abolishment of the anomalous reservation system,"[8] while Commissioner Leupp, years later, dilated on the value of Indian culture and the mistake of trying to make Indians over completely. Later critics were to comment feelingly on this zigzagging policy.[9] The system

[6] *Reports* of Commissioners of Indian Affairs, 1904, 23.

[7] *Ibid.,* 1905, 1.

[8] *Ibid.,* 1899, 7.

[9] Phelps-Stokes Fund, *The Navajo Indian Problem,* 118.

seemed normal to the whites who had devised it, but they could collect pressure groups and vote a change. The Indians were a helpless football for each well-meaning newcomer, and to this may be attributed some of their withdrawal and secrecy.

In the nineties, few people had recognized the zigzagging difficulty. Emphases were on more appropriations, more improvements, and better employees. In our account of these developments on the Navajo reservation, we must go back a few years before the turn of the century. Charles Vandever may be taken as the starting point for the new type of agents who were better prepared for their positions, even though there was still no Civil Service. After Vandever came the unfortunate Shipley (1890–93) who tried to carry out the orders of Congress about compulsory schooling with decided lack of success. Lieutenant Plummer (1893–94) came from Fort Wingate to fill the gap after Shipley resigned and was popular with the Indians, as were most military men. He took a group of Navajos to the World's Fair where they saw the white people "like ants" and revised their opinion that the whites might some day be driven out of the country. Constant Williams, another military man (1894–98), turned in the usual competent report, and Hayzlett, the civilian who succeeded him, could assure Washington of excellent conditions. These were the last agents of an undivided Navajo reservation. After them, one man was not expected to handle all the People.

Most of the agents mentioned bad weather and loss of crops, for the weather cycle had turned inclement again. In 1895, flour had to be issued in response to the plea that the Navajos were starving. The government decided to build more irrigation ditches, in the hope that the barren land could somehow be made to produce sufficient food. A large ditch was finally dug from the San Juan River, the most important source of water in the area, and there a little farming community was started, with a government farmer in charge. The arrangement worked so well that another farmer was stationed at the west of the reservation in 1901.

It was this sort of personal contact to which the Navajos responded. When a matron was stationed at San Juan, they flocked to her house, sometimes thirty-nine in one day.[10] Presently she was joined by a Methodist missionary. All reports were loud in praise of these two women who had no equipment but their own primitive kitchen and occasionally a barrel of clothes or some seeds from the East. Nevertheless, they presented civilization to the Navajos much more effectively than the schools of that day.

The horror of school was slowly fading. But the changing attitude was not immediately felt, since in 1903, out of a population of 23,000, there were 300 children in school. These were divided among three schools, all boarding schools, of course, since there was never a center to which children from the scattered huts could walk every day. The violent discussions of future years about day and boarding schools had not yet begun. Families who had a chance to know the white officials as friends were becoming less apprehensive. This was evidently the case with Emma De Vore, the kindly woman superintendent at Little Water, for in 1905 she wrote: "The past year was the first in the history of the school that it was not necessary for me to go to the camps to collect pupils."[11]

More friendliness between whites and Indians was having its effect, and here a large part was being played by the Christian

[10] *Reports* of Commissioner of Indian Affairs, 1892, 210.
[11] *Ibid.*, 1905, 169.

missionaries. St. Michaels Catholic Mission, established in 1898 by the Franciscan Fathers,[12] was to grow, with its affiliated boys' school, into a famous institution, both for teaching and research.[13] In 1897, the Episcopalian Mission of the Good Shepherd founded a small hospital at Fort Defiance. There was a Methodist missionary at San Juan, there were Baptists at Two Gray Hills, and other missionaries had been invited by trader Hubbell to Ganado. The unhurried, parental interest which the Navajos received from these workers was invaluable to a people who could not understand the impersonal government attitude.

The government, too, was trying to work more closely with the Indians. In 1903, a Court of Indian Offenses was set up, like those on other reservations. To this court the Indian police brought domestic relations cases and reservation squabbles. There were three native judges, appointed and paid by the government. Agent Shipley said their decisions were so sensible that he never had to reverse them. As one who, later, saw their informal but eminently wise procedure, I endorse his judgment, and so did later investigators.[14]

By 1903, the Navajo agency had become a great sprawling territory of over nine million acres, too large for one agent to handle. Gradually it was divided into five reservations, with an agent in each one.[15] The men who had held long terms of office in the different Navajo agencies approached to some extent the

[12] Mission schools for the Navajos were: St. Joseph's Roman Catholic school, opened 1903 in connection with St. Michael's Mission by the Sisters of the Blessed Sacrament boarding school for boys and girls: Rehoboth, Dutch Reform, near Fort Wingate, boarding school for boys and girls; Ganado, Presbyterian, began with informal day classes, 1901, day school, 1910, and boarding school for both sexes, 1912.

[13] See the translations by Haile in the bibliography.

[14] Phelps-Stokes Fund, *The Navajo Indian Problem*, 73.

[15] The five Navajo agencies were: Southern Navajo, the original agency, with headquarters at Fort Defiance; San Juan, later Shiprock, established, 1903;

People's idea of leader and guide, although most of them acted on the assumption that the white man's way was completely right. Still, they worked hard to get tools and waterworks for their charges. Ditches and windmills were put in at points where the barren land looked worth exploiting. (The Hogback ditch was installed in 1906, and when it was damaged by rains, the Indians worked without pay to repair it.)[16] The Navajos were given paid work on the new buildings, the one telephone line, and the few roads for which there was money. When Superintendent Hunter at Fort Defiance secured aid for Navajos in a blizzard, they made him a moving speech, ending "We thank the mother who bore him."[17]

It was Hunter who decided that the Navajos should, at last, have more self-government. He divided the barren area of Leupp, where he was then agent, into a number of "chapters" and asked the Navajos from each one to send representatives to a council. Representative government, majority vote, and elected officers were a new thing to the People. Their ancient councils, as far as they had any, had included all the adult men of an area who met night after night, speaking in low voices and with long pauses until they reached a unanimous decision. No government business, however, could wait for such a slow procedure. The chapter meeting was instructed to elect president, vice-president, and secretary, and to vote as the white men did. Old Navajos say that, of course, the decisions of the chapter were made outside the meeting and by the old method. Nevertheless,

Western Navajo, with agency at Tuba City, established in 1901; Leupp, an extension bought in 1901, jurisdiction established in 1908; Eastern Navajo, with agency at Pueblo Bonito, later Crownpoint, New Mexico, established in 1907. The Hopi agency, which had been administered with the Navajo since 1884, was separated in 1902.

[16] See the report of Agent Hunter, in archives at Window Rock.
[17] Records at Fort Defiance.

this beginning of self-government was a heartening thing, and the idea spread to all the reservations. One chapter near Gallup built its own chapter house during a cold winter, over six hundred men working without pay to thaw the adobe with bonfires and melt snow for water.

Agent Perry tried to deal with the problem of pasturage for the sheep. It was obvious that pasturing could not go on forever on the same limited area. The sheep were growing thinner, and the wool yields were smaller. For years agents had been urging the Navajos to dispose of some of their useless display horses, but here the People were adamant. "If there were no horses, there would be no Navajos." The next best thing would be to improve the sheep. Perry imported Rambouillet bucks, hoping that animals could be bred fewer but larger. Unfortunately it turned out that the lambs born were too large for the little *churro* ewes, and even when the breeding was successful the wool was too curly and greasy to be used in Navajo weaving. The breed was changed again and again, until, by 1933, scarcely an example of the old *churro* could be found.[18] More useful was sheep dipping for scabies which was introduced in 1907.[19] Anyone who has seen the gay crowds around a sheep-dip today and heard the women laugh as they push the struggling animals along the disinfecting trench must realize that here was one unalloyed benefit.

The tempo of government activity was accelerating. There was still no over-all plan for the Navajos, except that they must be educated for self-supporting citizenship. For this, it was assumed that government schools were the means. It would have

[18] James O. Grandstaff, "Evaluating Fleece Characteristics of Navajo Sheep from a Breeding Standpoint," *Rayon Textile Monthly,* (October–November, 1941).

[19] Ruth Underhill, *Here Come the Navaho,* 276–77.

been better if, at this point, there had been some simple arrangement such as served the white man in his pioneer days. The informal farmer-teacher, only a few grades ahead of the pupils
and willing to live with them in their homes, would have been
enough for the Navajos. But the days when such schooling
seemed sufficient to the whites were long past. For themselves,
they now wanted imposing school buildings and teachers trained
in "normal school." So trained teachers came out to the wilds,
prepared to induct the Navajos into the same middle-class life
which was their own ideal.

Between 1900 and 1925, nine boarding schools and two day
schools were set up on the reservation.[20] As early as 1893, agents
had been agitating for day schools, so that children need not be
taken from their parents. Still, the miles of desert that some
children would have to cross and the fact that families moved
two or three times a year were obstacles facing the establishment
of day schools.

So children willing to be educated were taken from their
movable camps to be gone for years. There was no more kidnapping, but when the school emissary arrived with his logical
appeals, children were likely to hide in the brush or disappear
from home and parents for weeks. Navajo parents, unused to
forcing or disciplining their young, turned unrevealing faces to
the officials and awaited the children's return.

The bleak, stone school buildings look grim enough today,

---

[20] Boarding schools on the Navajo reservation: Keams Canyon School for
Hopis, enrolled some Navajos, 1925; Little Water or Tohachi, 1900; Tuba City,
1901; Shiprock, 1907; Leupp, 1909; Chinle, 1910; Crownpoint, 1912; Toadlena,
1913; Wingate, 1925. Off-reservation schools which received Navajos were:
Albuquerque, New Mexico, 1881; Grand Junction, Colorado, 1886, closed 1911;
Santa Fé, New Mexico, 1891; Phoenix, Arizona, 1891; Fort Lewis, Colorado,
1892; Fort Apache, Arizona, 1893; Sherman Institute, California, 1902. Day
schools: San Juan, which was later Shiprock boarding school, and Moenkopi,
on the Hopi reservation.

but agents who had been appealing for school money since 1868 were proud of the renovated army camps or the soiled, brick buildings with their long, whitewashed corridors, their huge dormitories with barred windows, their schoolrooms, sewing rooms, and sometimes blacksmith and carpenter shops. There were not too many Navajo children who could "be induced or compelled to attend." Often those who did attend came from poor families who were relieved to get this means of free board and lodging. (A later commissioner complained that the boarding schools were no more than educational almshouses.)[21] Most children shunned the regimented life which was as different as possible from the serene, outdoor existence, where days, weeks, and even years were not divided into work times and play times. This was a period of stern discipline, even in white schools, and the reservation teachers, aghast at all the little savages had to learn in a short time, resorted to particularly stern measures. They kept their charges busy from dawn to bedtime, marching to meals, marching to class, and marching to "detail" work in kitchen, field, and shop.[22]

Here was another disadvantage in the mechanical gulf between whites and Navajos. Agents had long been urging that the Indians be taught some skills which would enable them to improve their homes and perhaps earn wages. If one youth at a time could have been apprenticed in some kindly blacksmith shop, or one girl in a home, this might have worked. But there were no shops or homes nearby, and the huge understaffed schools needed work from the children if they were to operate. So "industrial detail" often resulted in a girl washing tin dishes for two hundred children three times a day or a boy shoveling

21 Francis E. Leupp, *The Indian and his Problem*, 137.
22 Boarding school life for the whole Southwest has been feelingly described by E. E. Dale in *The Indians of the Southwest*, chapter 12.

manure or operating the mechanical bread mixer. One can imagine how much learning and incentive would be instilled in a raw desert youth after a year at boarding school.

"I hate to send this boy to school," one mother said. "I know I say goodby. He would come back a stranger."[23] Strangers indeed were the unfortunate school graduates, who returned to the earth-floored dwellings with clean clothes, shoes and stockings, a habit of bathing, and a reliance on mechanical aids. Most of what they had learned was impossible to put into practice, even if the family had been receptive. Almost any prospectus of those days, whether from government or missions, voiced the faith that the educated young Indians would return to the reservations as a generation of dedicated teachers, devoted to the improvement of their homes and families. But there is the fact that few people of any race choose a course of unselfish dedication. Also the young Navajos had to contend with the Indian attitude of reverence for age. Their families, completely settled in the life of medieval shepherds were not amenable to changes suggested by "educated" youngsters. A purification ceremony to take away the dangerous magic of strangers was given for the returned youth, and the family hoped that finding a mate for this misfit would not prove too impossible.

As for taking a job off the reservation—that spelled sheer misery, as it often does even today. The Navajo might know some English, but he had not learned the genial aggressiveness with which a white man pushes himself ahead in the world. Nor did he dream that, in order to make friends, he must "sell" himself. Used to the protecting presence of clan, family, and Navajo schoolmates, he simply waited for the group to carry him along. The group did not. Sometimes they laughed at him, an act which, to an Indian, means cruel criticism. Sometimes

[23] Lewis Meriam (ed.), *The Problem of Indian Administration*, 574.

they ignored him. Most often he was despised as a stupid Indian and was refused the good jobs or the desirable dwelling places. The result was that he went "back to the blanket," or he went to drink. In spite of all this, many Navajos tell today about the friendship and understanding they found at government schools and, even more, with the missionaries.

The mission hospitals filled an even greater need than the schools.[24] The Episcopalian hospital at Fort Defiance was opened before the government had any hospitals at all. The Presbyterian hospital at Ganado grew into an imposing institution, training Indian nurses from all over the country. Slowly the government continued building until, by 1933, it had eleven hospitals, on and off the reservation.[25]

The hospitals were rarely full, and disgruntled doctors complained that Navajos used them only as places to die. Sick Navajos were appalled by the impersonal loneliness of hospital life, by the strange food, and the busy doctors and nurses who left them alone except when treatment was necessary. They were used to the tender solicitude of a whole family, with everything they wanted to eat, and, as comfort and uplift, the long and beautiful ceremony by which the patient is brought hourly into direct communion with the spirits. It is no wonder that some patients who seemed grievously ill reported that when they left

[24] The Episcopalian hospital of the Good Shepherd, at Fort Defiance, was opened in 1897. When the government built a hospital at the fort in 1912, this institution switched to specialization in eye diseases. Since the government now has an enormous institution at the same place, the Good Shepherd acts as an orphan home and community center. The Presbyterian hospital at Ganado was founded in 1912. By 1940, it had 100 beds, by 1944, 150 beds.

[25] Government hospitals in 1933 were: Wingate (established by the army in 1889 and continued as part of the Indian school in 1926); Leupp, 1908; Shiprock, 1908; Tuba City, 1911; Fort Defiance, 1912; Crownpoint, 1914; Toadlena, 1926; Kayenta, 1927; Tohachi, 1927; Chinle, 1932; Winslow tuberculosis sanitarium, 1933. Several of these were closed during World War II for lack of staff and repairs.

the hospital and had a "sing" they recovered. Modern doctors agree that some of the intense faith generated by a Navajo chant might be good for any patient. Patients did, of course, die in the hospital, and when this happened even once, without the building or any of its equipment being burned, the Navajos were horrified. If the white people could endure this accumulation of evil, let them do so. The Navajos had long used the expedient of moving a dying person out of the house, so that it need not be burned. Now, thankfully, they let him go to the hospital. They let the government make him a coffin and the missionaries bury him with any service they liked, so that his family need not suffer the awful contamination with a corpse. It was not heartless. For the Navajo, a corpse lost its identity as a body belonging to a person they had loved and became a source of supernatural contagion.

During the first World War, Navajos were not drafted, but some of them fought alongside the whites and were officially thanked by President Coolidge. In 1924, in recognition of this service by them and by other Indians, the Supreme Court pronounced all Indians citizens, with the right to vote in federal elections. Arizona and New Mexico had literacy and wardship restrictions which would have debarred the Navajos, but as most of them knew nothing about elections and had never heard of the ruling, they were not troubled. In fact, they presented to travelers who were now visiting the West by train the ideal picture of a carefree, primitive people. It is true that the Navajos were using wheat flour for their squaw bread, and in every home coffee, sugar, and canned goods were eaten from white man's dishes and stacked on wooden boxes in lieu of shelves. And the monthly visit to the trader had become a necessity, supplying them with almost all of their food except mutton and goat and all their clothing except moccasins. But these were small things which did not alter the spiritual pattern of their lives. Psychologically, they lived in the Middle Ages.

How could they understand the impending change that was heralded by the addition of a few thousand dollars, the price of an oil lease, to the tribal treasury? Formerly, the Navajos had objected to any prowling by strangers among their beloved hills, where at least two prospectors had met their deaths. Now the tribe permitted test wells and the establishment of an oil company near Shiprock. Washington ruled that underground wealth was the property of the tribe and that the tribe should make the leases and receive the money. Therefore the tribe must be organized. Under the direction of former Governor Hagerman, of New Mexico, appointed as commissioner for the purpose, the men of each superintendency met to choose two delegates and two alternates for a council. The council met at Fort Defiance in 1923 and elected a chairman and vice-chairman, to conduct the tribe's business for four years.[26]

Who should be chairman but Henry Chee Dodge, the half-Navajo who had grown up in a white man's home, spoke English, and was acquainted with money! His life on the reservation had been a model of what any Navajo might do, were that Navajo an individualist, thrifty with money, and willing to adopt new methods good for business. In his farm clothes and turquoise necklace, Chee was already a familiar figure at ceremonies, urging school and co-operation with the government. He could have lived with the whites had he so chosen, but he cast his lot with the Navajos. Other mixed-bloods have done likewise and become leaders of many tribes. As modern problems began to confront the Navajos, they could be thankful for this one tribesman who understood the value of money, as distinguished from horses, and who made sure that the Indians got

[26] Archives at Window Rock.

their share. During his chairmanship, over one million dollars in royalties and bonuses was placed to the Navajos' credit in the United States Treasury.

The Navajos knew nothing, so far, about the fluctuation of prices and were unaware of the cycle of droughts which was now blowing dust storms over Oklahoma and Kansas and would soon be helping the sheep to destroy Navajo grazing land. The depression which was to cause an upheaval throughout America was still in the future. If one failed to count the number of undernourished families in the barren areas and saw only the prosperous groups, with their gorgeous costumes and their lavish ceremonies, one could picture the Navajos as living in a primitive golden age. Few people, however, have been able to remain long at such a pinnacle, and, with the Navajos, change was already at work. Even without the depression and dust storms, their own interests and desires would have led them away from the old system of simple sheepherding and farming. Trips outside the reservation were acquainting them with cars, with phonographs, and with kerosene stoves. Although they did not want the white man's way of life, they did want this wealth of his, not realizing that the two are an organic whole. In time they had to face this fact.

17: Time Catches Up with the Navajos

THE DOWN TREND

"SEND HELP! The Navajos are starving!" It seems almost unbelievable that this cry could have gone up sixty years after the Navajos came to the reservation and after they had once attained prosperity. Two inexorable factors were against them. One factor was the cycle of bad weather which every so often swept over the Southwest, confounding the conservationists and scientific farmers. The other factor was the population increase of the People themselves. They were too populous for the land. So it was in the 1920's.

Of course, all the Navajos were not starving. They, like other peoples of the earth, had their rich and poor. Poor Navajos were those whose lands were waterless, or those who were now off the reservation, in the lands of the railroad or homesteaders. In olden days, the poor Navajos would have gone forth to make their fortunes by raiding. Now they camped with clan members whose land was already too small for their own sheep. Legally they might have homesteaded like the whites, but, as has been mentioned, the technique of this procedure was beyond the ken of most Navajos. It was for them that the agents asked rations over and over again, even as late as 1947.

The rich Navajos were those who, in early raiding days, had established a right to some fertile bottom land which, according to the People's custom, no one disputed. Reports tell of a group of seven families who laid claim to six hundred acres of good land.[1] When the government put in an irrigation ditch, they had no idea they should share its benefits. "There are hundreds of instances" complained the supervisor of ditch construction, "where individual Indians claim as much as 500 acres of land ... and Navajo of a foreign clan cannot be induced to take up or farm the land so claimed."[2] Families like this, who had had the luck or foresight or pre-empt good lands, could rank as *ricos,* as in Spanish days. Thus, even in bad years, when poor Navajos were near destitution, there were heads of families who counted their sheep by the thousands and their horses by hundreds.[3] Poor young relatives gathered around them, much in the manner of an ancient Scottish clan around its chieftain. They tilled the land of their headman and tended his sheep on shares. Their reward was assistance at times of special expense, like a "sing" or a marriage.

Such a *rico* was the late Chee Dodge, the tribal leader during this period of Navajo history.[4] After the People's custom, his home was a cluster of three houses which were open to all his relatives. As one sat at his bountiful table, eating the standard Navajo banquet of roasted goat ribs, canned peaches, and coffee, young women in brilliant skirts served the meal and young men in Levis tramped in and out receiving instructions. The feudal atmosphere was almost like that of pre-Sumner days. Yet the houses were modern frame structures, not meant for destruction after his death. The young men were driving cars. More im-

[1] *Reports* of Commissioner of Indian Affairs, 1905, 167.

[2] *Ibid.,* 267.

[3] *Ibid.,* 1903, 126.

[4] Henry Chee Dodge died in 1948.

portant yet, Chee did not invest in useless horses, but bought cattle and hired pasture for them outside the reservation. Other Navajos might have followed in his footsteps, but they did not have his long experience with the white man's ways. They watched with awe as he bought farm equipment and sent a son to college, but they still preferred the earth-floored hut and the children at home, tending sheep or weaving rugs.

Chee himself told them that this life could not continue, and so did the government officials. The life depended on sheep, the sheep needed grass, and the grass was disappearing. It was time for a complete change, but the Navajos who had grasped so eagerly at sheep, at horses, and at weaving some three hundred years ago now seemed immovable. Perhaps it was because the suggestion was not their own. They admitted that the sheep were growing thinner and the wool clips were becoming smaller. In fact, the down trend had started in the 1890's, and a good year now and then could not disguise the steady drop. Although the tribe now had about one million dollars in the United States Treasury faithfully held at 4 per cent interest, this money could not make grass grow on bare rock or support three or four sheep where there was only nourishment for one.

Grass was disappearing from the reservation at an alarming rate. The sharp hooves which denuded the soil around a Navajo hut had been treading that same earth for over one hundred years. Herding methods were practically the same as those adopted from the Spaniards. Let the white man suggest that the pasture was being overgrazed beyond repair! Let them preach that the rams should be kept apart, so that lambs would be born only at a convenient time! The Navajos smiled at this tiresome talk. Especially they smiled when the white men argued that the children who tended the flocks ought to be in school, and that, anyhow a child of seven could hardly practice scientific animal husbandry. The People were not interested in such theories. The children were happy, which was more than could be said for most pupils in school. The flocks were happy, although it was true that they were getting thinner. As for the grass, the reason it did not grow was that ceremonies had not been practiced properly.

The white men, whose taxes paid for the ever-recurring rations, were not so calm. They now realized that they should have given the Navajos more land to begin with. But even so, it was not possible for one part of the country to operate at a medieval level while the rest cared for its land and its animals by new, scientific methods. The Southwest, no longer an unknown Great American Desert, was filling with towns and ranches. Americans were becoming aware that overgrazing and destruction of the soil in one part of the country meant floods and obstacles to irrigation in other parts. It was time to think of western problems in terms of the nation, not of the individual pioneer, or even the state. One of the most important of those problems concerned the Indian reservations, of which there were now over one hundred west of the Mississippi.

Particularly pressing was the case of the Navajos. While nearly every hogan still had its sheep and nearly every man his horse, and while splendid ceremonies still held the old way of life together, the general level of prosperity had dropped alarmingly. The largest annual income on the reservation (that of government employees near Fort Defiance) was $2,000, and the smallest, in the barren west, was $31.[5] Navajos who left the reservation to earn money were likely to return after a few months, too lonely to remain away. But they had spent their money. On the reservation, schools were still not filled to capacity. Many hospital beds stood empty though doctors reported that deaths

[5] Lewis Meriam (ed.), *The Problem of Indian Administration,* 449.

233

from tuberculosis took an enormous toll on the population.

The shocking facts were brought out by a survey, made at government request, by a group of research experts. The Meriam report, published in 1927, asked for better-trained and more sympathetic personnel, for doctors, hospitals, farm experts, care of the land, more opportunities for Indians, and more education, in day schools where possible.[6] Commissioner Rhoads and his assistant, Mr. Scattergood (1928–32), immediately began a slow and steady movement toward helping the Navajos into modern life. Events would not wait for them.

A new administration and a depression made radical changes in American life and in the Bureau of Indian Affairs, which became the Indian Service. The panic of 1929, the closure of businesses, and the spectacle of millions unemployed gave birth to a new phase in American thinking. Men and resources were both being wasted. Acres of soil were blown off the over-plowed fields of Kansas and Oklahoma, and the men who might have helped to build up the country remained in enforced idle-ness. The New Deal, with its program for national welfare, came in, and with it came a new Indian Commissioner and, for the Navajos, a change that amounted to revolution.

John Collier, who had been a social reformer all his life, was deeply sympathetic to the Red Man and full of imagination and enthusiasm.[7] Although Collier had before him a program of improvement for the Navajos, he had no way of knowing that President Roosevelt, who had appointed him, would be in office for almost four terms and that he could therefore make a twelve-year approach to the Navajo problem. He felt sure only that, for one presidential term, he had money and backing. And he

---

[6] Meriam (ed.), *The Problem of Indian Administration.*

[7] John Collier was Commissioner of Indian Affairs from 1934–45. See pamphlet, *The New Deal for the Indian,* published by the Indian Bureau, 1935.

believed that any plans he had for the Navajos must be pushed through before, perhaps, some reactionary was put in his place. The Navajos, therefore, were subjected to an accelerated program of betterment. Plans about the land, about education, and about self-government, which should have been slowly unfolding for forty years, had to blossom in four. The People were confused, then resentful, and, in the end, bitter, for this was not their method of change.

Yet from the white man's point of view, it looked as though good fortune was coming to the Navajos. They were to be given work exactly like the unemployed whites and to receive the same standard wage. To a white man, this meant mere subsistence; but to the Navajos, it meant wealth. The work provided had to be, if possible, something of a permanent benefit to the locality. In Navajo country, there was no question what this should be— soil conservation and waterworks. Young men were collected by the scores and set to work on ditches, wells, reservoirs, and dams. For the first time, Indians from remote parts of the reservation saw tractors and drag lines and even learned to use them.

This learning opportunity for Navajos can hardly be overestimated. The men worked regular hours, using tools and methods often quite new to them. Perhaps from this time, we can date the Navajo's interest in cars and his skill with them. In the evening, there were classes for workers who might want to learn a trade or make a start at English. It was a healthy start toward a new life, but it could not fail to mean injury to the old.

The wages were forty dollars a month, a small fortune to most Navajos, who handled no more than sixty or eighty dollars cash in a year. In the past, money in the hands of the people had undermined feudal systems, and so it did this time. Young men had once been glad to work for a kinsman for the reward of food, clothing, and help when needed. Now that close tie was broken as they accepted cash from the impersonal government. The close solidarity of the family suffered also. When a man had food and flocks, his kinfolk knew it and expected hospitality. When he had money, he could conceal the fact and fail in his duty. These disruptive forces began to work on the Navajos. The Civilian Conservation Corps and Emergency Conservation Work poured two million dollars a year into the reservation. Experts were called in to improve the health of the People and their animals, the conditions of their land and crops, and to advertise their craftwork, keep up its standard, and get better prices for it.

To bring them all together, a "Navajo capital" was planned at Window Rock, near Fort Defiance, where the gorgeous red rocks of Arizona would look down on buildings made of their own red stone. One of the first to be built was a great, octagonal council house where the tribal delegates could meet, under mural paintings by one of their own artists.

White people took fire at the idea. I have seen them breathlessly sitting among an audience of Navajos while an eloquent government speaker drew for them his picture of the future. It was winter, and the Navajos sat huddled in sheepskin coats and bright Pendleton blankets, their shaggy hair in buns, and here and there a long moustache drooping over the green and yellow blanket. When the speech was over and a Navajo rose to reply, all he said was: "Yes, but what about our sheep?"

They had consented to dip their sheep to get rid of ticks and disease. That they could understand, yet the mere stoppage of disease, the white men told them, was not enough. The numbers of sheep would have to be reduced if any were to have enough to eat. Even in 1869, when they had less than 40,000 sheep and goats, they had never found pasture enough. Now with 749,000, the situation was hopeless.[8] From early days, agents had been writing to Washington about this waste, for many of the horses were never used except for meat in lean years. The wild, shaggy horses need not be broken to bridle or harness, or even curried or fed. They roamed the mesas in herds, almost as wild horses had done before man came to America. As white men collect stamps or first editions, with no practical use, so the important Navajos collected horses up to the number of three, four, or even eight hundred. This spelled destruction for the grass, and carefully the experts explained: "One horse eats five times as much as a sheep and the sheep are starving. You must sell some horses."

The Navajos shook their heads. Sell what men live by—as well ask the white man to sell the beautiful house he had built, the first editions or the stamps he had collected! And what is this ridiculous witchcraft about one horse eating five sheep? Horses do not eat flesh. No Navajo ever disputed that statement of the experts which they did not understand. The habit of avoiding explanations with a white man was too ingrained. They put it down to the kind of insanity which seemed to afflict these strangers and which the Navajos must simply suffer.

It is ironic that, while the People were in this grim mood, they were getting some of the best service given to Indians anywhere. Would that forty years ago they could have had some of these attractive day schools, with a bus to bring children from their distant huts, and with blacksmith shops, shower baths, sewing machines, and laundry tubs for the use of their parents. Would that, when the first school was opened, children could have had these pretty reading books in English and Navajo and a Navajo assistant teacher to do the explaining about toilets and eating utensils and to help them in Navajo over the first dreadful difficulties of school. If, in those early days, there could have been

[8] Statistics from the Navajo Agency, Window Rock, Arizona.

237

radios at the trading stores, the People might have been enthusiastic about such talks as now came through the loud speaker, giving the news of the reservation. A simplified method of writing Navajo was worked out, and a weekly newspaper was published in their own language. It was hoped that many Navajos would learn to read it, since thus they could know what other men knew without the appalling difficulty of learning a foreign tongue. However, the Navajos, the great learners, had at this point set themselves against learning.

Here and there, it is true, there were sparks of personal contact, as when four medicine men were asked to help dedicate the new hospital or when an anthropologist tried to find out who were the chiefly leaders and to have friendly talks with them. Children did attend the pretty, stone schoolhouses, which were never full. Fathers and mothers did begin to use the shops and equipment. The men, who had always made their own clothes, bent over sewing machines as energetically as the women. However, they had neglected to tell the planners that they would be moving with the change of season, and sometimes the pretty schoolhouse was left empty practically one-half the year.

The reservation was divided into districts. The number of "sheep units" which each could support was determined, and the Indians were asked to get rid of the extras, whether this meant a horse that ate as much as five sheep, a cow that ate as much as four sheep, or even a sheep itself. Then those sheep which were left would grow fatter, have better wool, and bigger lambs. In the end, the money return might be even greater. Did they not see?

They did not even try to see. For them, this breakup of the old life was the end of the world. What matter if the government sowed new grass and provided model pastures? What if a sheep laboratory was set up near Fort Wingate, where every effort was made to study the Navajos' needs in wool and mutton and to breed an animal that would satisfy them! None of these farsighted measures counted, for the old, hammerheaded horses were carted off to the slaughter house, and their owners, instead of having "what men live by" had only some white man's money.

Sheep and goats were sold and slaughtered, too. A quota was established for each district, and no one could have a permit for more. Some, who had not yet begun their sheep owning, could not have any at all. It seemed inexpressibly horrible to think of coming back to the earth-covered hut and not to hear the patter of hooves and see the river of wooly backs pouring toward the corral.

The Navajos became sullenly obstinate. Yes, the new day schools looked nice, and the shower baths, irons, and sewing machines might be useful. Probably it was all some evil plot, and many of the Navajos refused to send their children. The proposal that the Navajos should organize as a tribe and then borrow money from the government as other Indians were doing was rejected. To statements on any subject, the answer was usually a grunt: "What about our sheep?"

The plans for Navajo betterment had stalled—in spite of schools and waterworks in a quantity which would have looked fabulous in 1868, in spite of new arrangements for the employment of Navajos, in spite of more earnest and intelligent officials than the People had ever had at one time! Even though an Indian Service doctor had discovered that sulfanilamide would cure the contagious eye disease that was bringing blindness to so many Navajos, the handsome hospital, where Navajos could get better care than many a white man, was not used to capacity. The wage money which, it was hoped, would salve the wounds of change, did not alter the attitude of the average Navajo. He was being hurried into a way of life which he had not chosen, and instead of enthusiasm, he felt misery.

We may pause here to ask whether such a change is ever accomplished without suffering. There is the case of the European immigrants who came to America intent on making themselves a part of the new country, yet they suffered as they and their children adapted at different speeds, and the new ways seem harder to accept than they had supposed. How much harder it would be for the Navajos who had no desire to adapt. Up to this time, they had been the student's ideal of a well-adjusted, primitive people. Now that they were leaving the status of the primitive, life was as bitter for them as for many another tribe. Perhaps there could be no better example of the difficulty involved when one people plans for another, no matter with what wisdom and benevolence. The Navajos were being asked to make the transition from the Middle Ages to modern civilization in one leap, and the transition, though delayed, was difficult. For them, this was the very dark hour before dawn.

Tom Burnsides, Navajo silversmith.
(Courtesy John Adair, Cornell University)

Rug designs supplied to Indians by Colenso,
trader to Navajos in 1890's.
(Photograph by Milton Snow, Courtesy U. S. Indian Service)

18: Ferment

To SOME PEOPLES, the Second World War meant the end of an era of wealth and power, but to others, like the American Indians, it often meant a beginning. Many of the American Indian tribes, like the Navajos, were at some stage of severance from the primitive life. Perhaps they had barely started the change, like the Pueblos, or perhaps they had bogged down part way, like the Sioux. The Navajos, too, might have bogged down if their bitterness about the sheep had not been assuaged. However, the war gave them a life so full that their bitterness was temporarily forgotten. In this war, America needed every man, and all Indians who could meet qualifications were drafted.

To a white American, this might mean the blighting of a career, with a change of living habits and mental attitudes sharp enough to drive him to neurosis. But to an Indian, army life seemed satisfactory and even enjoyable. Coarse foods, irregular hours, and lack of privacy were no hardship for the Navajos, and the mental attitude of a fighter was the identical one handed down from their ancestors for generations. Heretofore it had led only to frustration, but now it meant fulfillment. White officers have told me that no man in their commands took the

241

stress of war with greater calm than the Indian. What was more, the Red Man could now distinguish himself. He could perform the feats required of a soldier as well as any white man, and often better. This sloughing of the sense of inferiority was a glorious experience. Not only were the Indians not inferiors, but they were accepted as comrades. I remember the quiet burning joy with which a Navajo marine told me: "Us Marines are *buddies*. We stick together against *everybody*." That Indian might never in his life have had the chance to be a buddy to a white man. Now it had happened, and the gulf was bridged. The white world was no longer merely an abode of mysterious enemies, but a place one might enter.

Navajos volunteered for the armed services even before the draft. When, as citizens, they were drafted, they flocked to their registration boards, even the old men carrying guns and asking to be shown where the enemy was. Altogether, there were 3,600 Navajos in the United States Army, Navy, and Marine Corps, with a dozen Navajo women in the Women's Army Corps. They saw service in every theatre, and won nearly every type of decoration awarded.

Navajos in the United States Marine Corps performed a unique service. Their language, with its forms so utterly different from those of European tongues, was unknown to all enemy nations. It made an ideal code to be used in the signal corps. Two Navajos carrying portable telephones or two-way radio sets could convey messages across enemy lines with perfect assurance that this code would never be "cracked." Twenty-nine Navajos enlisted for this service and were trained all together as a platoon. They did service in the Pacific, and these youths who, perhaps, had never been more than one hundred miles from home came back speaking some Japanese and carrying samurai swords and silken kimonos. There were "code talkers" also in Sicily and Italy, as well as fighting men.

"I stopped in New York and Philadelphia on the way home," one sergeant told me, in the gentle Indian voice which can match the accents of the most cultured white man. "I had buddies there." With his leather gloves, his tailored blouse, and his well-polished shoes, this boy was returning to an earth-floored hogan. But not for long. Not only he, but his family would soon be wanting more comforts. The People were beginning, at last, to see what the whites worked for and what could be had. For better or for worse, the medieval way of life had been damaged beyond repair.

The output of weaving and silverwork diminished when it was found that any coarse labor would pay five or ten times as much. One trader calculated that the return a Navajo woman got for making a rug, with all the wool washing, carding, dyeing, spinning, and weaving, came to five cents an hour.[1] Families were moving away to work, or they were breaking up and sending out individual members, as they had never done before.

This might not have meant a permanent change in Navajo family life, for men before this had gone off to raid and war and come back to carry on the ancient family customs. It was money that made the difference. Money in a soldier's allotments meant that he must observe the white man's marriage laws. Up to now there had been little interference with the Navajo custom of frequent marriage and divorce without legal registration. Some men still had more than one wife. Yet the allotment system assumed that a married soldier had one wife and one legitimate family of children. Obviously it was not fair that a Navajo

[1] See *Urgent Navajo Problems,* a leaflet published in 1946 by Kirk Bros., Indian traders, at Gallup, New Mexico.

should have two or more families and get support for them all. The People, never blind to a practical problem, began to see why marriages and births should be registered and divorces carried out by a process of law. The government instituted a campaign with moving pictures to show why each Indian should take a "paper name" which he would keep all his life, instead of different names, changed after every important event.

There now were attempts for better planning in Indian work. Two big ordnance plants went up in the desert country near the reservation, and Navajo and Hopi Indians provided most of the working force. When trucks drove up to the workshops in the morning to disgorge hundreds of young men and women in modern dress, it was plain that change had come to the Navajos, if only an outward one. They worked eight hours a day in the white man's manner (foremen said that they did not want to stop at noon); and when living arrangements had been completed by the employers, they went home to shower baths, wooden floors, and beds. One of the villages at Fort Wingate was given to the Navajo tribe when the war was over. The neat streets, houses, and government school will, it is hoped, afford an opportunity for those Navajos who wish to go out to work and live like white men, without going too far from home.

Money was coming into the reservation, both from wages and from soldiers' allotments. The first expenditures were of course, for silver ornaments, that portable wealth which can always be pawned with the trader and which meanwhile, enhances the family status almost as much as horses. Then came clothing which, for the men, meant magnificent cowboy costumes. Plush for the blouses which, for the last forty years, had constituted "native dress' was growing scarce. Some women bought expensive velvet, and one might see whole frocks of it on the streets of Gallup, topping off the sneakers which had

taken the place of moccasins. Navajo shrewdness ultimately dictated a change of style, and more and more Navajo women
could be seen in the costume of white, farm women.

In some hogans, stoves for wood or kerosene took the place
of the earthen hearth in the center of the floor. There were dishes,
glasses, and, perhaps, a movable cabinet. The building of new
houses went on gradually, since the People still clung to the idea
that a house must be deserted after a death. Instead of houses,
for a time, they bought battery radios and, above all, tenthhand
cars. Navajo boys often show a near genius in tinkering with
cars which their white brothers would throw on the junk heap.
No license was required on the reservation, and a speed of ten
miles an hour was at least better than horse and wagon.

Even the ceremonies were changing. Navajo chanters themselves admit to occasional alterations of procedure, after these
have been tried and proved not to bring misfortune. But, it may
have been the young people from boarding school who brought
the change in the Squaw Dance, the finale of the Enemy Way.
This is a purification rite performed for the benefit of those
Navajos who have had too much contact with strangers and
was in much demand after the war. The public dance, on the last
nights, symbolized the return of warriors after a raid, when the
women came to greet them and receive their trophies. Maidens
now invite youths to dance and receive a gift, of money. Within
my memory, each maiden modestly held her "warrior" by the
belt, circling round him, while he stood with folded arms. Now
couples often dance arm in arm, as they may have done at school.

A more sinister novelty was whiskey which sometimes
passed among spectators and dancers, too. Navajos had always
bought whiskey since the first railroad brought it within their
reach, and the federal law, passed in 1802 at the request of the
Indians themselves, was practically unenforceable. Whites who

have been through a prohibition era, may understand this. They should realize, too, the sense of inferiority which weighed on a Navajo man, particularly a soldier, when he was denied service at a bar where his comrades drank freely. The exchange of expensive bottles of bad liquor in dark corners of Gallup streets went on apace. The liquor difficulty was mounting to an impossible pinnacle which would need attention after the war, like many other Navajo problems.

Even the Navajo attitude toward death began to waver. Scores of whites had tried to convince the People that the dead body of a loved one need not spread evil and that photographs and memorials to the dead can be beautiful and consoling. Resolutely the Navajos had kept to the idea that any contact with the dead is dangerous. Yet bodies of white soldiers were being brought home and buried with ceremonies which brought honor to all connected with them. Should the Navajos refuse this honor? The leaders were brought together and asked whether they wished a war cemetery for Navajo heroes. They hesitated, but desire for prestige overcame the ancient taboo. For the war dead, at least, public burial was accepted. The first Navajo killed in a training plane was buried with ceremony, under the American flag.

The Navajos experienced four years of this accelerated life, and then the war was over. Soldiers and war workers all over the country were drifting back to a world which seemed to have nothing for them, but with the Navajos, this emptiness was particularly miserable. Now they wanted money, better housing, more possessions, and, particularly, education. War had done what at least a half century of argument had failed to do. The Navajos were ready for school.

But the schools were not ready for them. The poor state of repair and the lack of seating capacity of schools on the reservation became a scandal, once it was known. There were twenty-one thousand children of school age and less than six thousand enrolled in all schools, federal, mission, and public![2] Hasty work began to make up for some of the lack. Money was appropriated for repairing the old schools and for building new ones wherever the population justified it. This program could never bring schools to all the People before their growing children had passed school age. There were concentrated programs for children over twelve in Indian boarding schools all over the Southwest, and there were special courses for the veterans who could not go to college because of lack of preparation.

Such measures would have seemed lavish forty years ago. Now they were merely a drop in the bucket of Navajo needs. These needs touched every phase of life, for all phases had been slowly worsening, as the People increased in number and received no plan for change which they cared to accept. The old still drew comfort from their ceremonies, but the young who had been away so much had lost faith. There were now over thirty Christian churches on the reservation, with some devoted converts. Yet the attitudes of Christianity still seemed foreign to the People, who had no belief in a better life from which mankind had fallen. They had no words for penance, pardon, and sacrifice, and only a very vague conception of these ideas. Their aim had never been eternal bliss, but only to be happy and loved in this present life.[3]

At this transition stage, they became acquainted with the *peyote*[4] cult, which had swept through the plains a few gener-

[2] Statistics from the Navajo Agency, Window Rock, Arizona.

[3] This subject was treated at length by Gladys A. Reichard in "The Navajo and Christianity," *American Anthropologist,* Vol. LI (1949), 56–71.

[4] For statements on peyote, see *Science,* Vol. CXIV, 582–83. Detailed descriptions of peyote meetings have been given by Omer Stewart in *Washo-Northern Paiute Peyotism,* University of California Publications on Archaeology

ations ago, and whose emissaries were now penetrating the Southwest. This cult, involving the eating of a narcotic cactus, Anhalonium lewinii, has been excoriated by Christian missionaries and viewed with alarm by government officials. Yet I, who have attended many of the ceremonies, can see reasons for it as a transition stage between old beliefs and new. I have sometimes wondered if the Indians, with their lack of background for a theology involving sin and penance, could not be approached simply with a creed of brotherly love, as a basis for Christian living. No Christian church has been willing to present such a fraction of its theology, but the Indians have done it for themselves. *Peyote,* runs their creed, has appeared to them as a symbol of righteous living and love to all the world. And, mark, it appeared *only to Indians.* They did not have to be converted by any white man.

The cult, organized in the last century as the Native American Church, uses the cactus as a sacrament. Its bitter, green "buttons," like thorny brussels sprouts, can be chewed fresh. Or the dried root can be minced and brewed like tea. At the meetings I have attended, each person took eight buttons in the course of a night. The effect is one of mild hallucination, as one listens to drum and rattle with eyes fixed on a small fire. Objects appear rimmed with rainbow colors. Space measurements are slightly blurred, and time seems to lag. There is no desire for violent action. Instead, one sits quiet, with a sense of general euphoria.

These gatherings had something of the atmosphere of a

---

and Ethnology, Vol. XL, No. 3 (1939), 63–142 and *Ute Peyotism,* University of Colorado Studies, Series in Anthropology, Vol. I, 1948. Also see J. Slotkin, *Menomini Peyotism,* Transactions of the American Philosophical Society, Vol. XLII, Pt. 4, 1952. In *Saturday Review,* February 6, 1954, Aldous Huxley recommended the use of mescalin instead of alcohol and tobacco. A doctor and an anthropologist, consulted by the magazine, did not go so far as this, but the doctor stated: "Its dangers are probably minimal."

Christian prayer meeting, though held in a tepee, with earthen altar and incense of tobacco smoke. The Navajo songs, which once hymned the plants and animals in the old Indian manner, were now versions of Christian supplication.

> *Jesus God, Only One!*
> *Pity me, pity me!*

They were interspersed with testimonials, some from people who had been healed by faith and some from those inspired to lead a better life. Such a naïve approach to a new theology seems little more deviant than that of early barbarians in Ireland or Scandinavia or even of Europeans in the Middle Ages, who pictured the twelve disciples as gorgeous princes with swords and helmets.

The objection to the *peyote* cult is its supposed bad effects on health and morals. Here psychologists and biochemists who have experimented with the plant are rarely in agreement with its accusers, or, at least, the more violent of them. *Peyote* contains some eight alkaloids, of which the predominant one is mescalin. Experiments have been made on this substance and are still going on, so that full knowledge about it is for the future. So far, the statement has been made that, taken in moderate quantities (up to 350 milligrams), it has no effects beyond those mentioned above. The heightened sensitivity to sound and color which it induces may help to produce a vision, the Indians' ancient method of communion with the supernatural. The usual eight buttons can hardly go as far as this, for experiment shows them to contain only some 107 milligrams of mescalin, or a third of the quantity necessary for true hallucination. Moreover, these are taken at long intervals, which always reduces the effect of a stimulant.[5]

[5] Spaeth and Beske, *Berichte*, Vol. XLVIII, Berlin, 1935. Experiments now

The danger from *peyote* is an overdose. White experimenters who have taken 700 milligrams of mescalin have felt faintness and shortness of breath, like that experienced at high altitudes. *Peyote,* so far, has never been known to kill a human being and has not been proved habit forming. Elaborate research now being undertaken may finally give us the complete facts. Meanwhile, the federal government has not found sufficient reason to condemn it as a narcotic. Several states, however, forbid its importation, including New Mexico and Arizona. Supposedly, exception is made when its use is religious, but this line is hard to draw. There are individuals who eat *peyote* outside the meetings, and for these people there is danger, just as there is for those who make a habit of alcohol. The remedy, perhaps, is the same as that for alcoholism—provide the patient with a new, absorbing interest.

Alcohol was taking high toll among the Navajos in the postwar years. So it was with many a white man, and for the same reasons. They had no work and no money. Ever since 1933, money had been coming to the reservation, from civilian conservation work, war work, and soldier pay. Now the last soldier had used up his twenty dollars a month, which was meant to support him while he looked for a job. Most of the Navajos had no jobs. In spite of years in the army, they were not prepared for work in the white man's sense. Not only were they not clock-trained, but also were innocent of techniques for getting ahead. Whites who grew impatient at these faults forgot that their own ideas of work had been developing under pressure for a hundred years and more. Navajo training had been eighty years of dependence on Uncle Sam. And now that they felt ready to emerge from the larval stage, they had no wings with which to fly.

being carried on at Colorado General Hospital, Denver, have so far given similar results. Others are in process at the University of Michigan, Ann Arbor, Mich.

19: Last Call for Help
from the Navajos

"SEND HELP! The Navajos are starving!" If
the reader feels this plea to be repetitious, so
did the Navajos, so did the Washington offi-
cials, who had heard it at intervals ever since 1868. Sometimes it
had been a loud complaint, sometimes a mere note in an agent's
report. Rations, agricultural improvements, and land purchases
had not served to silence it. Now, in 1947, it caught the attention
of the press and was broadcast through the country.

Of course, not all the Navajos were starving, or ever had
been. It was the poor who were undernourished, while the rich
Navajos were doing well. Even the poor, the officials sighed,
would be better off if they had saved their war money or if their
men had taken the jobs available. Finally, there were other Indians and even white Americans who had the same problem.

Such corrections barely registered in view of the details published day by day. Here was a group of American citizens living
in earth-floored huts, like peasants of the Middle Ages. Scores
of families, without the mutton and goat meat which had once
been daily fare, were existing on a diet of fried bread and coffee.
The rate of tuberculosis was one person in ten, whereas for the
rest of rural America it was one in eighteen. Treatment for

251

trachoma had practically stopped during the war, and now the disease was on the increase. Once large numbers of Navajos had refused treatment for these ills. But now the problem had grown too serious, and sick people were willing to come to hospitals. But the six hospitals on the reservation could treat only about one-half the people who needed medical aid. The number of aged, crippled, and blind was piling up. Once these unfortunates had been cared for by their large, united families. Perhaps the care had been none too good, and, indeed, many of the crippled had died at birth or in infancy. Now their number had increased, and this load was more than the impoverished People could carry. The states of Arizona and New Mexico, none too rich anyway, considered that their social security did not apply to Indians.

The country was shocked. Many citizens had never heard of this tribe of over fifty thousand people in faraway New Mexico, yet the contributions poured in, from clubs, churches, communities, and private individuals. Tons of clothing and caravans of trucks laden with food began to arrive at the agency. It was strange to see a Navajo woman in a fur coat, mounting her horse to drive a flock of sheep. It was stranger to see the boxes of evening gowns and silver slippers, whose only use was to bring a few dollars from the neighboring Mexicans. The chairman of the council was silent when a package, specially addressed to him, revealed a carefully packed lipstick. Thus America expressed her understanding of the Indian problem.

Officials and, later, Red Cross workers brought some order out of the flood of temporary good will. But this was no permanent solution to the Navajos' future. Nor did any of the old remedies hold a solution. The sheep program was a success—technically. The sheep were fewer but bigger and better, and they were bringing in more money than the small flocks of former days, but the money came to fewer people. How were the rest to live? Millions had been spent on improving the reservation, but even so there was not water and land for all. Land had been added to the full extent possible. The three and one-half million acres of treaty land had increased to fifteen million acres. Even that was not sufficient for 55,000 people, the Navajo population in 1947. And the Navajos were increasing at the rate of one thousand a year.[1]

The eighty-year-old problem rose up in stark finality. How were all the Navajos to live on the reservation? The answer was: they cannot. Other means of support must be found.

This answer came after a thorough survey made by order of the Indian Service, which, in 1947, was an entirely different organization from that started in the country's ungainly youth, when scandal and inefficiency in government were as common as adolescent pimples. While the Indians' attitudes, understanding, and abilities had been improving, the Indian Service had been developing likewise. Now every new employee but the commissioner had to pass a Civil Service examination which often included questions meant to detect prejudice against Indians. But more than that, the Indian Service now included specialists in soil conservation, livestock care, farming, and other lines of modern activity helpful to the Indians. Based on an investigation of every phase of Navajo economics, a "long range program" was evolved which embodied a new way of life for the Navajos.

If the Navajos were ever to be anything other than picturesque pensioners, their way of life had to be changed again. The old trinity of sheep, land, and People must be left to the few who had decent pasturage. Even farming, granting the fullest possible use of irrigation, would support only a fraction of

[1] J. A. Krug, *Report on the Navaho.* For statistics in this chapter consult Krug's book.

the People. Other Navajos had to be educated to practice modern trades. This would mean opening small businesses wherever possible on the reservation—garages, shops, tourist motels, mines for the low-grade coal there, and even roads to serve all these. In short, the picturesque land would be modernized and so, in time, would most of the People.

The improvements on the reservation would run into more millions than had ever been spent on the Navajos. Even so, the land could hardly support more than 35,000 people, or about one-half of the growing tribe. No more land could be bought from white ranchers, and even if it could, should the government keep on buying, year after year, as thousands of new Navajos were born? There was only one solution. One-half the tribe had to obtain a living off the reservation.

Here was the real blow to the old way of life, appalling to many Navajos and whites. Yet the People had moved before and grown stronger. It is not parting from the land of mesa and canyon which meant tragedy for the Navajo, but the severing of his little strand of life from the fabric of the group, with its complex ties of friendship and duty, its joy in shared belief and ceremony, and its sense of belonging. No Navajo can have these comforts of the spirit when he goes to live among white men, even friendly white men. Usually white men are not friendly: Indians are often excluded from restaurants, hotels, and theatres, and children in a public school are likely to shun Indian children. Adult whites relegate the Indian and his family to the slums, and the worst among them consider the Indian legitimate prey for the thief and the bootlegger.

In spite of their new feeling for money, few of the People wanted to live permanently in the white man's world. When work was found for them, they sometimes dropped it and returned without a word of explanation. To the white man, brought up to make his own way and expecting some years of hard grind on the road to success, this seemed to indicate laziness and lack of will power. He did not realize that the Indian saw little success ahead. For the Indian, without training or stimulus, the grind might go on for life.

A plan on which the Indian Service placed more hopes was for the Indians to leave the reservation in groups. On the lower Colorado River, where irrigated land produces six crops of alfalfa a year, there is a reservation of 100,000 acres, set aside long ago for tribes along the Colorado River and its drainage. Some Navajos and Hopis are now located in this area. The small local tribes, Mohaves and Chemeheuvis, had held council meetings and agreed to make room for these people of completely different backgrounds and speech, setting aside 75,000 acres for them. The government is cleaning and irrigating the land of all groups, acre for acre. Veterans of any of the four tribes may have forty acres, with a crop already planted and may borrow $5,000 from the government for machinery and household goods. Twenty-four Navajo families had moved in 1947, and in a few years many had paid off their debts. Others would come as soon as the land was prepared. They would face separation from relatives, but not from tribesmen. Perhaps this group approach to a new way of life is the least painful. It may mean contributions to American life, just as such contributions have already been received from Little Italy and Little Israel.

So much for Navajo economy. Other needs of the People and other Indians all over the country were being deeply felt. In the late 1940's, seventy or eighty years after the reservations had been set aside, the whole Indian problem was being reviewed carefully. Were the Indians to go on forever being wards of the government, set apart as a special group and treated differently from other American citizens? The Federal government, since the 1860's, had been talking about relinquishing its service to the Indians and turning them over to the states. This did not mean "closing" the reservations, which are held tax-free for the Indians as a treaty obligation. It meant that the states would now maintain schools, hospitals, and other facilities and open them to near-by whites as well as Indians.

This had not been possible in early days, when the western states were new and sparsely populated. It was now time that Indians should cease to be set apart and regarded almost as objects of charity. The move, however, could not be made cheaply. Washington, which fifty years ago could not afford a few dozen plows, was now contemplating expenses which would involve millions. The treaties would be kept to the letter. Reservation land would remain tax-free, and the states would be reimbursed for their expenses. All treaty obligations would be paid in land or money, before the turnover. Since the government, the supreme authority, cannot be sued without its own permission, a court of claims was set up so that tribes might make out a case for their rights and sue. The Navajos took advantage of this permission. They prepared to prove that the reservation given them by treaty was far smaller than the land they once occupied. It was a case for skilled argument, but the Navajos of 1947 did not need coyote pollen to make them eloquent. With the consent of the secretary of the interior, they drew on the oil money being kept for them in the treasury and hired a lawyer.

This was the first drastic move the Navajos had ever made as a tribe. In the old warring days, they had acted as small units, under independent leaders. When they refused to adopt a constitution and protested against sheep reduction, it had been a matter of digging in where they were, rather than advancing. Now they had the heady feeling of opposing Washington, even with Washington's permission and at great expense. Later might

Navajos at the sutler's store, Fort Sumner.
(Courtesy Army Signal Corps)

Street scene at Fort Sumner.
(Courtesy National Archives)

A committee of the Navajo Council in session.
(Photograph by Milton Snow, Courtesy U. S. Indian Service)

The late Chee Dodge, former chairman of the Navajo Council, inspects work displayed by the Navajo Arts and Crafts Guild.
(Photograph by Milton Snow, Courtesy U. S. Indian Service)

come the nostalgia for protection and expert services, perfected through years of experience. Meanwhile, a new event worked toward pushing them into the modern world. Off-reservation Indians achieved the vote.

Since 1924, all Indians had been assured of voting privileges by the federal government, but some states had laws which nullified this right. Arizona forbade the privilege to illiterates, and both Arizona and New Mexico ruled out "persons under wardship," among whom were minors, the insane, and—technically —Indians. In 1947, under the guidance of the Indian Service, two test cases were fought and won. Off-reservation and literate Indians were assured the right to vote in both states.

Thus the government, some eighty years after the Indians had been relegated to reservations, began to take thorough cognizance of their problems. The best experts available had given their advice, and Congress, instead of ignoring it, was preparing to spend enormous sums to put it into practice. It is useless to lament that this should have been done eighty years ago, for then the country was unprepared for such measures, the public was not aware of the Indian problem, and the money and the knowledge were not available. While Washington and its citizens had been growing and learning, the Navajos had grown also. No longer were they willing to stand before the agent's desk, awaiting such largess as he was authorized to give. Through periods of suffering and incertitude, they had developed their own ideas.

They now had a representative body, prepared to exert pressure in the American manner. True, it was still an informal group, whose acts had to be approved by the Indian Service. This was because, years ago, in the "no sheep" era, they had refused to organize like other tribes. Now they began to talk about the project while the superintendent, with the sanction of

Washington, encouraged them. These first steps were uncertain. The real Navajo leaders were still the old "long hairs" who remained back on the reservation, while the young men who could speak English sometimes formed a front. The debates often went on for days until a unanimous decision could be reached, for that had always been the People's custom. But the disposal of a few ownerless horses still seemed a more important subject for debate than the spending of a few thousand dollars for poor relief.

The council, inexpert and disunified as it was, began to show a new spirit of independence. The trader, long a friend and almost a parent, was outraged at the proposal that he pay rent for the land he used. A new missionary group, full of devotion and desire to serve, could hardly believe that it was refused any land at all. The Indian Service which had labored so long and so painfully found that, instead of its expert help, the Navajos sometimes turned to their paid lawyer. These were not growing pains, but the violent gestures of a people fighting towards independence and responsibility. These were the years of ferment when the medieval way of life had failed, and the Navajos were stumbling toward something new. They were ready for a fourth beginning.

20: Fourth Beginning: the Navajos Today

NEW HORIZONS

In the 1940's, the Navajos were reported starving. Their beautiful, arid land was too poor to support the population, and it was thought that half of the people must find a living elsewhere. Twenty years later, the population had almost doubled and the reservation was the richest in the United States. Oil had been discovered there. Between the years 1961 and 1964, the Navajo Tribe had received in bonuses and exploration fees one hundred million dollars. In that same period, the birth rate had soared. In 1967 agency records showed the population to be 110,000,[1] but speakers, both white and Indian, placed it as high as 115,000 or even 120,000.

The money was not distributed to individuals. For one thing, it would not go far among some 100,000 people. For another, there had been examples elsewhere of per capita distribution whose main result was drunkenness and disorganization. Therefore, the Tribe, with advice from government agents, set about putting the reservation in order. Already the Indian Bureau had plans. A long-range program was being developed for improving the Navajo reservation and the smaller Hopi area which it surrounded. Millions of dollars were to be spent for land man-

[1] According to the Bureau of Indian Affairs Agency at Window Rock.

agement, roads, health, education, and employment, along with surveys to map the possibilities ahead. Now the program would not be carried out by a beneficent government battling alone to convince a reluctant people what was good for them. Navajos and government co-operated, the Navajos furnishing heavy machinery and men while the Bureau paid expenses and provided the plans. These plans were duly laid before the Navajo Advisory Council and were not put into effect until they had the chairman's signature.

The chairman was an important official, with a house at Window Rock, near the residences of the government employees. He was elected, like the President of the United States, every four years in November, as were the vice-chairman, four judges, and seventy-four councilmen. All had salaries and travel money, the salary of the chairman in 1966 being $18,000 a year. The Tribe employed a secretary-treasurer, a corps of policemen, rangers, and various other assistants, as well as non-Indian lawyers and other specialists. Tribal relations with the Indian Bureau meant not the taking of orders but discussion in committees. Often these committees were headed by a Navajo. Their membership might include not only Bureau experts but specialists from the state governments of New Mexico and Arizona, perhaps even Washington.

As a result, Navajoland is no longer a wilderness of rocks, brush, and piñon where tourists are warned not to venture without full information. Now paved roads connect the main settlements. The longest highway, crossing from east to west through magnificent scenery, is likely to become a favorite part of the route between Chicago and Los Angeles. In the open country, where once the only moving objects were sheep and shepherds, one can often see heavy machinery and truckloads of men engaged in digging and fencing. Water can now be brought to areas that looked hopeless before by lining ditches with concrete and digging rain-water reservoirs—one reservoir even has a rubber lining. Land can be cleared for farming by burning and dragging out the brush and piñon, then reseeding, perhaps by plane. Low-cost housing is being set up for rent by the Tribe to its members. Civic centers are built for local meetings. The Navajos are pushing and being pushed into the modern world.

Most of them want the change. They listen eagerly to radio talks in their own language from Flagstaff and Gallup. They wear modern clothing. A few still live in windowless hogans, but someone in the family connection always has a truck in which the whole group can visit a near-by town, go to the movies, and perform the one act which is the same for a Navajo as for a white man—drinking liquor at a bar. The law against the sale of liquor to Indians was repealed after World War II. Indian soldiers believed it unfair that they should share everything with their white buddies but the celebrations, from which they were turned away as though they were children. "It will be a bath of blood for a while," one government agent remarked. And it is true that a number of persons with few outside interests in the new life have taken to this one escape. The Council has forbidden the sale of liquor in the reservation. Their hope is the same as that of workers in many white communities—that better education, better health, and more employment may substitute achievement for escape.

Health, education, and employment are not as easily produced as new roads and ditches. In fact, Navajo health is still below that of other rural areas in the country. Raising health standards and changing habits mean not only medical care but education. The U.S. Public Health Service has plans for improvement of Indian health, since it has taken over the responsibility from the Indian Bureau, already overburdened with too many functions. Navajos have become more willing to co-operate, for they have learned that there is a group of diseases which their own health healers cannot handle. Even at other times, they appreciate the cleanliness and the regular food of the hospitals. Many women now go to a hospital at childbirth and for advice about ailing children.

There are five big hospitals on the reservation and one in Gallup. Away from the settlements are health centers and smaller health stations for treatment and dental care. Health education is stressed in schools, and dentists and extension workers tour the reservation. Some Navajo girls are being trained as nurses, but there are no Navajo doctors yet—that is, doctors trained in the white man's schools. But the Navajo chanter sometimes sings for patients in the hostpital. In one remote settlement, a group of doctors from Cornell University set up a community project in which they collaborated with the local healers to work on the health of the whole group.

The People may be only partially convinced that good health demands the change of so many habits that have served them for centuries. On the subject of education, however, they are not only convinced, they are dedicated. World War II opened Navajo eyes to the fact that many of the white man's good things could be earned only with education. Immediately there went up from the reservation a cry that was unanimous and insistent: "Give us more schools!"

This was a chance for the educators, even though it meant a hurricane of planning. Schools that had been standing half-empty were filled beyond capacity. New ones were erected as fast as possible, and, in remote parts of the reservation, trailers were used. Older children were sent all over the country to any Indian school which had room. In Utah, a huge army hospital was taken over for the teen-agers who must not be allowed to live longer without some rudiments of schooling. Parents who had once held out against separation from their children, now patiently took over the children's chores. They knew what they wanted.

Most hopeful for the future was the opening of public schools to Indians. When children went to school in the towns, the Tribe outfitted them with clothing and the government reimbursed the state for the extra expense. Dormitories were furnished where the young scholars could stay in town for the week, returning home for the week end to renew family contacts. By 1946, there were 16,000 Navajos in public schools and 19,000 in government schools, with a few still cared for by missions.

Public school was no easy matter for children from homes where there were no books, where the elders of the family knew nothing of world geography or world history. It was generally admitted that Indian children, with their lack of English, were at least a year behind the white children, and educators considered the problem carefully. Summer meetings of teachers were held. A handsome school building at Window Rock was turned over by the government to a Navajo corporation for use as an experimental school for Indians.

The problems are even greater for Navajos going to college. The Tribe maintains a scholarship fund for boys and girls who pass the requisite examinations. The Indian Bureau and private sources provide other scholarships. But the high-pressure intake of information and the new group life send some college students home in discouragement. The universities at Tempe, Arizona, and Provo, Utah, make special provision for Indians. In 1966, six hundred Navajo boys and girls were attending college. A number of graduates are school teachers on the reservation and one is a principal.

These are forward-looking moves, but they refer mostly to the future. In the present, many families are living in one-room huts and look with discontent on the radios, the plumbing, the good clothes, and good jobs which appear to be the birthright of every American citizen. For themselves, there are sixteen million acres of land, valuable mostly as scenery, for the oil money is diminishing as surveys are completed. Aged and dependent tribal members receive the same welfare payments as other American citizens. In 1967 the agency gave the number of employed individuals, male and female, between the ages of eighteen and twenty-five as 48,995. As recently as 1961 researchers reported in horror that the average family income was no more than $200 a year. That did not include the few sheep or the corn, beans, and squash which a family might raise. It did not include long visits to relatives or many a meal received in return for small services. And it ignored the luxury of a nine-day "sing" when, besides being fed, one has the comfort of companionship and the sure blessing of the spirits.

Some Navajos really make money. These are the craftsmen who work silver and the women who weave beautiful rugs. The Tribe has an Arts and Crafts Guild which features these unique products, no two ever alike. But the amount of time required to make each article seems ridiculous when one thinks of the millions of somewhat similar articles produced in factories. It seems so to the Navajo's, and therefore they buy cloth and ornaments in the cheap stores in town. Their own rugs and jewelry have become collectors' items, but there are not many collectors in the country.

Must the Navajos leave the reservation, as was suggested twenty years ago? Some are trying it on the government system that was instituted at that time. The Bureau has established relocation offices in six cities, and there seems to be a constant movement to and fro, especially by young couples. The money attracts. The routine and the bleakness of life, without kin or

ceremony, repel. There has been talk of inviting outside indus-
tries to the reservation. Yet, until recently, no industry was at-
tracted to the waterless country. One possibility there was, at
Red Lake, where Captain Dodge long ago held his give-away.
There the Tribe owns a sawmill, managed by an outsider, of
course, but employing 450 Navajos. The reservation has one
favored corner, where the San Juan River loops down from the
north. Here outsiders have set up a uranium plant, a vanadium
grinding mill, and an electric power plant, all of which employ
a few Navajos. Another electric plant is in the offing which may
take hundreds more. None of this activity, however, provides
a solution for the Navajo money problem.

The government has an answer—the same one which has
been proposed for all Indians since land was first reserved for
them: farming. Once it was ridiculous as a livelihood for a large
number. Now the San Juan River offers possibilities for irrigation undreamed of a century ago. Navajo men do not scorn this
work as the buffalo hunters did. For nearly a thousand years, they
raised some corn, beans, and squash in favored places after the
time-honored manner their men had learned from the Pueblos.
Perhaps some of their own poetic imagination went into the
ritual sung by the planter, as he moved clockwise around his
field, from the center out:

> *In the middle of the wide field,*
> *I wish to put in*
> *White corn I wish to put in.*
> *Soft goods and hard goods*
> *I wish to put in.*
> *Good and everlasting ones*
> *I wish to put in.*[2]

2 W. W. Hill, *The Agricultural and Hunting Methods of the Navajo Indians*
(Yale University *Publications in Anthropology, No. 18*), 63.

"Good and everlasting ones" were the seeds, while "soft and hard goods" were the woven cloth and jewelry which would come, eventually, to any hard-working man.

The Navajo did not usually plant things to sell nor did he expend much effort on his garden. He left its fate to the summer rains, some sketchy irrigation, and the few tools he was likely to get from the yearly treaty payments. True, that treaty had promised productive land for each family. But Washington officials had had no idea of the aridity of the reservation or the impossibility of large-scale irrigation, given the resources and the knowledge of 1868. And the Navajos, at Fort Sumner, had refused the labor and responsibility of community irrigation.

Now irrigation is proposed on a scale undreamed of in 1868. A dam has been built in the San Juan River, producing the largest man-made lake in the United States. A survey by a firm of experts looks toward the watering of 110,000 acres with small farms for a thousand Navajo families. The farms, of course, must raise crops for sale. The families must pay rent to the Tribe, buy seeds, and pay irrigation charges. That means a bounce into new lifeways for people who, only a short time ago, scarcely handled $200 a year in cash and who dropped work without a qualm when a nine-day ceremony was in prospect. The Navajos will need training, admit the sponsors of the plan. In fact, small projects of the kind were begun in the 1950's with families settled for two years on an irrigated tract and promised a farm of their own on "graduation." Some families stuck out the course, but others found it not to their taste. As a result, the surveying firm reported that the Navajos were not yet ready to handle commercial farming. They like the work, but for the present the Tribe probably would find it advantageous to hire non-Indians as managers.

That likely will be only an interim measure, for, as this

volume has shown, the Navajos have displayed great determination in learning new skills—when they wanted to. The survey report goes on to suggest food-processing and other projects which could spread out from the farming area and bring the Tribe some thirteen million dollars a year.

Would this mean the end of the old Navajo life? A section of The People is standing out vigorously against too much change, and perhaps they can steer the plans along ways that will not sacrifice too many of the old values. From 1962–66 the chairman was a man who might be called a Progressive, a former navy man and radio announcer. He was re-elected in 1966, on a platform demanding a recognized constitution and religious freedom. The constitution means bringing the Navajos definitely into line with most other tribes which incorporated and wrote constitutions years ago. The Navajos refused this well-meaning government arrangement because of their anger about the sheep. Now they want their official organization to have more recognition. And this big tribe is gaining recognition in many ways, for elected officials in the states of New Mexico and Arizona are paying attention to their wishes. Navajos now vote with the whites on election day. They have been citizens, like other Indians, since 1924, but certain voter requirements of the two neighboring states prevented their voting. Now these requirements have been removed, and the Navajo attitude may grow politically important in the Southwest.

The demand for religious freedom might have surprised our Founding Fathers, who, when they wrote the Constitution, were probably thinking of Protestants and Roman Catholics. What the Navajo Progressives want is freedom for the Native American Church, whose ritual includes eating of the peyote cactus. New Mexico and Arizona, like many other states, have laws against importing this cactus except for scientific and religious purposes. The Navajo Council has forbidden it entirely; yet for the last four years meetings have been held quietly. The amount of peyote consumed is barely enough to produce the hallucinations reported from its use. What happens to The People is their union under the supernatural helper which came to Indians and not to whites. The all-night meetings in an old-time hogan mean an inspired fellowship which is all The People's own. For its members, the Native American Church stands in the same position as the white men's churches, and it inculcates the same morality. There are now many denominations on the reservation. Most of the Navajos, some of the peyote group, belong officially to one, though they may keep up the native ceremonies as well.

The Christian rituals appeal to them as an addition to their own. A recent photograph of a Navajo wedding showed the bride and groom in church, the bride's dark complexion and ebon hair beautifully set off by white dress and veil. (Old-time Navajos, it may be mentioned, never wore white. It was not suitable for their work and too hard to keep clean.) Navajo young people still take part in the "Squaw" or War Dance. They also flock to jazz sessions in the towns, and some even form their own bands. They elect a beauty queen and send a candidate to the national contest for Miss Indian America. At an earlier age, they are enthusiastic members of Boy Scouts, Girl Scouts, and 4–H Clubs.

Time was when a tourist, asking information from a Navajo, was met by a blank stare or a turned back. Now it has dawned on some of The People that guiding tourists, setting up campgrounds for them, or serving at motels and gas stations may be pleasanter tasks than farming. In fact, "tourism" is bringing money into several reservations whose chief asset is scenery. Navajoland now has thirty-two campgrounds with tables and fireplaces and two motels with restaurants. The wooded wilderness of the Chuska Mountains which once could be penetrated only on horseback now has an automobile road. Its charming little lakes, instituted for water control, have been stocked with fish by the government, as have other and larger lakes which now have boats for hire. The imposing pinnacles of Monument Valley are segregated in a park, which has rangers and an entrance fee.

The great inrush of visitors comes in the autumn at the Navajo Fair. Then a huge acreage near Window Rock is jammed with cars, Indian and white, from all the neighboring states. The crowds which stream through the gates for three days can see exhibits of Navajo crafts and a Navajo farming. They can buy hot dogs and soft drinks and watch a famous comedian on television. A tourist gazing at the throng in blue jeans and cotton frocks inquired, "Where are the Indians?"

The Indians are making their fourth beginning.

Bibliography

I. *Unpublished Material*
Haile, Berard. The Story of the Navajo Shooting Chant.
Reichard, Gladys A. Story of the Male Shooting Chant.
Wheelwright, Mary C. Bead Chant.
———. Coyote Myth.

II. *Federal Documents*
Annual Reports of the Board of Indian Commissioners, 1869–1932.
Annual Reports of the Commissioner of Indian Affairs, 1838–1950.
Board of Indian Commissioners. *The Indian Bureau from 1824 to 1924*. Washington, 1925.
Simpson, Lieut. J. H. *Journal of a Military Reconnaissance from Santa Fé, N. M., to the Navajo Country, 1849*. U. S. 31 Cong., 1 sess., Senate Exec. Doc. 64, 1849–50. In *Report* of Secretary of War.
U. S. Census Office. *Indians Taxed and not Taxed*. 11th Census *Report*. Washington, 1890.
U. S. Congress. *Report of the Joint Special Committee on the Condition of the Indian Tribes*. Washington, 1865, 1867.

III. *Books and Pamphlets*
Adair, John. *The Navajo and Pueblo Silversmiths*. Norman, University of Oklahoma Press, 1945.
Amsden, Charles A. *Navajo Weaving*. Santa Ana, Fine Arts Press, 1934.
Bailey, Flora. *Some Sex Beliefs and Practices in a Navaho Community*. Peabody Museum *Papers*. Cambridge, 1950.
Bancroft, H. H. *History of Arizona and New Mexico, 1530–1888*. San Francisco, History Company, 1874–89.
Benavides, Fray Alonso de. *The Memorial of Fray Alonso de Bena-*

vides. Translated by Mrs. E. E. Ayer, annotated by F. W. Hodge and C. F. Lummis. Chicago, 1916.

Bolton, Herbert E. *Spanish Explorations in the Southwest, 1542–1706.* New York, C. Scribner's Sons, 1925.

———. *Coronado, Knight of Pueblos and Plains.* Albuquerque, University of New Mexico Press, 1949.

Bourke, John G. *The Medicine-Men of the Apache.* Bureau of American Ethnology *Ninth Annual Report.* Washington, 1892.

Boyce, George A. *A Primer of Navajo Economic Problems.* U. S. Department of Interior, Navajo Service. Window Rock, Arizona (mimeographed), 1942.

———. *Reports* on Education to the Navajo Tribe. U. S. Department of Interior, Navajo Service, Window Rock, Arizona (mimeographed), 1945–48.

Brew, John Otis. *Archaeology of Alkali Ridge, Southeastern Utah.* Peabody Museum *Papers.* Cambridge, 1946.

Browne, J. Ross. *Adventures in the Apache Country: A Tour Through Arizona and Sonora.* New York, Harper & Bros., 1869.

Bunzel, Ruth L. *The Pueblo Potter.* Columbia University *Contributions to Anthropology,* No. 8 (1929).

———. *Zuni Ritual Poetry.* Bureau of American Ethnology *Forty-Seventh Annual Report.* Washington, 1932.

Calhoun, James S. *The Official Correspondence of James S. Calhoun.* Edited by Annie Heloise Abel. Washington, 1915.

Carroll, H. B. and J. V. Haggard (tr. and ed.). *Three New Mexico Chronicles.* Albuquerque, Quivira Society, 1942.

Clark, Elizabeth P. *Report on the Navajo.* Home Missions, Council of North America (mimeographed), 1946.

Connelly, W. E. *Doniphan's Expedition and the Conquest of New Mexico and California.* Topeka, 1907.

Cremony, John C. *Life Among the Apaches.* San Francisco, A. Roman & Co., 1868.

Curtis, E. S. *The North American Indian.* 20 vols. Cambridge, Harvard University Press, 1907-30.

Dale, Edward E. *The Indians of the Southwest*. Norman, University of Oklahoma Press, 1949.

Davis, W. H. *El Gringo, or New Mexico and Her People*. New York, 1857.

Driver, Harold E. *Girls Puberty Rites in Western North America*. Culture Element, *Anthropology Records*, Vol. VI, No. 2. Berkeley, University of California, 1941.

——. *Southern California*. Culture Element, *Anthropology Records*, Vol. I, No. 1. Berkeley, University of California, 1937.

——. *Yuman-Piman*. Culture Element, *Anthropology Records*, Vol. VI, No. 3. Berkeley, University of California, 1941.

Elmore, Francis H. *Ethnobotany of the Navajo*. Albuquerque, University of New Mexico and School of American Research, 1944.

Franciscan Fathers. *An Ethnologic Dictionary of the Navaho Language*. St. Michaels, Arizona, St. Michaels Press, 1929.

Gladwin, H. S. *Chaco Branch Excavations at White Mound and in the Red Mesa Valley*. Gila Pueblo, Globe, Arizona, 1945.

Goddard, Pliny L. *The Beaver Indians*. American Museum of Natural History *Papers*. New York, 1916.

Grandstaff, James O. *Wool Characteristics in Relation to Navajo Weaving*. Washington, U. S. Department of Agriculture, 1942.

Hackett, Charles W. (ed.). *Historical Documents Relating to New Mexico, Nueva Vizcaya and Approaches Thereto, to 1773*. Washington, Carnegie Institution of Washington, 1937.

Haile, Berard. *Some Cultural Aspects of the Navajo Hogan*. U. S. Indian Service (mimeographed), 1937.

——. *Origin Legend of the Navajo Enemy Way*. Yale University *Publications in Anthropology*, No. 17 (1938).

——. *Origin Legend of the Navajo Flintway*. Chicago, University of Chicago Press, 1943.

——. *Navajo War Dance*. St. Michaels, Arizona, St. Michaels Press, 1946.

——. *The Navajo Fire Dance*. St. Michaels, Arizona, St. Michaels Press, 1946.

———. *Navajo Sacrificial Figurines*. Chicago, University of Chicago Press, 1947.

———. *Starlore Among the Navajo*. Santa Fé, Museum of Navajo Ceremonial Art, 1947.

Hall, Edward Twitchell, Jr. *Early Stockaded Settlements in the Governador, New Mexico*. Columbia University *Studies in Archaeology and Ethnology*, 1944.

Hammond, George P. *Don Juan de Oñate and the Founding of New Mexico*. Santa Fé, El Palacio Press, 1927.

——— and Agapito Rey (tr. and ed.). *Gallegos Relation of the Rodriguez Expedition to New Mexico*. Albuquerque, Historical Society of New Mexico, 1927.

Hawley, Florence M. *The Significance of the Dated Prehistory of Chetro Ketl, Chaco Canyon, New Mexico*. Monograph Series, Vol. I, No. 1, University of New Mexico *Bulletin* (1934).

Hewett, Edgar L. *Chaco Canyon and its Monuments*. Albuquerque, University of New Mexico Press, 1936.

Hill, Willard W. *Navajo Warfare*. Yale University *Publications in Anthropology*, No. 5 (1936).

———. *The Agricultural and Hunting Methods of the Navajo Indians*. Yale University *Publications in Anthropology*, No. 18 (1938).

———. *Navajo Salt Gathering*. Anthropology Series, Vol. III, No. 4, University of New Mexico *Bulletin* (1940).

Hill-Tout, C. *British North America*. Toronto, 1907.

Hodge, Frederick W. (ed.). *Handbook of American Indians North of Mexico*. Smithsonian Institution, Bureau of American Ethnology, *Bulletin* No. 30. 2 vols. Washington, 1907, 1912.

Honigman, John J. *Ethnology and Acculturation of the Fort Nelson Slave*. Yale University *Publications in Anthropology*, No. 3 (1946).

Hrdlicka, Ales. *Physiological and Medical Observations Among the Indians of Southwestern United States and Northern Mexico*. Bureau of American Ethnology *Bulletin* No. 34. Washington, 1908.

Huscher, Betty H. and Harold A. *The Hogan Builders of Colorado*. Gunnison, Colorado Archaeological Society, Inc., 1943.

James, George Wharton. *Indian Blankets and Their Makers*. Chicago, 1914.

Jenness, Diamond. *The Sekani Indians of British Columbia, Canada*. Canadian Department of Mines and Resources, Anthropological Series No. 20, *Bulletin* No. 84 (1937).

——. *The Sarcee Indians of Alberta*. National Museum of Canada, *Bulletin* No. 90 (1938).

Keur, Dorothy L. *Big Bead Mesa*. Society for American Archaeology *Memoirs*, No. 1, (1941).

Kirk, Ruth F. *Navajo Indian Welfare*. New Mexico, Department of Public Welfare (mimeographed), 1945.

Klein, Julius. *The Mesta, A Study in Spanish Economic History, 1273–1836*. Cambridge, Harvard University Press, 1920.

Kluckhohn, Clyde. *Navajo Witchcraft*. Peabody Museum *Papers*. Cambridge, 1944.

—— and Leland Wyman. *An Introduction to Navajo Chant Practice*. American Anthropological Association *Memoir*, No. 53 (1940).

—— and Katherine Spencer. *A Bibliography of the Navaho Indians*. New York, J. J. Augustin, 1940.

—— and Dorothea Leighton. *The Navajo*. Cambridge, Harvard University Press, 1946.

Krug, J. A. *Report on the Navaho*. Washington, 1948.

Kupper, Winifred. *The Golden Hoof*. New York, Knopf, 1945.

Ladd, Horatio O. *History of the War with Mexico*. New York, Dodd, Mead & Co., 1883.

Leighton, Alexander H. *Gregorio, the Handtrembler*. Peabody Museum *Papers*, Cambridge, 1949.

Leupp, Francis E. *The Indian and His Problem*. New York, C. Scribner's Sons, 1910.

Lipps, Oscar H. *The Navajos*. Cedar Rapids, Torch Press, 1909.

Luomala, Katherine. *Navajo Life of Yesterday and Today*. U. S. Department of Interior, National Park Service. Berkeley (mimeographed), 1938.

Mason, J. Alden. *Notes on the Indians of the Great Slave Lake Area.* Yale University *Publications in Anthropology,* No. 34 (1946).

Matthews, Washington. *Navajo Silversmiths.* Bureau of American Ethnology *Second Annual Report.* Washington, 1883.

——. *Navajo Weavers.* Bureau of American Ethnology *Third Annual Report.* Washington, 1884.

——. *The Mountain Chant.* Bureau of American Ethnology. *Fifth Annual Report.* Washington, 1887.

——. *Navajo Legends.* American Folklore Society *Memoir,* No. 5 (1887).

——. *The Night Chant.* American Museum of Natural History *Memoir,* No. 6 (1902).

Mera, H. P. *Navajo Textile Arts.* Santa Fé, Laboratory of Anthropology, 1947.

The following were issued by the Laboratory of Anthropology, Technological Series, Santa Fé:

——. *Ceramic Clues to the Prehistory of North Central New Mexico. Bulletin* No. 8, 1935.

——. *Navajo Blankets of the Classic Period. Bulletin* No. 3, 1938.

——. *The Slave Blanket. Bulletin* No. 5, 1938.

——. *Pictorial Blankets. Bulletin* No. 6, 1938.

——. *Wedge Weave Blankets. Bulletin* No. 9, 1939.

——. *The Zoning Treatment in Navajo Blanket Design. Bulletin* No. 12, 1940.

——. *The Chinlee Rug. Bulletin* No. 13, 1942.

——. *Navajo Twilled Weaving. Bulletin* No. 14, 1943.

——. *Navajo Woven Dresses. Bulletin* No. 15, 1943.

——. *Cloth Strip Blankets of the Navajo. Bulletin* No. 16, 1945.

Meriam, Lewis, et. al. *The Problem of Indian Administration.* Baltimore, 1928.

Mindeleff, C. *Navajo Houses*. Bureau of American Ethnology *Seventeenth Annual Report*. Washington, 1898.

Moore, J. B. *The Navajo*. Crystal, New Mexico, 1911.

Morss, Noel. *The Ancient Culture of the Fremont River in Utah*. Peabody Museum *Papers*. Cambridge, 1931.

Newcomb, Franc J. and Gladys A. Reichard. *Sand Paintings of the Navajo Shooting Chant*. New York, J. J. Augustin, 1937.

Oakes, Maud. *Where the Two Came to Their Father*. New York, Pantheon Books, 1943.

Parsons, Elsie Clews. *Pueblo Indian Religion*. 2 vols. Chicago, University of Chicago Press, 1939.

Parsons, Elsie Clews (ed.). *Hopi Journal of Alexander M. Stephen*. 2 vols. Columbia University *Contributions to Anthropology*, 1936.

Phelps-Stokes Fund. *The Navajo Indian Problem*. Phelps-Stokes Fund, 101 Park Ave., New York, 1939.

Priest, Loring B. *Uncle Sam's Stepchildren: The Reformation of United States Indian Policy, 1865-1887*. New Brunswick, Rutgers University Press, 1942.

Reichard, Gladys A. *Social Life of the Navajo Indians*. Columbia University *Contributions to Anthropology*, No. 7 (1928).

———. *Spider Woman*. New York, Macmillan Co., 1934.

———. *Navajo Shepherd and Weaver*. New York, J. J. Augustin, 1936.

———. *Dezba, Woman of the Desert*. New York, J. J. Augustin, 1939.

———. *Navajo Medicine Man*. New York, J. J. Augustin, 1939.

———. *Prayer: The Compulsive Word*. New York, J. J. Augustin, 1944.

———. *The Story of the Navajo Hail Chant*. Privately printed, New York, 1944.

———. *Navajo Religion*. 2 vols. New York, Pantheon Books, 1950.

Reiter, Paul. *The Jemez Pueblo of Unshagi*. Monograph Series. Vol. I, No. 5, University of New Mexico *Bulletin* (1938).

Sabin, Edwin L. *Kit Carson Days, 1809-1869*. 2 vols. New York, Press of the Pioneers, 1935.

Sapir, Edward and Harry Joijer. *Navaho Texts.* Iowa City, Linguistic Society of America, University of Iowa, 1942.

Seymour, Flora W. *The Story of the Red Man.* New York, Longmans, Green & Co., 1929.

Stallings, W. S. *Dating Prehistoric Ruins by Tree Rings.* Santa Fé, Laboratory of Anthropology, *Bulletin* No. 8 (1939).

Stevenson, James. *Ceremonial of Hasjelti Dailjis.* Bureau of American Ethnology *Eighth Annual Report.* Washington, 1891.

Steward, Julian. *Ancient Caves of the Great Salt Lake Region.* Bureau of American Ethnology *Bulletin* No. 116. Washington, 1937.

Thomas, Alfred B. *Forgotten Frontiers.* Norman, University of Oklahoma Press, 1932.

———. *After Coronado.* Norman, University of Oklahoma Press, 1935.

———. *The Plains Indians of New Mexico, 1751–1778.* Albuquerque, University of New Mexico Press, 1940.

———. *Teodoro de Croix and the Northern Frontier of New Mexico.* Norman, University of Oklahoma Press, 1941.

Twitchell, Ralph E. *The History of the Occupation of New Mexico.* Denver, Smith-Brooks Co., 1909.

———. *The Leading Facts of New Mexican History.* 5 vols. Cedar Rapids, Torch Press, 1911–17.

Underhill, Ruth M. *Ceremonial Patterns in the Greater Southwest.* American Ethnological Society *Monographs,* XIII, 1948.

———. *Here Come the Navaho.* Lawrence, Haskell Institute (U. S. Indian Service), 1953.

———. *Red Man's America.* Chicago, University of Chicago Press, 1953.

Van Valkenburgh, Richard. *A Short History of the Navajo People.* Window Rock, Arizona, U. S. Indian Service (mimeographed), 1938.

———. *Dinebikeyah.* Window Rock, Arizona. Mimeographed for the Navajo Service, 1940.

Vestal, Stanley. *Kit Carson: A Happy Warrior of the Old West.* Boston, 1928.

Wheelwright, Mary C. *Tleji or Yehbechai Myth.* The House of Navajo Religion *Bulletin,* No. 1. Santa Fé, 1938.

———. *Myth of Sontso.* The House of Navajo Religion *Bulletin* No. 2. Santa Fé, 1940.

———. *Eagle Catching Myth and Yohe, or Dead Myth.* The House of Navajo Religion *Bulletin,* No. 3. Santa Fé, 1945.

———. *Navajo Creation Myth.* Museum of Navajo Ceremonial Art, *Navajo Religion Series,* No. 1. Santa Fé, 1942.

———. *The Hail and Water Chants.* Museum of Navajo Ceremonial Art, *Navajo Religion Series,* No. 2. Santa Fé, 1946.

Woodward, Arthur. *A Brief History of Navajo Silversmithing.* Museum of Northern Arizona *Bulletin,* No. 14. Flagstaff, 1938.

Wyman, Leland. *Sandpaintings of the Kayenta Navaho.* University of New Mexico *Publications in Anthropology,* 1952.

———, and S. K. Harris. *Navajo Indian Medical Ethnobotany.* University of New Mexico *Bulletin,* Anthropological Series, Vol. III, No. 5 (1941).

———, with W. W. Hill and I. Osanai. *Navajo Eschatology,* University of New Mexico *Bulletin,* Anthropology Series, Vol. IV, No. 1 (1942).

———, and Flora L. Bailey. *Navajo Upward-Reaching-Way.* University of New Mexico *Bulletin,* Anthropology Series, Vol. IV, No. 2 (1943).

Wissler, Clark. *The Social Life of the Blackfoot Indians.* American Museum of Natural History *Anthropological Papers,* Vol. VII, 1912.

IV. *Periodicals*

Adair, John, and Evan Vogt. "Navaho and Zuñi Veterans: A Study of Contrasting Modes of Culture Change," *American Anthropologist,* Vol. LI, No. 4 (October-December, 1949).

Amsden, Charles A. "The Navajo Exile at Bosque Redondo," *New Mexico Historical Review,* Vol. VIII, No. 1 (January, 1933).

Bailey, Flora. "Navajo Foods and Cooking Methods," *American Anthropologist,* Vol. XLII, No. 2 (April-June, 1940).

Bartlett, Katherine. "Hopi History, II: The Navajo Wars," Museum of Northern Arizona *Museum Notes,* Vol. VIII, No. 7 (1936).

Bender, A. B. "Military Posts in the Southwest, 1484-1860," *New Mexico Historical Review,* Vol. XVI, No. 2 (April, 1941).

Bloom, Lansing B (ed.). "Bourke on the Southwest," *New Mexico Historical Review,* Vols. VIII–XIII (1933–38).

Bloom, Lansing B., and Lynn B. Mitchell. "The Chapter Elections of 1672," *New Mexico Historical Review,* Vol. XIII, No. 1 (January, 1938).

Blumenthal, E. H. "An Introduction to Gallina Archaeology," *New Mexico Anthropologist,* Vol. IV, No. 1 (1940).

Blunn, Cecil T. "Improvement of the Navajo Sheep," *Journal of Heredity,* Vol. XXXI, No. 3 (1940).

———. "Characteristics and Production of Old Type Navajo Sheep," *Journal of Heredity,* Vol. XXXIV, No. 5 (1943).

Burton, Estelle B. "Volunteer Soldiers of New Mexico and Their Conflicts with Indians," *Old Santa Fe,* Vol. I, No. 4 (April, 1914).

Creer, Leland H. "Spanish-American Slave Trade in the Great Basin, 1880-1853," *New Mexico Historical Review,* Vol. XXIV, No. 3 (July, 1949).

Farmer, Malcolm F. "Navajo Archaeology of Upper Blanco and Largo Canyons," *American Antiquity,* Vol. VIII, No. 1 (July, 1942).

Goldfrank, Esther. "Irrigation Agriculture and Navajo Community Leadership: Case Material on Environment and Culture," *American Anthropologist,* Vol. XLVII, No. 2 (April–June, 1945).

Grandstaff, James O. "Evaluating Fleece Characteristics of Navajo Sheep from a Breeding Standpoint," *Rayon Textile Monthly,* (October–November, 1941).

Gwyther, G. "An Indian Reservation," *Overland Monthly,* Vol. X, No. 2 (February, 1873).

Haines, Francis. "The Northward- Spread of Horses Among the Plains Indians," *American Anthropologist,* Vol. XL, No. 3 (July–September, 1938).

Hall, Edward Twitchell, Jr. "Recent Clues to Athapascan Prehistory in the Southwest," *American Anthropologist,* Vol. XLVI, No. 1 (January–March, 1944).

Harrington, John P. "Southern Peripheral Athapaskawan Origins, Divisions and Migrations," *Smithsonian Miscellaneous Collections.* Vol. C. Washington, 1940.

Hibben, Frank C. "The Gallina Phase," *American Antiquity,* Vol. IV, No. 1 (July, 1938), 131–36.

———. "The Pottery of the Gallina Complex," *American Antiquity,* Vol. XIV, No. 3 (January, 1949).

Hill, Willard W. "The Hand Trembling Ceremony of the Navajo," *El Palacio,* Vol. XXXVIII, Nos. 12, 13, 14 (1935).

———. "Navajo Rites for Dispelling Insanity and Delirium," *El Palacio,* Vol. XLI, No. 14 (1936).

———. "Some Navaho Culture Changes During Two Centuries," *Smithsonian Miscellaneous Collections,* Vol. C. Washington, 1940.

———. "Some Aspects of Navajo Political Structure," *Plateau,* Vol. XIII, No. 2 (October, 1940).

———. "The Legend of the Navajo Eagle Catching Way," *New Mexico Anthropologist,* Vols. VI, VII (1944).

———. "Navaho Trading and Trading Ritual, A Study of Cultural Dynamics," *Southwestern Journal of Anthropology,* Vol. IV, No. 4 (Winter, 1948).

Hilzheimer, Max. "Sheep," *Antiquity,* Vol. X, No. 38 (June, 1936).

Hodge, Frederick W. "The Early Navajo and Apache," *American Anthropologist,* Vol. VIII, No. 3 (July, 1895).

———. "The Name Navaho," *Masterkey,* Vol. XXIII, No. 3 (May, 1949).

Hoijer, Harry. "Classificatory Verb Stems in the Apachean Language," *International Journal of American Linguistics,* Vol. XI, No. 1 (January, 1945).

Hubbell, John Lorenzo. "Fifty Years an Indian Trader," *Touring Topics,* Vol. XXII, No. 12 (December, 1939).

Huscher, Betty H. and Harold A. "Athapascan Migration via the Intermontane Region," *American Antiquity,* Vol. VIII, No. 1 (July, 1942).

Keur, Dorothy L. "A Chapter in Navaho- Pueblo Relations," *American Antiquity,* Vol. X, No. 1 (July, 1944).

Kidder, Alfred V. "Ruins in the Historic Period in the Upper San Juan Valley, New Mexico," *American Anthropologist,* Vol. XXII, No. 4 (October-December).

Kluckhohn, Clyde. "Some Personal and Social Aspects of Navaho Ceremonial Practice," *Harvard Theological Review,* Vol. XXXII, No. 1 (1939).

Letterman, Jonathan. "Sketch of the Navajo Tribe of Indians," Correspondence of the Smithsonian Institution, *"Annual Report* of the Board of Regents. Washington, 1855-56.

Malouf, Carling and A. Aline. "The Effects of Spanish Slavery on the Indians of the Intermountain Region," *Southwestern Journal of Anthropology,* Vol. I, No. 3 (Autumn, 1945).

Malcolm, Roy L. "Archaeological Remains, Supposedly Navaho, from Chaco Canyon, New Mexico," *American Antiquity,* Vol. V, No. 1 (July, 1939).

Matthews, Washington. "The Gentile System of the Navajo Indians," *Journal of American Folklore,* Vol. III (1890).

Mera, H. P. "Some Aspects of the Largo Cultural Phase," *American Antiquity, Vol.* III, No. 3 (January, 1938).

Morice, A. G. "The Unity of Speech Among the Northern and the Southern Dené," *American Anthropologist,* Vol. IX, No. 4 (October–December, 1907).

Opler, Morris. "Southern Ute Pottery Types," *Masterkey,* Vol. XIII, No. 5 (September, 1939).

Page, Gordon. "Navajo House Types," Museum of Northern Arizona *Museum Notes,* Vol. IX, No. 9 (1937).

Pepper, George. "Native Navajo Dyes," *The Papoose,* Vol. I, No. 3 (1903).

Reeve, Frank. "The Federal Indian Policy in New Mexico, 1858–1880," *New Mexico Historical Review,* Vol. XII, XIII (1937–38).

———. "The Government and the Navajo," *New Mexico Historical Review,* Vols. XIV, XVI, XVIII (1939, 1941, 1943).

Reichard, Gladys A. "Linguistic Diversity Among the Navaho Indians," *International Journal of American Linguistics,* Vol. XI, No. 3 (July, 1945).

Sapir, Edward. "Internal Linguistic Evidence Suggestive of the Northern Origin of the Navaho," *American Anthropologist,* Vol. XXXVIII, No. 2 (April–June).

Scholes, France V. "The Supply Service of the New Mexican Missions in the Seventeenth Century," *New Mexico Historical Review,* Vol. V, No. 1 (January, 1930); No 2 (April, 1930).

Stewart, Omer C. "The Navajo Wedding Basket—1938," Museum of Northern Arizona *Museum Notes,* Vol. X, No. 9 (1938).

———. "Navajo Basketry as Made by Ute and Paiute," *American Anthropologist,* Vol. XL, No. 4 (October–December, 1938).

Tschopik, Harry Jr. "Navaho Basketry," *American Anthropologist,* Vol. XLII, No. 3 (July–September, 1940).

———. "Taboo as a Possible Factor Involved in the Obsolescence of Navaho Pottery and Basketry," *American Anthropologist,* Vol. XL, No. 2 (April–June, 1938).

Van Valkenburgh, Richard. "Navajo Common Law," Museum of Northern Arizona *Museum Notes,* Vol. IX, No. 10 (1937).

Weltfish, Gene. "Prehistoric North American Basketry Techniques and Modern Distributions," *American Anthropologist,* Vol. XXXII, No. 3 (July–September, 1930).

―――. "Preliminary Classification of Prehistoric Southwestern Basketry," *Smithsonian Miscellaneous Collections*, Vol. LXXXVII. Washington, 1932.

Wyman, Leland and Flora L. Bailey. "Navajo Girl's Puberty Rite," *New Mexico Anthropologist*, Vol. VI (1943).

Index